Reflect to
Create!

The Dance of Reflection for
Creative Leadership, Professional
Practice and Supervision

ELAINE PATTERSON

Reflect to *Create!*
Published and Produced 2019 by IngramSpark
Cover and text design: meadencreative.com
Editor: Emma Dickens
Proofreader: Fiona Screen
ISBN: 978-1-9164560-0-6

All proceeds will be gifted to help support the achievement of the 2030 United Nations
Global Goal No. 4 for Sustainable Development. Global Goal No. 4 is the goal for
Quality Education which is aiming to ensure inclusive and equitable quality education and
promote lifelong opportunities for all by 2030. Please see www.globalgoals.org for more
information.

At the still point of the turning world.

Neither flesh nor fleshless;

Neither from nor towards;

At the still point, there the dance is,

But neither arrest nor movement.

And do not call it fixity,

Where past and future are gathered.

Neither movement from nor towards,

Neither ascent nor decline.

Except for the point, the still point,

There would be no dance, and there is only the dance.

T.S. Eliot from 'The Four Quartets'

Life is a dancer and you are the dance.

Eckhart Tolle

In Honour of my Mother:
Pearl Patterson
22nd January 1929 to 6th December 2011.

Dedicated to:
People who work with people everywhere who give of themselves to make the world a better place.

My Heartfelt Thanks to:
Edna Murdoch who has taken me to the heart of supervision, Karyn Prentice who has shown me how to bring my work alive, and everyone who I have ever worked with or spoken to whose gems of inspiration and wisdom are reflected in your own ways in my writing.

My Love to:
My sister Laura who always supports me, my husband Steve who always encourages me, and my daughter Naomi who always inspires me. They have walked with me word by word.

Sometimes

Sometimes
if you move carefully
through the forest,

breathing
like the ones
in the old stories,

who could cross
a shimmering bed of leaves
without a sound,

you come
to a place
whose only task

is to trouble you
with tiny
but frightening requests,

conceived out of nowhere
but in this place
beginning to lead everywhere.

Requests to stop what
you are doing right now,
and

to stop what you
are becoming
while you do it,

questions
that can make
or unmake a life,

questions
that have patiently
waited for you,

questions
that have no right
to go away.

David Whyte[1]

CONTENTS

PART 1: The Philosophy

PART 2: The Practices

CHAPTER 6
Seeing Anew

CHAPTER 7
Relating to the Whole

The *Flow*

CHAPTER 8
Initiating the Invitation

CHAPTER 9
The Art of Listening

CHAPTER 10
Finding Freedom

The *Denouement*

CHAPTER 11
Crafting Focus

CHAPTER 12
Working Wisely

CHAPTER 13
FeedForward

CHAPTER 14
Supervision

Resources

FOREWORD

I am delighted to write a foreword for this book. I have known Elaine Patterson for many years; she makes a significant contribution to the CSA Diploma in Supervision and to the discourse on new forms of leadership and professional practice. To say she is passionate about adding to this discourse is an understatement. Her thinking arises from sound business experience, Masters level research and from years of professional supervision with leaders, coaches and supervisors in many parts of the world.

We have become used to rather urgent descriptions of 21st-century leadership challenges – evidenced by the volume of concern and advice about how to operate wisely in a 'global, virtual and diverse' world. There are many responses to these challenges and the growth of professional supervision (reflective practice) for leaders and coaches is one of them. So this book is a timely and practical resource for anyone who wants to raise their game and respond more skilfully to the complexities of the workplace.

A quick look at Amazon tells us that 'reflection' is frequently mentioned in contemporary business and leadership literature: there are many titles that are reflections on something. However, in this book we are invited *into* reflection and into an anatomy of reflection itself – reflection as a 'natural gateway to learning'. Reading through the chapters of this book, I found myself wondering how many of us actually know how to reflect, or respect the potency of reflective processes. As I read, I was constantly thinking, 'But, of course!' and wondering why I had not already seen what is revealed in these pages. But then, that's partly why we read books – to increase understanding, to be guided by someone whose research has unearthed something useful.

One of the great pleasures of reading this book is the sense it gives you that the author has become so immersed in her subject that she really can bring something new to the current business and leadership conversation – a way to name and highlight the rewards of intelligent reflection. It has been a joy to follow Elaine's explorations and be rewarded with many original insights on reflection as well as a host of exercises for those who will take up the challenge of becoming a skilled reflector.

Reflect to *Create!* subtly and powerfully works on the reader; we are drawn deeply into reflection even as we read about the reflective process. Reading this text, therefore, is to participate in what is being created before our very eyes and to be affected by it – that is to say, we naturally begin to reflect on reflection. And we are drawn into this process by the ever-deepening insights of this radical work: radical, because this is not a 'how-to' book, though there are many original exercises to experiment with. Rather, it is more a 'become-it-from-the–roots-up' sort of book. That's part of the gift of Reflect to *Create!* – Elaine knows that only becoming it will do. And she echoes many contemporary thinkers when she says, 'more of the same is no longer enough'.

The marriage of research into reflection with an imaginative use of the dance metaphor, is a wonderful invention. The introduction of dance moves to explain the key elements of reflective process is both surprising and purposeful. We can all relate to 'retreat, reflect and return' – hints of the Gay Gordons dance on the page! This is a brilliant way to invite the reader into reflection and to take seriously the idea that these processes are 'our natural gateways into learning, innovation and creativity'. This is reflection laid bare. The use of dance moves helps the reader to embed key moments in the rhythm of reflecting. This begins with 'stop', where stopping is understood to be strategic withdrawal at moments of enquiry, difficulty or complexity. In our busy 21st-century lives, as we hurtle from one complexity to another, we need sufficient awareness to be able to 'stop' at regular intervals: stop and reflect.

There's plenty here for those who want the hard facts and figures, and the book teems with practical exercises. Those who learn through more holistic presentation are superbly guided by a lively text well supported by illustrations that powerfully enhance meaning. In addition, Elaine has mapped her thinking onto the well-established Theory U presence model, which was developed by Otto Sharmer and Peter Senge. Many readers will be familiar with this model and as it is used here, it gives resonance to the reflective processes that are uncovered in these chapters. It quickly becomes obvious how deep reflection ensures that we create a new thought, idea or solution. At this level, reflection is an intentional practice and Elaine shows clearly how transformative it is to work consciously with the reflective process so that WHO and HOW we are, in work and life, is continually developed. Many contemporary commentators are encouraging leaders to find ways to become their best selves – to achieve the 'post-conventional consciousness' that enables us to bring our best to the table. Reflect to *Create!* is a powerful contribution to this discourse.

In this generous and delightful book, Elaine shows how to become a natural reflector and amply illustrates the pressing need for leaders, coaches and people professionals to 'pause, retreat, reflect and return'. This is a book I will keep on my desk and I encourage the reader to do the same. There is so much to explore here and I welcome this superb contribution to the literature on leadership, professional practice and supervision.

Edna Murdoch
CEO Coaching Supervision Academy Ltd.

PREFACE

Turning and turning in the widening gyre
The falcon cannot hear the falconer;
Things fall apart; the centre cannot hold;
Mere anarchy is loosed upon the world,
The blood-dimmed tide is loosed, and everywhere
The ceremony of innocence is drowned;
The best lack all conviction, while the worst
Are full of passionate intensity.

'The Second Coming' William Butler Yeats[2]

Why Now?

This book is dedicated to leaders and people professionals everywhere who are looking for new and different ways to live and work. Never before have we as individuals, families, organizations and societies faced so many changes from so many sides. Technological, psychological, ecological, economic, societal and political weather fronts pound the shores of our very being and blur the horizons we seek. And leaders, people professionals and development practitioners are responsible for helping others to live with such uncertainty, whilst also learning to live the questions themselves with generosity, courage, compassion and wisdom. As Rainer Maria Rilke wrote:

> Do not now seek the answers, which cannot be given you because you would not be able to live them. And the point is, to live everything. Live the questions now. Perhaps you will then gradually, without noticing it, live along some distant day into the answer.[3]

Why Me?

My love of reflection was forged by the dinnertime conversations we used to have when I was growing up. School was always hard. I had spent my preschool years in Holland where we learnt through play. When we returned to the UK, I found myself constantly trailing behind, always playing catch-up. This was compounded by my dyslexia which did not get diagnosed until my fifties.

I did enough to be able to read History at Bristol University and went on to be accepted onto the prestigious NHS National Management Training Scheme for high flyers. But what I very quickly discovered was that although theory, textbooks and technical skills or competence might be helpful, they were not enough to lead wisely, with courage and compassion.

This was not taught at any of the business schools I went on to attend. Instead I began to appreciate that I needed to understand the central relationship between WHO I was in the moment by moment because this shaped HOW I worked and the impact I made. I came to realize that reflection – and reflective learning – enabled me to work on this central dynamic. As David Whyte wrote:[4]

> We shape our self
> to fit this world and by the world are shaped again.

Twenty years on in 2003, I left my Board post to go on adoption leave and subsequently to train as an executive coach and thinking partner, and then as a supervisor.

In 2007, at an Association of Coaching book launch, I was lucky enough to meet Edna Murdoch, Co-Founder of the Coaching Supervision Academy. I felt an instant connection and asked Edna if she would become my Coaching Supervisor. This was the start of a wonderfully rich creative working partnership which has fueled and inspired my practice ever since. I also want to thank Karyn Prentice as we joyfully partner together as PattersonPrenticeDesigns to bring the work we love to do to the world.

I am very clear that my journey from novice to master coach with a flourishing practice was only made possible by the supervision I received and the reflective practices I developed. These were made all the more necessary as we negotiated the joys, trials and tribulations of parenting a child with very complex special needs.

In my practice I also noticed that many leaders and people professionals were really struggling to thrive in and navigate our new VUCA world as more and more complaints about professional practice seemed to be lodged, and as more and more corporate scandals seemed to hit the news headlines.

The phrase VUCA was beautifully coined by Bob Johansen[5] to describe the volatility, uncertainty, complexity and ambiguity of our new post-industrial post-conventional world. My own experiences as a wife, mother, sister, aunt, practitioner, leader and citizen made living these challenges both personal and universal. My MA research was inspired by the fact that, in the existing literature, I could not find an answer to the question, 'Can reflection and reflective practice help leaders to lead?' The stage was set for my research and this book.

My Research Findings

The answer to that question was yes.[6]

I discovered that reflection is innate and very natural to us. I discovered that reflection's deep dive processes of retreat, reflect and return are our natural gateways to learning, innovation and creativity. I discovered that reflection has the power to put us in touch with the wisdom of our own humanity and the humanity of others, which can free us to create and transform ourselves and the world around us. Excitingly, I discovered that reflection is an act of creation – to bring something new into the world or to reshape what already exists – where more of the same is no longer enough. From this I coined the phrase Reflect to *Create!*.

The *Reflect to Create!* Dance Map

I started to see Reflect to *Create!* as a holistic philosophy, with practices which are expressed as a dance with a *Prelude* and three core dance sequences. These are:

| *The Opening:* | **Retreat's Rest and Release** |
| *The Flow:* | **Reflection's Fertile Void** |

and

| *The Denouement:* | **Return's Harvest and Action** |

I then started to define three dance steps for each move and to bring these alive with a variety of practices for practitioners to flow in and out of depending on where they were and what they needed.

I want to create a movement to change hearts and minds about what is needed and what can help in today's world. I want to help bring reflection out of dusty classrooms or stale accreditation frameworks and to make it essential, fun and mainstream for people who work with people. I want to us to rally to Václav Havel's impassioned address as president of the Czech Republic to the Joint Session of the US Congress in March 1990:[7]

> The salvation of this human world lies nowhere else than in the human heart, in the human power to reflect, in human meekness and in human responsibility. Without a global revolution in the sphere of human consciousness, nothing will change for the better in the sphere of our being humans, and the catastrophe toward which the world is headed – be it ecological, social, demographic or a general breakdown in civilization – will be unavoidable.

Your Invitation

This book invites you to dance through the mysterious and potentially liberating rollercoaster world of Reflect to *Create!*

These pages will show you how the processes of retreat, reflect and return – the slowing down, the tuning in and sense making – allow us to let go of our assumptions and access our own humanity and wisdom in service of our clients, teams, organizations or communities.

You will emerge with a clearer understanding of how you can develop your own creative and reflective practices. You will find the ways and means for yourself to embrace the complexities, vulnerabilities and opportunities inherent in the 21st century.

The book blends the latest thinking and research from disciplines including relational dynamics, mindfulness, adult learning theory, appreciative inquiry, systemic thinking, Eastern philosophy, the arts and the natural world.

It has been designed to enable you to dip in and out as you require, and is divided into three parts:

Part 1   **The Philosophy:** setting the stage, outlining the 'Bigger Picture', the imperative for Reflect to *Create!* and the choreography of Reflect to *Create!*.

Part 2   **The Practice:** choreographing the Reflect to *Create!* dance, introducing the *Prelude* and the three subsequent core dance sequences – *The Opening*, *The Flow* and *The Denouement* (with their nine dance steps and associated practices) – to unlock your natural powers for reflective learning and *creativity*.

Part 3   **The Resources:** signposting you to additional reading, references and resources.

Each chapter is brought alive with stories, insights, quotes, and poems.

Each chapter will end with some reflective questions for you, to bring your reading back to you, your life and your work.

* * * * *

Reflective Questions

1.   What attracted you to this book and why?

2.   What do you hope to discover which might support and resource you and your work?

PART 1
The Philosophy

INTRODUCTION: SETTING THE STAGE
On Work

It's life Jim, but not as we know it.

Mr Spock[1]

Change and challenge are everywhere. Tidal waves of deep societal, economic, business, organizational, technological and ecological upheaval are stretching us to our core. At no time in our history have we faced so much disruption on so many fronts. This can seem to be threatening the very essence of who we are, how we think, how we relate and how we work.

How we choose to live these questions of purpose, identity and agency in our virtual and actual VUCA world will determine our fate: our ability and our choice to either sink, paralyzed by muddle, blame and confusion, or swim creatively in a sea of innovation, potential and possibility.

Leaders, coaches, supervisors, Human Resources, people professionals, social entrepreneurs and development practitioners are all working on the frontline of these seismic shifts. Whatever their role, sector, culture or country, people are starting to notice that what got them – and their clients – to where they are in their professions, in their organizations or in their lives is not what is going to keep them there; and more of the same is no longer enough. They are sensing that a different response, shaped by engaging in more imaginative conversations, is urgently needed. As Albert Einstein wrote:[2]

> Problems cannot be solved from the consciousness which created them.

My interviews with leaders and people professionals across many different sectors in many different countries have conclusively shown that reflection and reflective learning can unlock our vast potential and creativity in these uncharted waters. Reflection, they report, had helped them to learn how to become their best selves through making sense and then making meaning of their experiences. Reflection had helped them to move through their work and life by celebrating what is working but also by finding new and creative ways through seemingly intractable problems. It has helped them to find the space within themselves to challenge old paradigms whilst at the same time constructing new possibilities and directions.

Today's Realities

Johansen[3] has helpfully coined the acronym VUCA to describe today's world. VUCA is shorthand for volatility, uncertainty, complexity and ambiguity; and whilst leaders and professionals have always worked in VUCA worlds what is now new and different is the scale, rapidity and intensity of the changes. It is this scale, rapidity and intensity, in an increasing globalized, virtual and diverse world, which now consigns predictive planning, yesterday's logic, and linear thinking to the scrap heap.

A quick look at what researchers are saying gives us a feel for the challenges we are facing into:

- Only 15% of leaders sampled showed a consistent capacity to innovate and successfully transform their organizations[4]

- Only 30% of CEOs are confident that they have the talent needed to grow their businesses[5]

- 89% of employees admit that they do not have the skills or knowledge to do their jobs[6]

- 13% of employees are actively engaged (and twice that number would actively sabotage their employer)[7]

- 58% of new executives fail within 18 months of taking up post[8]

- Only 8–12% of those who attend formal training translate their new skills into measurable performance[9]

- 75% of organizations report that they struggle with overwhelmed employees[10] and people now check their cell phones almost 150 times a day, with busy professionals focusing for only 7 minutes at a time[11]

- The poorest 40% of the world's population accounts for 5% of global income and the richest 20% accounts for 75% of the world's income[12]

and

- We are using 150% of our planet's capacity to sustain our current levels of consumption[13]

The 2015 report by ?WHAT IF! Innovation Partners[14] reported that almost 72% of leaders admitted that their organization was too reliant on fading revenue streams; that 58% of teams were failing to lead for innovation; and that 28% of leaders believed that their current business model was not sustainable.

Facing into the Pressures of People Work

Within this wider context, the work of leaders and people professionals is a huge privilege and also a huge responsibility; and it can also be lonely.

Our clients allow us the honour of inviting us into their lives often at times when they feel most confused – when the way is not clear, or when they feel stuck or challenged. And it is here that we bear witness to their greatest excitements and potentially deepest vulnerabilities. The work can be fascinating, joyful and effective *and* – often at the same time – it can also be full of challenge, frustration, and worry. In the interviews people said, for example:

'I am so twisted out of shape I do not know who I am anymore.'
Senior NHS Leader

'All my creativity has been crushed out of me.'
Senior Utilities Trainer

One leader said:

It is thrilling, but it is also lonely, frightening and sometimes I do not sleep at night with worry. I have to work with my vulnerabilities and worries about the re-organization: Are we going in the right direction? Will this be good for business?... and then see the worry and fear in the eyes of my team ... and still get through the day.

One counsellor said:

There are days when I feel swamped by the sadness and grief, which my clients bring to the sessions. I empathize, I hold the space, I do my best...but at the end of the day I just collapse completely exhausted and empty.

When leaders and professionals miscue, a lot of potential damage can occur, as a Head of Service from a Local Authority recalls:

I remember our Chief Executive had organized an Away Day to help us get to know each other and how to work with each other. The elephant in the room was his Deputy who – bottom line – had been over-promoted. The Facilitator was completely lost and out of their depth with the anger and pent-up emotions within the team, which had got subverted. The day ended with relationships worse than they started and it took over a year for all of us to repair the fallout. Dreadful. Never again. Ever since then I have been very wary of stage-managed interventions.

As people practitioners we do ourselves and our clients a potentially dangerous disservice when we are not sufficiently resourced ourselves to be able to:

i.   Create and then hold a safe space for the exploration of often difficult and contradictory raw emotions

and

ii. Take risks ourselves in order to fully embrace our shared humanity, what it means to be human and what it means to work with another human being.

WHO we are and HOW we hold ourselves as we work is the key we hold – or withhold – to facilitating learning and transformation in others.

Why WHO you are is HOW you Work

This central dynamic is why the trademark phrase 'WHO you are is HOW you coach' from Edna Murdoch at the Coaching Supervision Academy has now been extended by me to read 'WHO you are and HOW you are being in this moment is HOW you lead, coach, supervise, learn and work.'

This central relational dynamic between 'WHO you are' and 'HOW you are being in this moment' and 'HOW you work' is the golden thread, which runs through all people work. It is the inquiry into this central dynamic – in all of its many guises – which sits at the heart of Reflect to *Create!*. As Gardner wrote:[15]

> Our state of being is the only real source of our ability to influence the world.

Reflection is the process. Reflection helps us to rewire and re-sculpt our brain's hardwiring so we can choose WHO we want to be moment by moment. Reflection creates the conversational dance, space and place which enables us to inquire into – and learn from – this central dynamic as it is plays out across the past, present and future. Reflection is where our role meets our soul, and each can converse with the other. Here, both separately and together, can each be shaped.

This was also supported by my research in which all the leaders had ultimately concluded that learning to lead was actually first and foremost a radical act of learning to know and lead themselves.[16] They realized that by first learning how to relate and connect with themselves they could better relate and connect with others and their world. It was from this place of authentic connection that they could truly discover what was needed from them and how they could best respond. As Edna Murdoch writes:[17]

> My experience is that operating alongside all of our professional trainings, our thinking, tools and models, is the personhood of the practitioner – our humanity matters, as does our maturity, our open-heartedness and our generosity of spirit.

'Facing into our own humanity' is a lifelong personal and professional journey: in order to allow in the creativity of the human heart and a richer deeper connection with all of life, we must first let go of our controlling strategizing ego. As Carl Jung advised:[18]

> Learn your theories and techniques as well as you can, and then be prepared to set them aside when you meet the miracle of the living soul in front of you.

On Reflection

Learning is experience.
Everything else is information.

Albert Einstein[19]

In the literature on adult learning, development and change, reflection and reflective learning are often seen as the poor relation – an add-on in development programmes or in team meetings. Reflection is either bypassed or has become the last resort in our frantic rush to action. Facing overload and overwhelm, practitioners convince themselves that they do not have time to reflect. But learning how we learn is WHO we are. As human beings we are naturally programmed to explore, to learn, to adapt, to evolve and to create – if the conditions are right. There is a lovely story of when a reporter asked the Dalai Lama how he found the time to meditate.[20] The Dalai Lama's answer is as true for reflection as it is for meditation. He said,

> You should meditate for at least 20 minutes a day … Unless you are too busy and then you should meditate for an hour.

In our hearts, minds and souls, we know that more of the same is no longer enough. As Peter Drucker wrote:[21]

> In times of turmoil the danger lies not in the turmoil but in facing it with yesterday's logic.

In our turmoil, we have lost sight how of reflection and reflective practices can be the way to supporting, resourcing and inspiring us to become our better selves and hence to do our best work.

> Here is Edward Bear, coming down the stairs now, bump, bump, bump, on the back of his head, behind Christopher Robin. It is, as far as he knows, the only way of coming downstairs, but sometimes he feels there really is another way, if only he could stop bumping for a moment and think of it.
>
> *Winnie the Pooh* A.A. Milne[22]

Please note that 'Reflection' is often confused with 'thinking' and 'mindfulness'. This potential confusion is addressed in the Glossary.

What are the Main Triggers for Reflection?

My research showed that reflection is usually a response to an experience or set of experiences that are inviting us to stop and think more deeply. Discontinuity or a threat in the face of the unknown (like a promotion), or a perceived danger (like an inspection visit) proved to be the biggest instigators. Participants said they were triggered to reflect when:

'I feel an unease'

'I feel a discomfort'

'I feel that my peace is being disrupted'

'I feel an irritation – with a noise going on in my head'

'I notice something new and surprising and my antenna start twitching'

or

'My body's barometer tells me'

The key triggers for reflection were found to be:

1. When we need to address our blind spots and shadows: when we do not know what we do not know

2. When we need to learn: when we need to become aware of what we do not know but want to know

3. When we need to know ourselves: when we need know what we do know but do not want to know

4. When we are stuck, face difference or new difficult decisions and choices: when we do not know how to respond, what to do or where to go

5. When we face overwhelm: when we need to catch up with ourselves – we need to process what has happened or is happening to find meaning and purpose

6. When we feel stressed, isolated or lonely: when we need to know how to feed and nourish ourselves for the long haul

7. When we need to be more creative: when what we know is no longer enough or sufficient and a change of some sort is needed

8. When we need to be authentic or true to ourselves: when we need to close the gap between WHO we want to be and HOW we are actually BEING and HOW we are actually SHOWING up for ethical, courageous and compassionate practice

9. When we need to be fully human and BE ourselves: when we want to become more of WHO we truly are, realize our highest potential and find our place in the world

My research found that there was a big impact in not reflecting. These were quantified as losses in understanding, energy, creativity, productivity and a diminution in the quality of relationships and decision-making.

Misunderstanding Reflection

My research also found that whilst the participants described their own experience of the benefits of reflection as:

'Alive, fluid and full of movement'

'I love finding the aha moment – it is a bit like finding a dopamine hit'

'I love to find the link between things'

or

'I really value the personal space to think to carry me forward into the next phase'

They also acknowledged that reflection was almost seen as 'a dirty word' and 'counter culture'. It was perceived to be 'something wooly and off-putting', 'something dull and static', 'irrelevant' or something more associated with fault-finding and blame than creativity. One leader said,

'The bosses had put comfy sofas around the building but people were scared to use them for fear of being seen as not busy enough.'

The work of Descartes, Newton and others revolutionized science and the means of production, but it also allowed separatist linear thinking to dominate the organization of our professions, education, firms and society. Whilst bringing vast wealth and technological breakthroughs its transactional, mechanistic and reductionist approach has come to dominate. The capacities and capabilities needed today are not those forged in the factories and schools of the industrial revolution. Today's challenges cannot be solved using yesterday's logic.

Something different is needed. Something more.

Reflect to *Create's!* Dance for Inner Transformation

I have now come to define reflection thus:

Reflection and Reflect to *Create!* is our dance with the rhythm of our experiences. Reflection enables us to make sense and then to create meaning of our experiences of the past in the present, the present in the present and the emerging potential of the future which is already here in the present for new insights. Reflection supports us in our quest for wisdom.

Reflection is a learning process which at its best engages the subtle multi-layered, multi-dimensional faculties of our minds, bodies, hearts and souls to release or reshape what is already present, or to create anew in order to develop more generative patterns of thinking, relating, doing and being . These enable us – in our relationships with others and with our world – to survive, thrive and flourish.

Reflect to *Create!* gives us the choreography, disciplines and practices to discover our inner truth and wisdom for change and transformation.

Reflection taps into our innate love of storytelling – our very human need to make sense of, then take meaning from, the stories of our experiences. At its heart, reflection is a dialogic inquiry and relational practice which invites us – either on our own or with others or via a combination of the two – to explore the essence of who we are, who we are becoming and how we work. Reflection mirrors ourselves in the world and the world in us. Reflection is grounded in the wisdom of our own humanity, in our shared humanity with others and in the interconnectedness of nature and all living things. Reflection paradoxically both grounds us and frees us to become our better selves for inspired work and fulfilled living.

The quality of our reflection is shaped by what we choose to pay attention to and what we intend as we pay attention. Both our attention and our intention are honed through the craft of reflective practice.

Reflection is personal and voluntary. It cannot be imposed or outsourced because learning and change start from the inside out. Its fruits can lead to profound shifts within ourselves, and through us in our relationships and in our agency to do good work, which is also work that we love to do.

The good news is that reflection is innate and natural to us, and can also be nurtured and developed. Regular reflection and reflective practice – and the reflective learning which they generate – can give us the generous thinking, feeling and sensing of time and space needed to rigorously inquire into our experience, challenge our stories and see into our processes. From this we have the opportunity to create new mindsets, relationships and behaviours, which can serve us better.

Ancient philosophers and thinkers have long understood the power of reflection but today this powerful learning methodology has become overlooked. Leaders and professionals cannot command people to become more reflective or creative, but they can create the conditions to liberate fresh thinking and innovation.

For David Whyte[23]

The field of human creativity has long been a battlefield between the upper world we inhabit every day and deeper untrammelled energies alive in every element of life. The world of commerce has, until now, run a mile from this hidden world: organizations have often seen these underground and seemingly eccentric desires as a source of continual disruption into their production and purpose.... The American corporate is tiptoeing for the first time in its short history into the very place that dedication, creativity and adaptability must come: the turbulent place where the soul of an individual is formed and finds expression.

How we create the invitation to the dance is the key to creative leadership, professional practice and supervision.

* * * * *

Reflective Questions

On Work

1. How is the VUCA world affecting you and your work?

2. WHO are you becoming in response either by accident or by design? How is this showing up in HOW you work?

3. Can you think of any leaders or practitioners who in your opinion are surviving and thriving in our VUCA world? What are you noticing? How do you think they are they achieving this? What do you feel you could learn from them?

On Reflection

4. What does reflection mean to you – and for your work?

5. Do you reflect?

6. How do you reflect?

7. What prompts you to reflect?

8. Do you feel you have time for reflection?

9. What are the costs to you and your work of not reflecting?

10. Can you think of any leaders or practitioners who in your opinion are reflective practitioners? What difference is it making to them and their work? How do you think they are achieving this? What do you feel you could learn from them?

CHAPTER 1
The Dance

Learning emerges from discovery, not directives; reflection, not rules; possibilities, not prescriptions; diversity, not dogma; creativity and curiosity, not conformity and certainty; and meaning, not mandates.

Dr. Stephanie Pace Marshall
Founding President and President Emerita, Illinois Mathematics and Science Academy[1]

The Reflect to *Create!* dance forms a metaphor for the processes of learning, change and transformation.

The Genesis of Reflect to *Create!*

Reflect to *Create!* appeared as a flash of insight one early summer's morning in August 2013. I was on holiday on the Isle of Wight with my family. I had made myself another cup of coffee and rubbed the sleep from my eyes. I pored over the mountains of my analysis. The data had come from six questions I had asked my research participants. The questions had been:

- How do you define reflection?

- What are your processes of reflection? (What? How? Where? and When?)

- What are your triggers for reflection?

- What helps or hinders your reflection?

- What benefits do you get from reflection?

- What advice or recommendations – if any – would you offer for the development of future leaders?

Suddenly I saw the underlying pattern. While the more traditional benefits were cited – enhanced self-awareness, improved relationships, finding renewed purpose – it was equally clear that reflection had also freed leaders to work with reshaping what already existed or birthing what was new in the following ways:

- to unlearn in order to learn or relearn something,

- to discover new insights or ideas,

- to find new ways of working,

- to design new products or services or

- to reshape what already exists.

As one leader said,

'Reflection is the gateway to possibilities.'

My conclusion was that at its heart reflection is an act of creation.

The Gestation of Reflect to *Create!*

It felt like a homecoming. I had used this idea as a navigational star throughout my life. Never accepting unfairness or the status quo, from very early on some form of reflection had reframed and redesigned how I worked and lived. It also felt true for my work with my clients and our conversations together. Working at a subterranean level I began to realize that the hope contained within Reflect to *Create!* had been an invisible golden thread both guiding and holding our work together. I have always been inspired by Eckhart Tolle's phrase 'Life is a dancer and you are the dance.'[2]

So I decided to work with the universal metaphor of dance because we can all dance in some way or other. Dancing is innate and natural to us. Also the concept of a dance where we can also improvise for ourselves captures for me the freedom that reflection can give. This is also why I chose the dancer from from Step 6: Finding Freedom to grace the book's front cover!

Since my discovery that August morning, I have been honing Reflect to *Create!* into a meaningful and useful dance map for leaders and people practitioners.

Whilst Reflect to *Create!* has its own logic, the invitation is for it to be experienced as an organic lived process, freeing the practitioner to move in and out of the dance sequences, disciplines and practices as needed in the service of their own inquiries and learning. How and where each practitioner chooses to enter the dance – and how swiftly they move through it or return and repeat different steps – is an individual choice based on their style, where they are in their own learning journey, and the wider reasons and context for their particular inquiry.

Practices to enable leaders and people practitioners to flow back and forth between the three moves are offered in Part 2 – The Practice. These are to be used as needed. All of the dance moves, steps and practices can be returned to again and again as new and different insights emerge.

The Reflect to *Create!* Dance Map

The Reflect to *Create!* dance can be illustrated using a simple U as the container or crucible for learning and discovery. The U curve is a shape which is used to describe a change process in many cultures. I also want to acknowledge the inspiration I have received from reading Otto Scharmer's work and how this has helped me to choreograph my own design.[3]

Within Reflect to *Create!* there is a natural symmetry, a flow and an order to the moves. The simple U is designed as a tool to locate where you are on the learning curve. It is not a straitjacket. In any reflective learning process there will be many natural overlaps, iterations and returns as experience is explored in a continual cycle of conversation, inquiry and discovery. The quality of our participation in the dance is a function of how we tune into our faculties for paying attention, which are developed through the disciplines of reflective practice as described in Chapter 3.

The dance is in four moves:

The Prelude	
The Opening	Retreat's Rest and Release
The Flow	Reflection's Fertile Void
The Denouement	Return's Harvest and Action

The characteristics of these four dance moves are illustrated in the U curve diagram opposite:

The Prelude

The Opening
Retreat's Rest and Release
...Letting Go...

The Flow
Reflection's Fertile Void
...Into Stillness and Spaciousness...

The Denouement
Return's Harvest and Action
...Letting Come...

- Suspending Habits
- Seeing Anew
- Relating to the Whole

- Initiating the Invitation
- Art of Listening
- Finding Freedom

- Crafting Focus
- Working Wisely
- FeedingForward

The Reflect to *Create!* Choreography

The Prelude

The dance starts with a *Prelude*. This is an invitation to pause or to stop. Vulnerability is embraced. Reflective learning is messy. Reflection is always prompted by a question or an intuition, which invites a stopping. The practitioner then has a choice: to pursue the inquiry or close it off. The stopping heralds a shift into *The Opening:* Retreat's Rest and Release.

Fig 1: *The Prelude*

The Prelude

The Opening

Retreat's Rest and Release

The Retreat is the space for rest and release. The dictionary defines retreat as

'relinquishing a position'.[4]

The dance steps for Retreat are Suspending, Seeing and Relating.

Step 1:   Suspending Habits means suspending familiar scripts or old ways.

Step 2:   Seeing Anew means seeing what 'is' with all of our senses.

and

Step 3:   Relating to the Whole means sensing and connecting to the wider field.

These dance steps start to free us from our controlling egos and strategizing minds to create a spaciousness in our hearts, minds, souls and bodies to enable us to receive new information from the field.

Travelling down the left-hand side of the U involves building in the practices and disciplines for intentionally clearing our heads, hearts, bodies and souls – potentially for the new to emerge at the bottom of the U.

The purpose of the dance steps in *The Opening* is to invite the practitioner to redirect their focus and attention – and to come into relational presence with themselves, with others and with their world. The Retreat is a necessary and conscious preparation of the ground for *The Flow:* into Reflection's Fertile Void.

Fig 2: *The Opening* Retreat's Rest and Release

The Opening
Retreat's Rest and Release
...Letting Go...

- Suspending Habits
- Seeing Anew
- Relating to the Whole

The Flow
Reflection's Fertile Void

The Flow means stepping into the stillness and spaciousness of Reflection's Fertile Void to listen and to receive. This is the place where boundaries dissolve. This is the Fertile Void's primordial soup, which teems with life's universal, generative and creative potentiality and energies.

The dance steps for *The Flow* are:

Step 4: **Initiating the Invitation** means inviting our own inner knowing and wisdom to emerge.

Step 5: **The Art of Listening** means listening to what is waiting to emerge and tuning into latent possibility and potential.

Step 6: **Finding Freedom** means allowing ourselves to act as a channel for life's creative energies.

Sitting at the bottom of the U curve means building the practices and disciplines for deep listening, trust, imagination and invitation.

The purpose of the dance steps in *The Flow* are to invite the practitioner to connect with possibility, potential and creativity. Reflection's Fertile Void provides the inspiration and creativity for *The Denouement* Return's Harvest and Action which actualizes reflection's creativity and provides the practical steps for bringing the new into the world.

Fig 3: *The Flow*: Reflections' Fertile Void

The Flow
Reflection's Fertile Void
...Into Stillness and Spaciousness...

- Initiating the Invitation
- Art of Listening
- Finding Freedom

The Denouement

Return's Harvest and Action

Return is the place for harvesting, action, and feedforward. *The Denouement* is for testing and applying the discoveries and riches from *The Flow* back into the world. Choices, options and decisions are designed, formulated, tested and applied. The invisible is made visible. The implicit is made explicit. Feedback is given and received.

The dance steps for *The Denouement* are Crafting Focus, Working Wisely and FeedingForward

Step 7: **Crafting Focus** means taking the active steps to harvest, design, test and apply what has emerged.

Step 8: **Working Wisely** means making wise choices and decisions in service of life and work.

Step 9: **FeedingForward** means being open to feedback to better move forward.

Moving up the right-hand side of the U curve involves building the practices and disciplines for designing, testing, and experimenting.

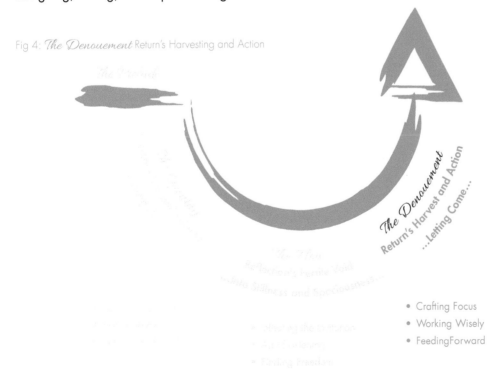

Fig 4: *The Denouement* Return's Harvesting and Action

The Denouement
Return's Harvest and Action
...Letting Come...

- Crafting Focus
- Working Wisely
- FeedingForward

* * * * *

Reflective Questions

1. What part of Reflect to *Create!* are you most curious or intrigued about and why?
2. What part of Reflect to *Create!* most resonates with you and why?
3. What part of Reflect to *Create!* are you feeling challenged by and why?
4. What part of the book would you like to go to now?

CHAPTER 2

On Creativity

Every child is an artist.
The problem is how to remain an artist as one grows up

Pablo Picasso[1]

Introducing Creativity

Like learning, creativity is natural. It is our inheritance. Creativity is an energy and a life force that defines us. Creativity is inherently who we are. As David Ulrich writes:[2]

> The urge to create – the unison of mind, body and heart, to express ourselves and our observations, our deepest longings, our greatest aspirations, joys and sorrows – is one of the basic human impulses. Every person has the potential to enter the stream of discovery and invention. Each of us has a vast wealth of resources that invite us to participate in the process of creation.

Moving beyond the given and known is one of the biggest challenges of our times. Unlocking and owning our creativity, then modelling this for others, is a great gift. At the heart of Reflect to *Create!* is showing how, through reflection and reflective practices, we can bring this gift into the world and make it mainstream. Because, as John O'Donohue writes:[3]

> Each of us is an artist of our days; the greater our integrity and awareness, the more original and creative our time will become.

This chapter will challenge current perceptions of what creativity is and how it works, and will confront the blocks, pain and joys of embracing our birthright.

What is Creativity?

The *Oxford English Dictionary* defines the word 'create' as 'Bring into existence, give rise to; originate'[4] and 'creativity' as 'Creating; able to create; inventive; imaginative; showing imagination as well as routine skill.'[5]

Creativity is the art of reshaping what already exists or bringing the new into the world. Creativity can be expressed as a new insight, a new way of working, thinking or relating, a new idea, a new product, a new piece of writing, art, theatre, music or dance. It can also be expressed in the choices we make minute to minute in what we choose to wear, eat, drink, speak, do and how we choose to be. WHO we uniquely are, is HOW we can uniquely create. As Martha Graham writes:[6]

> There is a vitality, a life force, an energy, a quickening that is translated through you into action because there is only one of you in all of time, this expression is unique. And if you block it, it will never exist through any other medium and will be lost.

Creative expression is not only concerned with who we *are* but also with who we are *about to be*. As Charles Du Bos wrote:[7]

> The important thing is this: to be able at any moment to sacrifice what we are for what we could become.

Creativity is a way of being and relating in the world. Reflection is the process. Creative insights can occur at any time but Reflect to *Create's!* choreography can guide and anchor you!

Reclaiming our Creativity

By challenging received wisdom and understanding the processes within us, we can reclaim our own innate creativity. There are four myths that can inhibit our creativity:

1.   Creativity belongs to the few

2.   Creativity is not welcome

3.   Creativity is not necessary

and

4.   'I might fail.'

Myth 1: Creativity Belongs to the Few

Popular culture has tended to present creativity as only belonging to the talented minority – people like Michelangelo di Lodovico Buonarroti Simoni (1475–1564), Pablo Picasso (1881–1973), Albert Einstein (1879–1955), William Shakespeare (1564–1616) or Martha Graham (1984–91). This has been fiercely challenged by Ken Robinson, amongst others, who wrote:[8]

> My starting point is that everyone has huge creative capacities as a natural result of being a human being. The challenge is to develop them. A culture of creativity has to involve everyone, not just the select few.

Myth 2: Creativity is not Welcome

The prevailing preference for the logical and the linear has pushed creativity's meandering messiness to the sidelines. Creativity has been starved of oxygen, light and space. As Rod Judkins, an artist, writer and lecturer, reflects:[9]

> At school, creativity was suppressed and crushed. It was something that teachers and authorities actually feared… They steered students away from it in the same way they steered them away from drugs, burglary or gambling. At art college it was completely different. The spirit was one in which mistakes

were good. Where you could try and fail. ... There was an air of freedom and release.

As Nick Udall writes:[10]

Unfortunately many of us have had creativity educated out of us. We are then socially conditioned to develop various mental and emotional filters (including the fear of failure) to maintain the status quo and keep us fearful of, and even blind to, what we don't know.

Myth 3: Creativity is not Necessary

There is an assumption that creativity is alien, that is not for us, that it is far removed from us and our daily lives, which are already overcommitted and overscheduled. As Rod Judkins has written:[11]

School and society have robbed us of our creative confidence. Although we are born with incredible imagination, intuition and intelligence, many people are not trained to use these powers.

Myth 4: 'I Might Fail'

Our egos and the part of us which needs rationality, order and control distrust creativity's innate spontaneity, imperfections, chaos and messiness. To embrace creativity means embracing risk and fear of perceived failure as new insights are explored and new approaches are prototyped. As Anup Kochhar says,[12] 'The fear of failure kills creativity and intelligence. The only thing it produces is conformity.'

Expertise is taught. Creativity is innate. Creativity is personal, forged on the anvil of our own experiences and perspectives. Creativity is therefore the ultimate form of self-expression. In daring to risk in this way we also dare to risk ourselves.

This legacy robs us of our natural inheritance and disconnects us from life's creative pulse.

The Music of Creativity: A Re-Frame that Frees

Reflect to *Create's!* choreography helps us to tap into the source of our natural creativity. There are six harmonies which form the backing music to Reflect to *Create!* These are:

Harmony No. 1 Living as a Creative Act

At a cellular level, living a human life is a creative act of constant birth, renewal, ageing, death and rebirth lived second by second as our bodies breathe and as we transition through different life stages. Living is also learning – a constant process of learning, unlearning and relearning in order to make sense of and take meaning from these natural cycles – as well as those imposed upon us.

At the root of our shared humanity is appreciating that we are all in a constant state of being created, which also makes us vulnerable. The only choice we have is to wholeheartedly embrace or stubbornly resist nature's natural creativity.

Harmony No. 2 Dancing with the Unknown

Creativity is a conversational dance between what we know and do not know. It is through Reflect to *Create's!* early moves that we can give ourselves the space and the permission to stop downloading our habitual thoughts, see with fresh eyes and touch the wider field or fertile void.

By letting go of what we think we know and who we think we are, we give ourselves the opportunity to experience other perspectives, other possibilities, and other potentials. This is the beginning of making the invisible visible, the unconscious conscious, and the unknown knowable. To quote Rainer Maria Rilke,[13] 'to live, embrace and dance our questions'.

As David Whyte writes in his poem 'Tobar Phadraic':[14]

Turn sideways into the light as they say
the old ones did and disappear into the originality
of it all. Be impatient with explanations and discipline the mind not to begin
questions it cannot answer.

Now you are alone with the transfiguration
and ask no healing of your own
but look as if looking through time,
as if a rent veil from the other
side of the question you have refused to ask.

Harmony No. 3 The Mystery of the Creative Process

Creativity and the creative process cannot be fully understood by the grasping ego or strategic mind. Creativity is a magical mystery tour, which works because it is elusive, because it defies the logic of the strategic mind and because it sidesteps the habitual and routine. Creativity is fed from our wandering, wondering, delight and surprise. As Pablo Picasso wrote, inspiration comes from everywhere:[15]

The artist is a receptacle for emotions that come from all over the place: from the sky, from the earth, from a scrap of paper, from a passing shape, from a spider's web.

Creativity works in us and through us. As Osho writes[16]:

The greatest are those who have been absolutely certain that they have been nothing but hollow bamboos and existence has been singing through them ... It has flowed through them ... and it has come from an unknown source.

The creative process holds its own inherent design but it is not a linear progression with a tight choreography. Rather it ebbs and flows with many iterations, returns and surges along the U-shaped curve of the Reflect to *Create!* process. Nick Udall equates the creative process to a rollercoaster ride. David Ulrich equates it to a river:[17]

> Like a river's journey, it contains broad currents of free-flowing movement, meandering streams that fuel its course, vigorous rapids and spirited falls, passages through perilous narrows, areas of inert stagnation, clear pools of polished stillness, and finally a place of union with the sea, merging with the source.

Each stage within the Reflect to *Create!* process asks for our full attention. Each stage with its different contribution to the creative process asks for a particular blend of somatic and soulful intelligences and energies.

Harmony No. 4 Touching the Fertile Void

When we let go of the ties that bind we step into reflection's generous inquiry, abundant curiosity and attentive listening. Here a fertile spaciousness opens up within us, which allows for a deeper consciousness which naturally connects us to the fertile void. This dissolves boundaries and enables us to see the emerging whole.

Creativity happens in the spaces in between our day to day busy-ness, when we allow ourselves to tune into a bigger spaciousness. This is allowing ourselves, to wander, get lost, to stand still and ponder for the new to emerge. As Leonard Cohen wrote his song 'Anthem':[18]

> Forget your perfect offering
> There is a crack, a crack in everything
> That's how the light gets in.

Becoming fully present to the here and now enables us to access a resonating co-creative frequency, which operates deep in our bodies to see and create anew. As Albert Einstein wrote:[19]

> A human being is part of the whole, called by us the 'universe', a part limited in time and space. He experiences himself, his thoughts and his feelings, as something separated from the rest, a kind of optical illusion of his consciousness. This delusion is a kind of prison for us, restricting us to our personal desires and to affection for a few persons nearest to us. Our task must be to free ourselves from this prison by widening our circle of compassion to embrace all living creatures and the whole of nature in its beauty.

This process of creativity working through us when we create the conditions around us to invite it in is beautifully captured by Danish sculptor Erick Lemcke:[20]

> After having worked with a particular sculpture for some time, there comes a certain moment when things are changing. When this moment of change comes, it is no longer me, alone who is creating. I feel connected to something far deeper and my hands are co-creating with this power. At the same time, I feel that I am being filled with love and care as my perception is widening. I sense things in another way. It is a love for the world and for what is coming. I then intuitively know what I must do. My hands know if I must add or remove something. My hands know how the form should manifest. In one way it is easy to create with this guidance. In those moments I have a strong feeling of gratitude and joy.

Harmony No. 5 The Science of Creative Insight

Creativity occurs in a place of aligned co-creative energy, when we connect with ourselves, with others and with the fertile void to see new patterns. As Karyn Prentice writes,[21] 'We are tuning forks picking up what deeply resonates within us.'

When we open ourselves to our experience a shift occurs. This shift is from the brain's left hemisphere's preference for the narrower focus to the right hemisphere's more spacious search for connections and meaning.[22]

Nick Udall writes that creative insight occurs through a chain of events in the brain when we have an issue which logic cannot solve. Using fMRI and ECH imaging, scientists have shown that we do think differently when creative insights occur. Creative insights are always initially fleeting or elusive, and occur when there is a shift in our brainwaves. As Nick writes, scientists have shown that an insight starts life as a transient dip in the activity in our prefrontal lobes, which opens us up to taking risks with the new. Then there is a burst of alpha waves at the back of our brains, which shuts down our visual cortex, cutting off distractions. This is quickly followed by a burst of gamma waves in our anterior superior temporal gyrus where we experience flashes of insight. Danah Zohar and Ian Marshall have also written that when bundles of neurons all over the brain oscillate simultaneously at similar frequencies of about 40 Hz then new levels of consciousness, or what they call the 'god spot', opens up to us.[23]

Harmony No. 6 Embracing Creativity's Rollercoaster Ride

Creativity requires us to risk ourselves. To risk what we think we know and who we think we are in the crucible of experience. To paraphrase Warren Bennis[24]

> Reflecting on experience is a means of having a … dialogue with yourself … What actually happened? … Why did it happen? … What did it do to me? … What did it mean to me? In this way one locates and appropriates the learning one needs, or more precisely remembers what one had forgotten and becomes, in Goethe's phrase the hammer rather than the anvil.

Creativity and Reflect to *Create!* requires us hold the mirror up to ourselves, our experience and to the world. To inquire, to be curious, and to risk ourselves as we find ourselves connecting more and more to our own source and to nature's source. To shed old baggage, patterns and identities as we adventure to seek to discover new lands, new connections, new vistas and new insights, which better serve us both in the present and going forward. As James Hillman writes of his 'Acorn Theory':[25] 'Each person bears a uniqueness that asks to be lived and that is already present before it can be lived.'

This is a journey of joy and vulnerability. The range of emotions that accompany adventure are experienced on this rollercoaster ride: shedding, letting go, and a reclaiming of our unique originality. To risk ourselves, to brave ourselves, to remember what we had forgotten, and to find our place of belonging in the world requires a support. We need an enabling ecosystem around us. As John O'Donohue writes:[26]

> Perhaps the art of harvesting the secret riches of our lives is best achieved when we place profound trust in the act of beginning. Risk might be our greatest ally. To live a truly creative life, we always need to cast a critical look at where we presently are, attempting always to discern where we have become stagnant and where new beginning might be ripening. There can be no growth if we do not remain open and vulnerable to what is new and different. I have never seen anyone take a risk for growth that was not rewarded a thousand times over.

Summary

We are as we respond. Creativity is always available to us at any time. Reflect to *Create!* gives us the process. Learning to see, be and attune to sources both within and without is our greatest challenge and our greatest opportunity.

* * * * *

Reflective Questions

1. How do you define creativity?

2. What stories were you told about your own creativity? How has this shaped your perception of your own creativity?

3. Which of the four myths, which block us from claiming our natural creativity, most applies to you? Are there others for you?

4. Which of the six harmonies are you most attracted to? And why?

5. What impact would reclaiming more of your innate creativity have for you? And for the people who you live or work with?

CHAPTER 3

Becoming a Reflect to *Create!* Reflective Practitioner

If you decide to live an unexamined life please do not take a job that involves other people

Parker J. Palmer[1]

Reflect to *Create!* is for any leader or people practitioner who wants to make a genuine difference and serve others well.

The dilemmas, grey areas of practice, and work we attract, often shine a light on our inner lives, holding a mirror to our own souls. Human work, which by definition embraces the human condition – with all of its joys, sorrows, anxieties and vulnerabilities – can be enlivening and it can be exhausting. As leaders and practitioners we therefore need to use reflection to attend to our own inner lives and wellbeing in order to stay 'fit for purpose'. This way, we can work wholeheartedly at integrating our roles and our souls – and role model this for the people we serve.

As Parker J. Palmer writes:[2]

> Our lives (as people practitioners) both deserve and demand reflection.
> We **demand** reflection because we must know what it is in our hearts, lest we do more harm than good. We **deserve** reflection because it is often challenging to sustain the heart in work … Inner truth is best conveyed by the language of the heart.

WHO We Are is HOW We Work – Joining Role and Soul

In people work WHO we are (and *how* we are moment by moment) is HOW we work. We are our only instrument.

Reflection and Reflect to *Create!* support us in honing this central dynamic because who we are is derived partly through a reflective, evolving and deepening sense of our own essence and an awakening to the interconnectedness of all living things. These discoveries shape what we choose to pay attention to, and how we are experienced by others as we work: the energy we transmit, the choices we make, the interventions we select, and the impact we make. This is because, as Howard Gardner wrote,[3] 'Our state of being is the only real source of our ability to influence the world.'

Or as Bill O'Brien, CEO of Hanover[4] said, 'The success of any intervention depends on the interior condition of the intervener.'

Our souls are the essence of our spirit and being. However, as David Whyte reflected:[5]

> The soul's needs in the workplace have been ignored because the path a soul takes to fulfil its individual

destiny is troublesomely unique to each person and refuses to be quantified in a way which can be put in a spreadsheet.

Dis-ease happens when we stop listening to the voices of our hearts and our souls. Reflect to *Create!* gets us back on track. When we are able to find ways to rejoin our own soul and role we can also inspire the clients and teams we work with to do the same.

The Heart of Reflection

Reflection is therefore the fundamental exploration of four core questions:

- WHO are you being and becoming and how does this show up in HOW you work?
- What are you choosing to pay attention to and what do you intend as you work?
- What are you sending out into the world and what impact is it having on others?

and

- What is the world sending back to you and what impact is it having on you?

Leaders and practitioners enable their clients and teams to let go, and work with not knowing, by renewing their hearts, minds, bodies and spirits through reflection.

Becoming a Reflective Practitioner

Reflect to *Create!* offers the inner disciplines and framework for this lifelong work. It is ultimately the creative unfolding and freeing of self which is also a spiritual unfolding. It is the process that turns information and knowledge into wisdom.

We cannot command ourselves (or others) to be more reflective or creative. But we simply allow ourselves to become Reflective Practitioners when we choose to commit to bringing alive the inner disciplines and practices of Reflect to *Create!* on a regular basis in our lives and work. Reflection and reflective practice keeps us alive, awake, and alert – and it cannot be outsourced.

Developing the Disciplines

> Through discipline comes freedom.
>
> Aristotle[8]

Reflect to *Create!* is simple but not easy. The relaxing of ego and stepping into the fertile unknown is exciting but can also be difficult and personally challenging. Background conditions and disciplines are therefore needed to start to gently develop our reflective muscles. As for any musician, dancer or athlete, leaders and people professionals also need warm-up exercises to prepare areas for attention.

For the new to be able to emerge and grow, we need to discover how to care for ourselves as we let go of old ways of thinking, seeing or relating which are no longer working. We also need to be able to role model this for others as we work 1:1, in our teams or across our systems and communities. For W. H. Auden:[9]

> The choice of attention – to pay attention to this and ignore that – is to the inner life what choice of action is to the outer. In both cases, a man is responsible for his choice and must accept the consequences, whatever they may be.

We cannot command or instruct ourselves to be more reflective, creative or brave. But we can design for ourselves – in ways which work uniquely for ourselves – the supporting disciplines, which open us up to new ways of noticing. As Michelangelo once said,[10] 'If the people knew how hard I had to work to gain my mastery, it wouldn't seem wonderful at all.'

These disciplines help us to re-wire and re-sculpt our brains – and our brains in our bodies. These disciplines recognize our learning is both an embodied and relational set of processes: we learn through and with our bodies and through and in the myriad of our many relationships in order to sense, read and understand our worlds.

Much has been written elsewhere on the biology and neuroscience of the evolution of our brain, mind and body.[11] This has included, for example, understanding cellular and brain development, the impact of stress on our brains and bodies, an appreciation of our multiple intelligences and how our early attachment patterns and key relationships can impact on our capacities to learn, unlearn and relearn.

Much has also been written on how the Enlightenment sought to compartmentalize, separate and divide us from ourselves and from others, and how much of our journey today is finding ways back to wholeness and integration.[12]

The good news is that reflection's disciplines can potentially enable us to develop new neural pathways in our bodies and in our brains to create new and different ways of relating, thinking, doing and being. Reflect to *Create!* is a way of finding within ourselves – and with the people we work with – the courage to step from

The Known <u>into</u> the New

Certainty <u>into</u> Possibility

Fixity <u>into</u> Flow

The Parts <u>over</u> the Whole

The General <u>into</u> the Unique

The Inanimate <u>to</u> the Animate

The Explicit <u>to</u> the Implicit

The Narrow <u>into</u> an open broad and deep Attention

Matter <u>over</u> Spirit

Blind Optimism <u>into</u> Actual Reality

Bureaucracy <u>into</u> Spontaneity

and from

Ego <u>to</u> Eco

where and when it is needed in our VUCA world.

This approach reclaims what leaders and people practitioners need to do *for themselves* in order to both survive and thrive doing the work they love. Background conditions and disciplines are offered here as the preparation for the dance. I have discovered that these disciplines give me the grounding and anchoring I need to consistently step into the unknown.

Invitation to the Dance

My experience has shown that five key disciplines are needed to create the favourable conditions where Reflect to *Create!* can flourish. As Steve Goodier writes:[13]

> When you assess your own life, consider it with the eye of a gardener. Underneath the surface lies rich, fertile soil waiting to nurture the seeds you sow. Even more than you can imagine will grow there if given a chance.

These are:

Discipline No. 1:	Making Your Commitment
Discipline No. 2:	Working with a Beginner's Mindset
Discipline No. 3:	Building Your Support
Discipline No. 4:	Developing Your Mindfulness Practices
Discipline No. 5:	Extreme Self-Care

Fig 5: Disciplines for the Dance

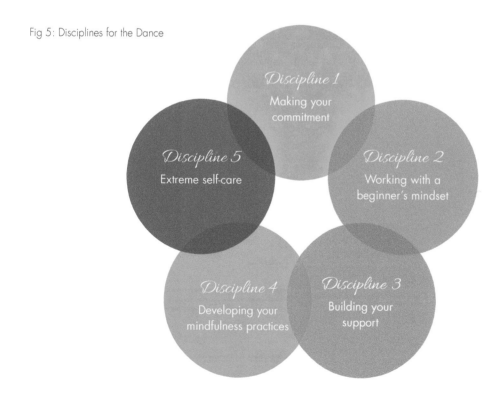

Discipline No. 1: Commit

My research showed that developing the habits of reflection had to be a personal choice – and could not be imposed. It starts with making the decision to invest in finding the disciplines which will support, nourish and resource us.

There is no blueprint or shortcut but the building blocks are:

✓ Making the decision to invest in yourself

✓ Deciding your intention and what you want from your investment

✓ Starting with where you are

✓ Experimenting with new approaches or refining old approaches until you find what works for you

and

✓ Being patient and kind to yourself in the process

As Johann Wolfgang Von Goethe wrote:[14]

> Until one is committed, there is hesitancy, the chance to draw back, always ineffectiveness. Concerning all acts of initiative and creation, there is one elementary truth the ignorance of which kills countless ideas and splendid plans: that the moment one definitely commits oneself, then providence moves too. All sorts of things occur to help one that would never otherwise have occurred. A whole stream of events issues from the decision, raising in one's favor all manner of unforeseen incidents, meetings and material assistance which no man could have dreamed would have come his way. Whatever you can do or dream you can, begin it. Boldness has genius, power and magic in it. Begin it now.

Discipline No. 2: The Beginner's Mindset

What we already know is necessary but not sufficient for today's VUCA world. As older certainties drop away we are forced into unknown territory where reliance on being yesterday's expert, specialist or authority can handicap, straightjacket and blind us. For Suzuki Shunryu,[15] 'In the beginner's mind there are many possibilities, but in the expert's there are few.'

Creativity needs freedom – freedom from the controlling mind, from history, from knowledge and from prejudice – to explore. For Dionysiu's ignorance is 'a luminous state of not knowing, where we are open and ready'.[16]

I have found that the building blocks for working with a Beginner's Mindset are therefore:

✓ Assume nothing

- ✓ Take nothing for granted
- ✓ Work with wonder and curiosity
- ✓ Notice when you are starting to get bored with the same old stories
- ✓ Follow your intuition
- ✓ Prepare to amaze, surprise and delight yourself
- ✓ Welcome the new
- ✓ Explore, experiment and play with what you know and don't yet know

As Joseph Henry wrote:[17] 'Seeds of great discoveries are constantly floating around us, but they only take root in minds (open and) well prepared to receive them.'

Discipline No. 3: Build Your Support

Creativity needs freedom but it also needs safety and support to flourish: places, spaces, processes and people

Where Reflect to *Create!* requires us to become vulnerable in the early moves it is critical that we deliberately design and build the supports and scaffolding around ourselves to hold us on our journey into deepening awareness and consciousness. These are ultimately journeys into our hearts and souls and being ready to perhaps ultimately discover the answer to the questions posed to us by the Chinese Sage Wu Wei Wu[18]:

> Why are you so unhappy?'
> Because ninety-nine percent of what you think,
> And everything you do,
> Is for your self,
> And there isn't one.

Finding a network of the places, spaces, processes and people to safely support us is extreme self-care. I have found that the building blocks are:

- ✓ Places means finding special places – like a favourite corner at home, a café, or an outdoor space – where we can relax, feel comfortable, be quiet, be inspired and be ourselves
- ✓ Spaces means finding the time in our hectic schedules to invest in being with ourselves and listening to ourselves
- ✓ Processes means finding questioning frameworks, habits, methods and mindfulness practices which work for us, our learning style and our lifestyle

✓ People means finding a network of colleagues, friends, coaches, mentors, supervisors and community that we feel we can safely trust to see, hear and be with us in our explorations. I have found that supervision has been critical and foundational for me here and is why in Chapter 14 I describe the role of the Supervisor as Reflect to *Create's!* dance partner.

The spaces, places, processes and people we choose must also offer us the safety, support and challenge we need for discovery and exploration.

- **Safety** because we need to feel that they are being safely held in our experimentation and risk taking

- **Challenge** because questioning and feedback is critical to innovation, exploration, accountability and staying on track

and

- **Support** because working in this way is demanding, lonely, exciting and exhausting and people practitioners need to be continually resourced for the long haul

Discipline No. 4: Mindful Practices

Mindfulness (or mind-emptying practices) help us to foster stillness and to pay refined attention to our experiences. I see mindfulness practices as like feng shui for the psyche – helping to clear the clutter of the everyday to get beneath the surface to detect the underlying patterns and discover deeper layers of meaning. For Dan Siegel,[19] 'Mindfulness is a form of mental activity that trains the mind to become aware of awareness itself and to pay attention to one's own intention.'

There is also mounting evidence that mindfulness boosts our creativity. Jack Kornfield describes how mindfulness helps us to:[20]

> Come alive through a growing capacity to release our habitual entanglement in the stories and plans, conflicts and worries that make up the small sense of self, and to rest in awareness. In meditation we do this simply by acknowledging the moment-to-moment changing conditions – the pleasure and pain, the praise and blame, the litany of ideas and expectations that arise. Without identifying with them, we can rest in the awareness itself, beyond conditions, and experience – and what my teacher Ajahn Chah called jai pongsai – our natural lightness of heart . Developing this capacity to rest in awareness nourishes samadhi (concentration), which stabilizes and clarifies the mind, and prajna (wisdom), that sees things as they are.

Mindfulness is burgeoning and we can be mindful and practice mindfulness in a myriad of different ways. The key is finding out what works for each of us. Forms of mindfulness are:

- ✓ Grounding, centring and meditation practices
- ✓ Yoga, t'ai chi and the martial arts
- ✓ Art, music, film, theatre and literature
- ✓ Walking and any form of exercise
- ✓ Massage, diet and wellbeing
- ✓ Spiritual and religious practices
- ✓ Hobbies like cooking, gardening, DIY, photography, craft and homemaking activities
- ✓ Being in nature
- ✓ Writing and journaling

My particular favourites are meditation, journaling, nature walks and sitting in silence in Quaker meetings. My research highlighted the value of journaling. It proved to be the most popular and cherished of the reflective disciplines. As one leader said, 'I just love using my lovely pens and lovely paper – my beautiful fountain pen and my beautiful book.'

As Joan Didion explained,[21] 'I write entirely to find out what I am thinking, what I am looking at, what I see, and what it means, what I want and what I fear.'

More inspiration can be found in the Resources section.

Discipline No. 5: Extreme Self-Care

Reflective learning is fun. It can also be challenging, daunting, frustrating and worrying.

Creating the disciplines and conditions for reflection is a radical act of self-care. We cannot do the work we love if we do not also love and take care of ourselves. As Howard Rheingold wrote:[22] 'Attention is a limited resource, so pay attention to where you pay attention!'

Take inspiration from the artist Susan Ariel Rainbow Kennedy who recommended us all to 'Invent your world. Surround yourself with people, color, sounds, and work that nourish you.'[23]

Or in the words of Arthur Ashe, top-ranked American tennis player in the 1960s and 1970s:[24]

Start with where you are.
Use what you have.
Do what you can.

Summary

Learning in this way is about attending to your preparation and support – as well as attending to that of the people you are working with. This is a necessity and a duty of care – not a luxury – for us in our VUCA world today.

* * * * *

Reflective Questions

1. Do you feel that you and your work demand and deserve reflection? And if so why?

2. What is the distance for you between your role and your soul?

3. Are you ready to become a reflective practitioner?

4. Which of the five disciplines is the most appealing and easiest for you to put in place? And why?

5. Which of the five disciplines is the least appealing and hardest for you to put in place? And why?

6. What do you need to do for yourself now?

PART 2
The Practices

I believe that we learn by practice. Whether it means to learn to dance by practicing dancing or to learn to live by practicing living, the principles are the same. In each, it is the performance of a dedicated precise set of acts, physical or intellectual, from which comes shape of achievement, a sense of one's being, a satisfaction of spirit. One becomes, in some area, an athlete of God. Practice means to perform, over and over again in the face of all obstacles, some act of vision, of faith, of desire. Practice is a means of inviting what is desired.

Martha Graham

Dance is the hidden language of the soul.
Nobody cares if you can't dance well.
Just get up and dance.
Great dancers are great because of their passion.

Martha Graham[1]

Part 2 offers just under two hundred different practices to bring Reflect to *Create!* alive. Each practice has been tried and tested. All can help to open our minds, hearts and will for creative action in a complex world. You are welcome to enter the dance at any point. Use what you need!

The following chapter explains the dancer's preparation for entering the Reflect to *Create!* dance. The moves start with a *Prelude*: an invitation to pause or to stop with a necessary embracing of vulnerability in order to learn. From the Prelude, the dance flows to *The Opening* Retreat's Rest and Release through to *The Flow* Reflections Fertile Void and coming full circle with *The Denouement* Return's Harvest and Action to begin again. Chapter 14 then concludes with an exploration of Supervision as a Reflect to *Create!* dance partner.

Reflect to *Create!* Choreography

Whilst Reflect to *Create!* has its own design logic, the invitation is for it all to be experienced as a flowing organic living process where there is no beginning and no end and where you are free to move in and out of the dance sequences and practices as needed in the service of your learning. All of the moves and practices can be returned to again and again as new and different insights emerge each time you step in and out of the flow of the dance as you too are constantly changing. How and where you choose to step into the dance – and how swiftly you move through the dance – is an individual choice based on your style, where you are on your own learning journey, and the wider reasons and context for your particular inquiry. I have found that – with practice – it becomes very easy to flow back and forth as appropriate in response to what is happening within you and in your external environment. With attentional intention, you can learn to finesse your dance steps in three dimensions: firstly, whilst you are in the experience – reflection in action; secondly, after the experience – reflection on action; and/or thirdly, in anticipation of experience – reflection for action.

> When the student is ready the teacher will appear.
>
> Buddhist proverb[2]

* * * * *

Reflective Questions

1. Start with where you are. Where are you?

2. What would be most helpful to you to attend to right now? And for your clients or team members?

CHAPTER 4
The *Prelude* to the Dance

We will go far away, to nowhere, to conquer,
to fertilize until we become tired.
Then we will stop and there will be our home.

Dejan Stojanovic[1]

The *Prelude* to the Dance starts by us courageously learning to stop when we do not know a specific answer or when we need to think more creatively about a question, issue or dilemma. We cannot learn if we are not prepared to make ourselves vulnerable in some way and we cannot make ourselves vulnerable without radical acts of self-compassion and self-care. This is because learning is harder if we do not feel nourished, resourced, and supported ourselves.

This chapter explores the practices for stopping, vulnerability and self-compassion.

Reflection always starts with a question or an intuition, which is inviting us to pause because it demands deeper exploration. Here we know that we do not know.

Often the question or intuition has surfaced through paying careful attention (see previous chapter). It could for example be how to approach a meeting, work with a difficult colleague or relationship, deal with a grey area of professional practice, clear obstacles, innovate or create something new, cope with mid-life or retirement. Or when we find ourselves on a plateau, stuck or frozen in some way. And here we can choose: to either pursue our inquiry or ignore it.

The Prelude

Stopping is often seen as counter-intuitive: as a weakness or a luxury that cannot be afforded. Stopping often feels contrary to the popular culture of go faster, be better, do more, hurtle on and hurry up – where efficiency, speed and instantaneous responses are prized over effectiveness. Stopping can be uncomfortable as it can strip us of the distractions we sometimes use to avoid deeper reflection. And stopping is also a radical act of self-care – as we cannot stop without giving ourselves both the permission and the time to do so. Stopping for David Whyte is a strategic withdrawal:[2]

> Withdrawal can be the very best way of stepping forward, and done well, a beautiful freeing act of mercy. Although withdrawal can look like a disappearance – withdrawal from entanglement can precede appearing back in the world in a very real way.

Reflection needs us to stop, to create the physical space for ourselves and the emotional, psychological and soulful space to explore. There we can tune out of the white noise and tune into what life is inviting us to work on. Here is why in the form of a Zen Kōan:[3]

Once, a long time ago, there was a wise Zen master. People from far and near would seek his counsel and ask for his wisdom. Many would come and ask him to teach them, enlighten them in the way of Zen. He seldom turned any away.

One day an important man, a man used to command and obedience, came to visit the master. 'I have come today to ask you to teach me about Zen. Open my mind to enlightenment.' The tone of the important man's voice was of one used to getting his own way. The Zen master smiled and said that they should discuss the matter over a cup of tea. When the tea was served the master poured his visitor a cup. He poured and he poured and the tea rose to the rim and began to spill over the table and finally onto the robes of the wealthy man. Finally the visitor shouted, 'Enough. You are spilling the tea all over. Can't you see the cup is full?' The master stopped pouring and smiled at his guest. 'You are like this teacup, so full that nothing more can be added. Come back to me when the cup is empty. Come back to me with an empty mind.'

There are many ways in which we can learn to stop. Here are six practices, which work for me.

Practice 1
Meditation: For Pausing, Grounding and Centring

Breathing Meditation is a key grounding and centring practice. I recommend that it is used – in a shorter or longer form – as the entry into all the other disciplines or practices. It has many forms and variations and can be adapted to suit your personal style and preferences.

For this Practice:

- Start by sitting in a comfortable upright posture

- Close your eyes (if that is comfortable for you)

- Rest the palms of your hands on your thighs

- Become aware of the ground or floor firmly beneath your feet

- Become aware of your hands on your thighs

- Become aware of your bottom on the chair

- Become aware of your spine, your shoulders, your neck and your chin which is tilting slightly towards your chest

- Become aware of your breath

- Follow each breath as you inhale and exhale

- Breathe in and out on the count of 2, then 3 and then 4

- Scan your body for any aches, pains or tensions
- Breathe into these areas
- Travel to your heart. Place the palms of your hands your heart
- Take 2 more deep breaths
- When you are ready return to the room

A pause gives you
breathing space
so listen
to the whispers
of the real you
waiting to happen.

Tara Estacaan[4]

Practice 2
Exercise: S.T.O.P.

Dr. Elisha Goldstein has developed the S.T.O.P. method. I have slightly adapted the approach for us.[5] For this Practice S.T.O.P. is a simple anagram for:

- Stopping
- Taking a breath
- Observing your experience (by checking in with your heart, mind, body and soul)

and then

- Proceeding by asking yourself what do I need to pay attention to right now?

Practice 3
Exercise: Setting Your Internal Thermometer

Your thermometer is a way of checking in with yourself to scan your energy and tiredness levels. For this practice:

- Start by visualizing your own thermometer or temperature gauge
- Decide on the optimum temperature for you where you are working in flow or at your best

- At intervals during the day scan your heart, mind, body and soul to see if you need to pause due to overheating, the start of feeling a little out of control, a confusion or tiredness

I use this practice regularly. I have made a commitment to myself that I will not make important decisions if I notice that my energy has dropped to below 80% at any point during the day.

Practice 4
Exercise: Stopping as a Diary Appointment

Time is energy. Your stopping cannot be outsourced! For this practice:

- Consciously diary in time at regular intervals over your day and/or over your week to intentionally stop, breathe and reflect

- Find your spaces and places, which inspire and support you

- Diary in shorter and longer times to work on more immediate and more strategic issues

- Set the intention to plan in time for a computer and social media detox!

Practice 5
Inquiry: What Do I Need to Stop Right Now?

Our hearts and our bodies know first. During Practice 1 or the longer meditations offered later invite yourself to notice:

- 'Where am I feeling tired or exhausted with myself, with others or what I am doing?'

- 'Where might I be feeling bored?'

- 'What is the conversation or conversations that I am having with myself and/or others that I need to stop?'

Practice 6
More Inspiration: Poetry Inviting Us to Stop

Poetry provides a language for bringing us home to ourselves. The famous poem by W. H. Davis called 'Leisure' is in praise of stopping.[6]

> What is this life if, full of care,
> We have no time to stand and stare.

No time to stand beneath the boughs
And stare as long as sheep or cows.

No time to see, when woods we pass,
Where squirrels hide their nuts in grass.

No time to see, in broad daylight,
Streams full of stars, like skies at night.

No time to turn at Beauty's glance,
And watch her feet, how they can dance.

No time to wait till her mouth can
Enrich that smile her eyes began.

A poor life this is if, full of care,
We have no time to stand and stare.

'The Gift Inside Us All (If We Did But Know It)' is a short poem I wrote to remind me to find my own oasis. I hope that it might help you to find yours.

Frantic and frenetic we risk crowding out the quiet knowing out of hearts, bodies and souls.

We stagger, we stumble and we lose our way,
When the answer lies in a simple no cost pause for breath,
A simple retreat to reflect and ponder,
To silence our inner professor, judge and jury.

A sacred place
Where we risk allowing ourselves to reconnect with our wise selves,
With the abundance of others and the generosity of our beautiful earth...
To then return to our own small lives that little bit more open,
That little bit more compassionate and
That little bit more creative.

Turn away from the phones, the computers, and the rush,
And find the quiet stillness inside you, which is always there
And which is your own secret garden,

Your private oasis,
Your beautiful sanctuary
And your wise guide as you go back out into the world.

The Opening Curtain:
Where Vulnerability Meets Self-Compassion

Vulnerability with self-compassion makes the dance possible.

Questioning makes us vulnerable and we cannot dance if we are not prepared to make ourselves vulnerable. Vulnerability like our love of learning and our innate creativity is at the core of our humanity. Vulnerability is not a weakness but our innate faculty for understanding life. The gifts of our not knowing and our imperfections are our doorways into making sense of our experiences.

The word 'vulnerability' comes from the Latin word 'to wound'. Half of life is about loss, disappearance and letting go. The only choice we have is whether to deny how life works – or embrace it. When we close ourselves off from our own vulnerabilities we also close ourselves off to the real conversations life is trying to have with us: we try to stem the pain and discomfort but in so doing we also risk closing ourselves off from compassion, connection and learning. For David Whyte vulnerability is not to be feared or shunned:[7]

> Vulnerability is not a weakness, a passing indisposition, or something that we can arrange to do without. Vulnerability is not a choice, vulnerability is the underlying, ever present and abiding undercurrent of our natural state. To run from vulnerability is to run from the essence of our nature; the attempt to be invulnerable is a vain attempt to become something we are not, and most especially to close ourselves off from our understanding of the grief of others.

For Brene Brown:[8]

> Owning our story can be hard but not nearly as difficult as spending our lives running from it. Embracing our vulnerabilities is risky but not nearly as dangerous as giving up on love and belonging and joy – the experiences that make us most vulnerable. Only when we are brave enough to explore the darkness will we discover the infinite power of light.

However, we need to meet our vulnerabilities with a generous and loving self-compassion to keep us in the dance, and to role model this for others. Our vulnerabilities without our self-compassion risk leaving us raw, exposed, frightened and stuck. Our self-compassion, without our vulnerabilities, risks leaving us complacent and blinded.

Self-compassion means giving ourselves kindness, acceptance and comfort within a secure base, which then grants us the courage to work with our own vulnerabilities and shadows without becoming swamped in criticism, blame, guilt or shame.

The eleven practices that follow are for Embracing our Vulnerabilities and Gifting Ourselves Self-Compassion.

Practice 7
Meditation: The Body Already Knows

This enables you to locate a wound inflicted on your younger self – which refuses to heal or grow older until it has spoken and been embraced. Learning to inhabit parts of our bodies, which are strange to us, helps us to access our own inner wisdom.

- Start with *Practice 1's* grounding and centring meditation.
- Settle into your body.
- When you are ready flow to the place where a vulnerability, a wound or trauma landed in your body.
- If you are feeling safe stay with it, feel it, touch it, see it, welcome it as a way back to healing.
- Journal or draw what you discovered and/or explore with a trusted practitioner.

Practice 8
Inquiry: Exploring Your Relationship with Vulnerability

Core questions for you to explore are:

- 'How do I choose to inhabit my vulnerabilities?'
- 'What is my relationship with my own vulnerabilities and those of the people I live and/or work with?'
- 'How do my vulnerabilities show up? How are they triggered? And what impact do they have on my daily and professional life?'
- 'How can I become a more generous citizen of loss?'
- 'How do I forgive myself and others?'

Practice 9
Reflection: Vulnerability as a Daily Practice

The rewards of vulnerability are embracing loss and also embracing joy, beauty, intimacy, creativity, wisdom and new ways of seeing, being and doing in our VUCA world. This practice invites you to design your life and work so that practising vulnerability becomes a daily exercise; and invites you to reflect on what this might look like and mean:

- for yourself
- for your work

- for your relationships
- for your contribution to the world

and

- for your legacy

Practice 10
More Inspiration: Poetry Inviting us into our Vulnerabilities

Here is a powerful invocation to embrace our vulnerabilities from Stephen Russell:[9]

> Vulnerability is the only authentic state. Being vulnerable means being open, for wounding, but also for pleasure. Being open to the wounds of life means also being open to the bounty and beauty. Don't mask or deny your vulnerability: it is your greatest asset. Be vulnerable: quake and shake in your boots with it. The new goodness that is coming to you, in the form of people, situations, and things can only come to you when you are vulnerable, i.e. open.

For Brene Brown:[10]

> Vulnerability is the birthplace of love, belonging, joy, courage, empathy, and creativity. It is the source of hope, empathy, accountability, and authenticity. If we want greater clarity in our purpose or deeper and more meaningful spiritual lives, vulnerability is the path.

Practice 11
Journaling: An Exercise in Self-Appreciation

This Self-Appreciation Exercise is a simple way of relating to what is good within ourselves. Everyone has aspects of themselves and their lives which are worthy of appreciation and which often get lost in the maelstrom of everyday life.

Self-Appreciation connects us to who we are – to ourselves and to all of life. Self-Appreciation is different to Self-Esteem in that Self-Esteem works to label and to separate us from each other by comparison and differentiation.

Write, draw or start a scrapbook to:

- Capture 10 things which you really like and appreciate about yourself
- As you write, draw or notice any discomfort you may be feeling. Inquire into this discomfort

and gently remind yourself that you are not looking to be 'perfect', 'better than...' or 'big headed' but want to appreciate and celebrate what is good in you.

- Use your meditation practice to help you to really own, appreciate and celebrate your own goodness.

- Return to your work over time and add to, or develop your list.

- Make your list your Talisman. Keep it in your bag. Take it with you as a reminder of WHO you truly are.

Practice 12
Exercise: The Criticizer, the Criticized and the Self-Compassionate Observer

This is an adaptation of the Three Chair Exercise from Gestalt Therapy. It is an exercise in listening to our Wise Compassionate Observer.

This practice invites you to set out three chairs or three mats in a triangle. If you are tight on space draw three circles in a triangle on a piece of paper.

Then:

- Think about an issue which is troubling you and often elicits harsh self-criticism.

- Designate one chair the Voice of Your Inner Critic; one chair as the Voice of the Part of You which Feels Judged and Criticized; and one chair as the Voice of your Wise Compassionate Observer.

- Go to the chair which represents the Voice of Your Inner Critic. Centre and ground yourself. Say out loud what the self-critical part of you is feeling and thinking. Notice the tone of your voice and the words you use. Notice also your feelings and what is going on in your body.

- Now go to the chair of your Criticized Self. Centre and ground yourself. Say out loud how you feel and what you think about being criticized, speaking directly to your Inner Critic. Again, notice the tone of your voice and the words you use. Notice also your feelings and what is going on in your body.

- Now conduct a conversation between Your Inner Critic and Criticized Self. Move between the chairs so that you embody the experience. Really try to experience each aspect of yourself so that each part of you knows how the other feels. Again, notice the tone of your voice and the words you use. Notice also your feelings and what is going on in your body.

- Now go to the Chair of the Wise Compassionate Observer. Centre and ground yourself. Call upon your deepest wisdom and intuition to speak to both the Inner Critic and Criticized Self. Allow your heart to soften. Speak with kindness, compassion, understanding and forgiveness. Again, notice the tone of your voice and the words you use. Notice also your feelings and what is going on in your body.

- Stop when you are complete. Centre and ground yourself. Step out of the exercise and identify any new insights you have gained. Reflect on your learning and set your intention to relate to yourself in kinder, healthier and happier ways in the future.

Practice 13
Inquiry: The Buddhist Arrow of Pain and Pleasure

The Buddhists teach that pain is inevitable but suffering is optional. They describe this using the metaphor of the Arrow (or *Sutta*) of Pain and Pleasure.

Physical pain and mental pain are differentiated. Physical pain is the first arrow and mental pain is the second arrow. Pain is an inevitable part of life. But when we want to deny, run away or escape from the first arrow of our pain, we create our own second arrow of mental suffering. Seeing this process as it happens and releasing ourselves from our own second arrow is an act of generous self-compassion. From whichever source it originates, pain is pain. The way we think about our pain turns pain into suffering. As for pain, so with pleasure. With a first arrow of a pleasurable experience we can inflict a second arrow of suffering by wanting to cling onto our pleasure whilst forgetting that all of life is impermanent.

This practice enables us to simply witness our pain (or our pleasure) by cultivating a patient, curious, and welcoming stance towards all that we experience. This equanimity is not a state of non-feeling but a state of freedom from habitual thoughts and blocks.

The steps are:

- Welcome your pain.

- Centre and ground yourself. Breathe deeply.

- Place your hand on your heart.

- Say to yourself, 'Everything is welcome.'

- Ask, 'How can I be with you (my pain) now?'

- Remember that the heart always welcomes 'what is' – and always has enough room to welcome all that is without criticism, attachment or judgement.

Practice 14
Exercise: Challenging Negativity and Isolation

Feeling unsure, vulnerable or negative at times is part of being human. Acknowledging how we are feeling, reconnecting to the human condition and asking ourselves what is now needed can remind us that we are not alone.

The steps for this Practice are saying to yourself and/or journaling:

1. 'It is hard to feel … right now.'
2. 'Feeling … is part of the human experience.'
3. 'What can I do to make myself happier in this moment?'

Practice 15
Exercise: Take a Self-Compassion Break!

Always remember that at any time you can push the pause button.

If you are feeling tired, stressed or uneasy you can always stop and take a break and do something which calms, inspires and/or relaxes you. Take a coffee, go for a walk, sit quietly, breathe, or pack your work away for another day.

Practice 16
Prayer: Serenity Prayer

The Serenity Prayer is a wonderful reminder to stay true to what we can and cannot change. Made famous by Alcoholics Anonymous, it reads:

> God grant me the serenity to accept things I cannot change,
> The courage to change the things I can,
> And the wisdom to know the difference.

Practice 17
More Inspiration: Poem for Self-Compassion

This beautiful poem by Mary Oliver called 'Wild Geese' reminds us that we do not need to be good.[11] We just need to be kind and true to ourselves.

You do not have to be good.
You do not have to walk on your knees
for a hundred miles through the desert, repenting.
You only have to let the soft animal of your body love what it loves.
Tell me about despair, yours, and I will tell you mine.

For Anna Quindlen:[12]

The thing that is really hard, and really amazing, is giving up on being perfect and beginning the work of becoming yourself.

Christopher K. Germer reminds us that:[13]

A moment of self compassion can change your entire day.
A string of such moments can change the course of your life.

* * * * *

Reflective Questions

Draw or journal your responses to the following questions:

Learning to Stop

1. On a scale of 0 – 10 where 0 is very poor and 10 is excellent how good are you at Stopping to properly reflect when you do not know what to do?

2. Which practice(s) for Stopping might work best for you? Do you have any other practices, which might work better for you?

Learning to Embrace Your Vulnerabilities

3. On a scale of 0 – 10 where 0 is very poor and 10 is excellent how good are you at Embracing Your Vulnerabilities?

4. Which practice(s) for Embracing Your Vulnerabilities might work best for you? Do you have any other practices, which might work better for you?

Giving Yourself the Gift of Self-Compassion

5. On a scale of 0 – 10 where 0 is very poor and 10 is excellent how good are you at Giving Yourself the Gift of Self-Compassion?

6. Which practice(s) for gifting yourself more self-compassion might work best for you? Do you have any other practices, which might work better for you?

Celebrating Your Progress

7. Revisit your responses as you work now and in the future with new questions so you can chart your progress.

The Opening
Retreat's Rest and Release

The Opening is the sequence designed to create the space within us (and our teams) to come into relational presence with ourselves, with others and with our world.

The Opening is a sequence of three dance steps, which are described in the next three chapters, and which should be considered together to help redirect attention and invite the opening of our hearts, minds, souls and bodies to receive new information from the field. The steps are designed to support and resource us to notice when we are 'in the grip' and how we can allow ourselves to open up to different ways of relating, thinking or doing.

These dance steps are

Step 1   Suspending Habits

Step 2   Seeing Anew

Step 3   Relating to the Whole

The Opening series is a necessary and conscious preparation for stepping into *The Flow* – Reflection's Fertile Void.

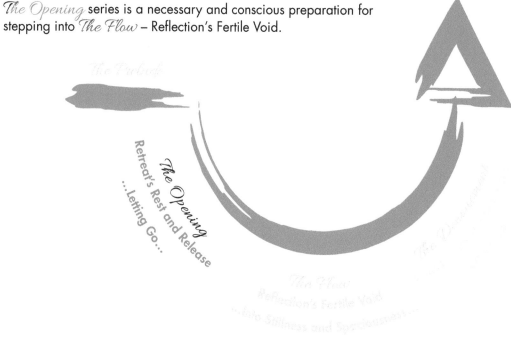

* Suspending Habits
* Seeing Anew
* Relating to the Whole

CHAPTER 5
Suspending Habits

While I dance I cannot judge, I cannot hate, I cannot separate myself from life. I can only be joyful and whole. That is why I dance.

Hans Bos[1]

The Prelude

The Opening
Retreat's Rest and Release
...Letting Go...

The Dénouement

The Flow
Reflection's Fertile Void
...Into Stillness and Spaciousness...

- **Suspending Habits**
  - Seeing Anew
  - Relating to the Whole
  - Initiating the Invitation
  - Art of Listening
  - Finding Freedom

This chapter presents the first of three 'dance steps' designed to help you find ways to let go of what no longer serves you in order to make the space for you to tune into what wants to emerge. For Jon Kabat-Zinn, letting go is a powerful inward manoeuvre to free ourselves. As he writes:[2]

Letting go is … a conscious decision to release with full acceptance into the stream of present moments as they are unfolding … to give up coercing, resisting, or struggling, in exchange for something more powerful and wholesome which comes out of allowing things to be as they are without getting caught up in your attraction to or rejection of them, in the intrinsic stickiness of wanting, liking and disliking. It is akin to letting your palm open to unhand something you have been holding.

Most of the time we are on auto-pilot. We are in the grip of impatient rush and hurry, drowning in a sea of data. We are ruled by routines, habitual mindsets, convenient assumptions, and patterns of behaviour. These have their place because they get us through the tasks of the day but they do not help us when we are faced with new, difficult or complex situations. We listen only to confirm what we think we already know. As Joshua Stone writes:[3]

We are not trapped by our thoughts.
What we generally do, however, is *create* thoughts that trap us.

To flow with the Reflect to *Create!* dance we must find ways to sidestep our scripts, our habits and our everyday selves. We need to find ways of recognizing when we are 'in the grip' in order free ourselves. We need to shift from the 'Me in It' frenetic isolation into a relational presence with others and with the wider system or whole, as well as with ourselves. The dictionary definition of 'Suspension' is: 'To keep in an undecided or inoperative state for a time, defer, temporarily annul, adjourn, or debar'.[4]

The first dance step of Suspending Habits can therefore be seen as a clearing of the ties that bind and a waking up to life. This is because, as David Wagoner wrote in his poem 'Lost', we are not lost but just need to rediscover ourselves.[5]

Stand still. The trees ahead and bushes beside you
Are not lost. Wherever you are is called Here,
And you must treat it as a powerful stranger,
Must ask permission to know it and be known.
The forest breathes. Listen. It answers,
I have made this place around you.
If you leave it, you may come back again, saying Here.
No two trees are the same to Raven.
No two branches are the same to Wren.
If what a tree or a bush does is lost on you,
You are surely lost. Stand still. The forest knows
Where you are. You must let it find you.

Practices for Suspending Habits

There are many ways in which we can start to free ourselves from the habitual thoughts, patterns and mindsets which inhibit, confine and trap us. The following twenty work for me and my practice.

Practice 18
Meditation: Body Scan for Noticing and Releasing Tension

This body scan meditation is a 40-minute guided mediation and is included in Week 1 of Jon Kabat-Zinn's eight-week Mindfulness Stress Reduction Programme (MSBR).

Many audio and Youtube downloads are available.[6]

How it works:

* The practice invites you to lay down on the floor with blankets and cushions to make sure you are comfortable.

* The practice opens with chimes.

* As the breath slows you are invited to bring systematic, intentional and open-hearted interest and curiosity to every part of your body.

* Starting with the toes on the left foot you breathe into the toes, sole, and top of the foot.

* You then move up the left leg from the ankle, to the shin, the knee and knee cap, to the thighs, the groin and left hip.

* From here you then move over to the toes on the right foot to repeat the sequence for the right foot, leg, thigh, groin and right hip.

* From here you move to the entirety of the pelvic region, including the hips again, the buttocks, the genitals, the lower back, and abdomen.

* From here you move to your upper torso – the upper back, the chest, ribs and the organs contained within the rib cage, the shoulder blades and then onto the collarbones and shoulders.

* From the shoulders you move to both arms, starting from the tips of the fingers and thumbs moving through each finger, the palms, the backs of the hands, the wrists, forearms, elbows, upper arms, armpits and returning to the shoulders again.

* Then you move to the neck, throat, and finally the face and head.

* Then you start to bring your awareness back to your surroundings.

- The practice finishes with chimes.

This healing meditation enables you to attend to and breathe into all of the different sensations you are experiencing in the different parts of your body. Holding the different sensations without judging or reacting to them lightens and frees us to differentiate the physical experience of discomfort, tension or pain from our emotions and thoughts. As Jon writes,[7] 'If you think of your body as a musical instrument, the body scan is a way of tuning it.'

Practice 19
Exercise: Stretches for Releasing Tension

The body keeps the score. By looking out for signs of tension and stress we can learn how to take early action to better support ourselves. Stretching can help to release tension. Here are a few examples of stretches that I always find useful and helpful. They are beautifully illustrated on www.wikihow.com.[8] However, listen to your body. Be gentle and never overextend. If you have any concerns seek medical advice. There are also many resources and books available on this. Choose what works for you.

- Neck tilts.
- Chin to chest stretches.
- Swinging arm stretch.
- Forward fold with the chest opening.
- Use a wall to do a standing neck stretch.
- Cobra pose to stretch and strengthen your neck muscles.
- Shoulder shrugs.
- Massage your trigger points.
- Use a foam roller to massage your neck muscles.
- Apply a heat pack to your aching muscles.
- Take a hot bath or shower.
- Plan in movement breaks and adjust your posture when sitting for a long time.

Practice 20
Exercise: Change Breath

If we are taken unaware by something that happens or is said, the Change Breath is a simple way that we can use to stop ourselves from unconsciously reacting to negativity or surprise. The Change Breath can be done anywhere. Here are the steps, which you can adapt wherever you are:

1. Straighten your back. Place the palm of your hand on your stomach if that is possible.

2. Take a slow deep breath in. As you do so visualize cleansing air entering your whole body. Pull the cleansing air down into your stomach. Feel your stomach expand outwards as this air circulates.

3. Then take a slow breath out. As you do so visualize any negativity or toxins leaving your body. Feel your stomach pull in as you exhale.

4. Repeat as many times as you need.

Practice 21
Exercise: Balancing Breath

When we are feeling under pressure for whatever reason the Balancing Breath is an easy technique, which brings us back to our calm centre. The Balancing Breath rebalances our energy and emotional systems.

Here is one way, which works for me. It may feel a little awkward at first but after a couple of attempts it will feel very natural. Find what works for you.

1. Place the thumb of your right hand on your right nostril.

2. Breathe in deeply and slowly through your left nostril. Send the breath through the whole of your body.

3. Hold your breath and close your left nostril with the third finger on your right hand.

4. Hold both nostrils closed for a few seconds.

5. When you are ready gently release the pressure of your thumb on your right nostril and breathe out slowly whilst keeping your left nostril closed with your third finger.

6. Take a deep breath through your right nostril, keeping your left nostril closed.

7. Hold both nostrils closed for a few seconds.

8. Open your left nostril and breathe out slowly.

9. Rest quietly taking a few deep breaths before continuing with your day.

Practice 22
Visualization: Seeing Thoughts and Emotions as Clouds

This visualization helps to remind us that we are not our thoughts or our emotions. It reminds us that we are not victims but are free to choose how we experience the world and the meaning that we might choose to attach to our experiences.

This is how the practice works:

- When you are next meditating or out exercising, picture your thoughts and emotions as fluffy clouds.

- Picture yourself as the vast blue openness of the sky. See the sky as you, your endless essence and your true self.

- As a thought or a feeling comes up, do not judge it. See the thought or feeling as simply 'just is' – as neither good nor bad.

- Simply put a name for the thought or feeling on a cloud and watch the cloud float away.

- As you do so remember that the clouds are not permanent. As the sky you are the backdrop to the clouds. Remember that you are free to choose whether or not you want to make your clouds dark and heavy so they block the sky, or light and fluffy so they float away.

Practice 23
Inquiry: Accepting the Inevitability of Change

For Jon Kabat-Zinn,[9] 'We can't stop the waves but we can learn to surf.'

Buddhism teaches us the three fundamental aspects of reality.[10] It teaches us that surrendering to these frees us to accept life as it is. Resisting these aspects leads to suffering. I work with these three Buddhist truths on a daily basis as part of my meditation practice.

The three aspects are:

1. Nothing exists that is permanent. Everything changes.

2. Nothing exists that is independent.

3. Nothing exists without a cause or reason.

The practice inquiry is:

- How might you surrender to these three aspects of reality?
- What might surrendering to these mean for you?

From the Yogi B. K. S. Iyengar we are reminded that:[11]

> Change is not something that we should fear.
> Rather, it is something that we should welcome. For without change, nothing in this world would ever grow or blossom, and no one in this world would ever move forward to become the person they're meant to be.

Practice 24
Inquiry: The Artificial Construct of a 'Self'

Buddhism also teaches the Four Noble Truths. The Four Noble Truths show us that suffering is caused by our grasping selves and that suffering starts to end when we realize that there is no self.

These Four Noble Truths are:[12]

First Noble Truth: Suffering is recognized as the actual state of our existence.

Second Noble Truth: Suffering's origins come from our grasping selves which cause us to behave selfishly.

Third Nobel Truth: Suffering ends when we realize that there is no self.

Fourth Noble Truth: Suffering ends as we start to cultivate the path of training the mind.

Buddha saw the consequences of our implementing the Four Noble Truths as being:

- We can overcome suffering to the extent that suffering is no more.
- We can eliminate the origins of suffering so that there is nothing to eliminate.
- We can actualize cessation so that there is no cessation.
- We can achieve the path to the point where there is no path to cultivate.

The practice inquiry is:

- How might you work with these Four Noble Truths?
- What might surrendering to these mean for you?

Practice 25
Visualization: Saying Goodbye to Your Baggage

There are many variations on this practice but here is the process that I follow:

- Begin by sitting comfortably with your back straight.
- Take three deep breaths.
- Feel your feet on the ground.
- Notice gently and without judgement whatever thought(s) or feeling(s) you are carrying (like anger, sadness, anxiety or tiredness).
- Allow yourself to just be.
- Now imagine holding out a beautiful golden bowl. Your bowl is your safe container.
- Allow yourself to give the bowl whatever thoughts and feelings are no longer serving you.
- Now see yourself saying goodbye and handing your bowl over to your God or to the One who forever loves you.
- Trust and believe that you can now let go and all can be well.

The metaphor of the bowl can be replaced by whatever metaphor or image works for you. Bags, suitcases and rucksacks work equally well! Sometimes writing your thoughts on paper and burning it in a safe place can also help.

A variation on this visualization is to give the bowl whatever thoughts or feelings are no longer serving you, to hand it over to your God or equivalent and then take back what is only yours.

Practice 26
Visualization: Surrender and Set Yourself Free

This visualization invites you to surrender whatever thought, feeling or situation is holding you hostage.

Play with the scenario by asking yourself:

- What would you feel like if you surrendered to this?
- What would happen?
- Spend 5 minutes dreaming of what your work or your life would be like if you did not have to worry about the outcome of the situation?

- What do you now need to do or how do you need to be with this situation now?
- What are your next steps?

Practice 27
Inquiry: Changing Your Storylines

We define ourselves by the stories we tell ourselves. The stories come from deep within us: our childhood memories, our unconscious scripts, and our own interpretation of what we see and experience. These stories can either confine us or set us free.

For this practice ask yourself:

- Am I boring myself with the stories I keep telling myself?
- Who would I be without that particular story or storyline?
- How would the story(ies) read if I was a faulty witness to my own story(ies)?
- How can I write a new chapter or design a different ending to my story(ies)?
- Which of my stories deserve and demand my immediate redrafting?

This is an extract from a poem Judy Brown wrote called, 'The Story That We Tell':[13]

The story that we tell
about what we must do
or be, or say,
deafens us to music
that is ours alone to play.

The story that is ours
to live completely
is a mystery to us –
because we are busy telling ourselves stories
that no longer fit –
until we wake one day
and see life with newly opened eyes,
full of surprise.

Practice 28
Exercise: Letting Go of What No Longer Serves

This reflective walking practice uses nature to help you let go. It was designed by PattersonPrenticeDesigns as part of the annual Autumn Equinox Retreat that we co-host at Tofte Manor in Bedfordshire.

This practice invites you find a garden, wood, field or mountain near you.

The steps are:

- Start by centring yourself. Take a few slow deep breaths. Feel the ground beneath your feet and take a 360° turn to absorb the natural world around you.

- Work with whatever question or inquiry comes to you. Take some time to feel your way into your inquiry. Journal it if you need.

- Now move to a spot which you feel offers you some insight into your inquiry.

- Here ask yourself *Question 1*:

  How do I face into/accommodate/be with loss?

Stay in that spot for about 15 to 20 minutes. Capture your insights in your journal. Photograph the spot, or pick up a stone or fallen twig or leaf to remind you of the spot. Notice what you leave behind.

- Now move to another spot. Here ask yourself *Question 2*:

  What does pruning and clearing mean for me?

Again journal, photograph the spot, or pick up a stone or a fallen leaf and twig from your spot.

- Now move to another spot. Here ask yourself *Question 3*:

  How do I find peace and ease with this/in this letting go? How might I welcome loss as a part of who I am and who I might be becoming?

Again journal, photograph the spot, or pick up a stone or a fallen leaf and twig from your spot.

- Now move to another spot. Here ask yourself *Question 4*:

  How could I respond creatively to what I have just explored and discovered in questions 1–3? How can I hold onto this so that it can enrich me and sow the seed(s) for the future?

Again journal, photograph the spot, or pick up a stone or a fallen leaf and twig from your spot.

- Rest a while in a beautiful spot.

Practice 29
Inquiry: Is Your Cup Half Full or Half Empty?

This practice encourages us to understand that our perceptions become our reality; that in our translation of events we can exercise a conscious choice.

As Shakespeare's Hamlet says to Rosencrantz in Act 2 Scene 2 of *Hamlet*,[14] 'Why, then, 'tis none to you, for there is nothing either good or bad, but thinking makes it so. To me it is a prison.'

For one anonymous writer, 'Life is not about waiting for the storm to pass, it's about learning how to dance in the rain.'

This practice:

- Invites you to stop when you feel you might be becoming negative for whatever reason.
- Reflect in the moment.
- Ask yourself, 'How am I choosing to interpret this?'
- Then ask yourself 'What else is possible?'

Practice 30
Inquiry: Understanding our Transactional Analysis Drivers

Transactional Analysis (TA) is one branch of modern psychology which studies the psychology of human relationships.

TA was first developed by the psychiatrist Dr. Eric Berne.[15] Eric developed his own observable ego states of Parent, Adult and Child, which reflect an entire system of thoughts, feelings and behaviours. Eric argued that these ego states get expressed as 'transactions' between people and are the fundamental units of social communication, interaction and relationship. TA is the study of these interactions in order to support the development of healthier relationships.

This practice explores the part of TA which describes our five unconscious Drivers. These Drivers are overplayed strengths. Awareness of our Drivers can help us to recognize when we might be in their grip and develop our own approaches, which can bring us back into balance.

Our TA drivers are: the 'Be Strong!' Driver; the 'Be Perfect!' Driver; the 'Please Others!' Driver; the 'Hurry up' Driver; and the 'Try Hard!' Driver. In essence, their overplayed strengths are:

- For the Be Strong! Driver: 'don't show your vulnerability' and 'don't ask for help'.

- For the Be Perfect! Driver: 'don't make mistakes' and 'don't take risks'.

- For the Please Others! Driver: 'don't be assertive' and 'don't stay no'.

- For the Hurry up! Driver 'don't relax' 'don't take too long or waste time'.

and

- For the Try Hard! Driver 'don't give up' and 'don't ever be satisfied'.

For this practice:

- Firstly breathe deeply to ground and centre yourself.

- Decide which Driver or Drivers you might automatically default to when you are under stress for whatever reason.

- Breathe deeply again. Be kind to yourself. Remember that your default is an overplayed strength, which is triggered by certain situations or contexts.

- Now draw two columns. Label the left-hand column 'How this Driver Serves Me' and right-hand column 'How this Driver Does Not Serve Me'. Fill out the columns.

- Breathe deeply again.

- From here, gently remember the physical sensations you first feel in your body when you are being triggered. Journal what you notice.

- Breathe deeply again.

- Now journal your different ways that you can be with this Driver.

- Practice, practice, practice…!!

Practice 31
Inquiry: Understanding Your Judgement, Cynicism and Fear Blocks

Joseph Jaworski in his inspirational book *Synchronicity – The Inner Path to Leadership* talks of his own odyssey in the wilderness.[16] Here he gives a personal account of facing into the three key blocks to our learning.

These are:

- Voices of Judgement
- Voices of Cynicism

and

- Voices of Fear

They were first described in a book which he co-authored called *Presence – Exploring Profound Change in People, Organisations, and Systems.*[17]

When they are triggered:

- The Voice of Judgement closes down our minds to new insights, ideas and thoughts
- The Voice of Cynicism closes down our hearts to love, vulnerability and compassion
- The Voice of Fear closes down our ability and our will to take action

For this practice:

- Firstly, breathe deeply to ground and centre yourself.
- Decide which of the three Voices is the loudest, most persistent or most easily triggered in you, when, where and how. Expand or find other words to describe 'Judgement', 'Cynicism' and 'Fear' which might work better for you.
- Breathe deeply again.
- Now in your journal draw or describe what this Voice looks and feels like for you and when it wants to speak.
- Breathe deeply again. Remember to be kind to yourself. Remember that we are all human.
- Now draw two columns. Label the left-hand column 'How this Voice Serves Me' and right-hand column 'How this Voice Does Not Serve Me'. Fill out the columns.

- Breathe deeply again.
- From here, gently reconnect with the physical sensations you first feel in your body when this Voice wants to speak. Journal what you notice.
- Breathe deeply again.
- Now journal the different ways that you can be with this Voice.
- Practice, practice, practice....!!

You may want to repeat this practice for the other two Voices to really understand your resistors, how they show up and how you want to work with them.

Practice 32
Inquiry: Lessons from Cognitive Behavioural Therapy

This practice borrows from the ABCDE mnemonic from Cognitive Behavoural Therapy (CBT) to suspend and reframe negative self-talk with more realistic and adapted self-talk. CBT is a solution-focused talking therapy for rational, emotional and behavioural adaptation.[18]

To use this practice:

- Firstly, breathe deeply to ground and centre yourself.
- Now choose your A: The Activating Event. This is an issue, a conversation, a behaviour or a relationship which is troubling you.
- Take a Change Breath.
- Now look to your B: Your Belief System. Journal asking yourself 'What are the thoughts and beliefs that underpin my reaction to x?' Do not judge your beliefs.
- Take a Change Breath.
- Then go on to examine your C: The Emotional Consequences of A and B. Journal asking yourself 'What the emotional consequences and impacts of my current thinking?'
- Take a Change Breath.
- Now move to your D: Disputing Your Irrational Beliefs. Journal asking yourself 'What other more realistic, adaptive and helpful thoughts and beliefs might exist here?'
- Take a Change Breath.
- Finally move to your E: The Effects of Changing Your Interpretation of Events. Journal asking yourself 'With D. what might now be possible?'

Practice 33
Inquiry: See Challenges as Opportunities for Learning

Pema Chodron invites us to see our challenges as our greatest teachers.[19] As she writes:

> Feelings like disappointment, embarrassment, irritation, resentment, anger, jealousy, and fear, instead of being bad news, are actually very clear moments that teach us where it is that we're holding back. They teach us to perk up and lean in when we feel we'd rather collapse and back away. They're like messengers that show us, with terrifying clarity, exactly where we're stuck. This very moment is the perfect teacher, and, lucky for us, it's with us wherever we are.

For this practice:

- Firstly breathe deeply to ground, centre and calm yourself.

- Bring to mind something that went less well that you had hoped, did not go as planned or where you feel you were not your best.

- Visualize yourself wrapping your inquiry in beautiful wrapping paper. Visualize your inquiry as a loving gift to yourself.

- Breathe deeply again to calm and centre yourself.

- With loving self-compassion ask yourself:

  ○ 'What went well?'

  ○ 'What went less well?'

  ○ 'What is mine/my responsibility here?'

  ○ 'What do I need to own?'

  ○ 'What is my learning?'

  ○ 'How may I repair, sort or remedy if this is appropriate?'

  and

  ○ 'How will I behave next time?'

- When you are ready, acknowledge the gift you have given to yourself. If it feels right wrap it up again and hand it back to the Universe in your golden bowl or suitcase from Practice 25.

As Winston Churchill put it,[20] 'Success is the ability to go from failure to failure without losing your enthusiasm.'

Practice 34
Meditation: Awakening Your Heart

Fear makes us want to protect ourselves and our hearts. This is a practice called 'tonglen' which is described by Pema Chodron in her book *Start Where You Are: A Guide to Compassionate Living*.[21]

To do this practice:

- Sit comfortably. Breathe slowly and deeply. Centre yourself.

- When you are ready, with your next in-breath imagine that you are breathing in a texture which is hot, heavy and dark.

- With the next out-breath imagine that you are breathing out a texture that is cool, light and white.

- Repeat this pattern until you have developed a calm synchronized rhythm.

- Then when you are ready breathe in whatever is troubling you without analysis or judgement along with the imaginary texture, which is hot, heavy and dark.

- Then with the next out-breath breathe out a sense of kindness, spaciousness and clarity along with your texture, which is cool, light and white.

- Repeat this pattern until you feel a dilution or dispersal of whatever was troubling you.

- Extend a wish that others similarly troubled find ease and peace. Keep extending your net of compassion to include as many people as you comfortably can.

Practice 35
Prayer: Forgiveness Prayer

Forgiving ourselves and others sets us free. Forgiveness releases us from the past, freeing us to move on with our lives.

For this practice:

- See self-forgiveness and your forgiveness of others as a gift to yourself.

- Give yourself the opportunity to express how you feel. Write a letter to yourself.

- Write down how you experienced that which you want to forgive.

- Write down the impact of holding onto your anxieties, worries, resentments, guilt, shame or anger.

- Own what has happened.

- Reflect to extract the learning.

- Repair what needs repairing.

- When you are ready, move on by safely burning your letters and returning the ashes to the earth.

- Say a Forgiveness Prayer to yourself as you do so. This one is adapted from Jackee Holder's book *Soul Purpose*[22] but there are many available on the internet:

I am released from fear,
I let go of bad feelings and resentments about myself and about others.
I return to love myself, and others, who are also human.
We are all learning all of the time. Learning means that we can all trip up and
make mistakes from time to time.
I am now free to explore and reach my highest potential.
I am now free to be my best self.

- If you notice that shadows remain remember to be kind to yourself and repeat the practice when you feel ready.

Practices of forgiveness are acts of self-compassion and compassion for others. Our capacity to forgive grows through generosity and practice.

For the poet Alexander Pope,[23] 'To err is human, to forgive, divine.'

Practice 36
Exercise: Looking After Your Health and Wellbeing

I have found that surrendering is easier for me if I am rested, relaxed, fit and healthy. I have realized that the practice of surrendering can use up huge reserves of physical, emotional, intellectual and spiritual energy. This means that paying attention to and acting on what your body needs is critically important to avoiding sub-optimal health and burnout. As 1 Corinthians 6:19-20 has it,[24] our bodies are our temples. When we respect and treat our bodies as temples we obtain physical, emotional, intellectual and spiritual blessings.

For B. K. S. Iyengar:[25]

Look after the root of the tree, and the fragrant flower and luscious fruits will grow by themselves. Look after the health of the body, and the fragrance of the mind and richness of the spirit will follow.

Buddha said,[26] 'To keep the body in good health is a duty, otherwise we shall not be able to keep our mind strong and clear.'

For this practice, review your current balance of work, rest and play:

- Centre and calm yourself
- Complete an audit of your wheel of life. Rate yourself from 0 to 10 where 0 is under-supported and 10 is fulfilled under the following headings:
  - Health, Fitness and Exercise
  - Fun and Leisure
  - Family and Friends
  - Support networks
  - Learning
  - Spirituality
  - Work and Career
  - Finances

This exercise works best if you do not overthink it. Just go with your gut instinct. Adapt the headings for you. Please note that there are many online tools. Find one that works for you.

- Against each score write down your reasons for your score.
- Decide what actions are needed if you want to either maintain or shift your scores up or down.
- Check in regularly with your progress.
- Rescore yourself every quarter to chart your progress. Be kind and patient with yourself.

Practice 37
More Inspiration: Encouraging You to Suspend Your Habits

Here are some inspirational quotes and poems to support you in your surrendering and letting go. Brene Brown reminds us:[27]

Shame, blame, disrespect, betrayal, and the withholding of affection damage the roots from which love grows. Love can only survive these injuries if they are acknowledged, healed and rare.

As Rumi the 13th-century mystic wrote:[28]

> Beyond our ideas of right-doing and wrong-doing,
> there is a field. I'll meet you there.
> When the soul lies down in that grass,
> the world is too full to talk about.
> Ideas, language, even the phrase 'each other'
> doesn't make sense any more.

John O'Donohue extends hopefulness in this extract from his poem 'A Blessing for One Who Is Exhausted':[29]

> You have been forced to enter empty time.
> The desire that drove you has relinquished.
> There is nothing else to do now but rest
> And patiently learn to receive the self
> You have forsaken for the race of days.

Finally, David Whyte reminds us in an extract from his poem 'What to Remember When Waking' that:[30]

> You are not a troubled guest on this earth,
> you are not an accident amidst other accidents
> you were invited from another and greater night
> than the one from which you have just emerged.
>
> Now, looking through the slanting light of the morning window
> toward the mountain presence of everything that can be
> what urgency calls you to your one love?
> What shape waits in the seed of you
> to grow and spread its branches
> against a future sky?

* * * * *

Reflective Questions

1. What are your reflections from reading this chapter?
2. Which of the twenty practices are you most drawn to and why?
3. Which of the twenty practices are you least drawn to and why?
4. What are you going to action now?

5 SUSPENDING HABITS

CHAPTER 6

Seeing Anew

The Opening

Originality is simply a pair of fresh eyes

Thomas W. Higginton[1]

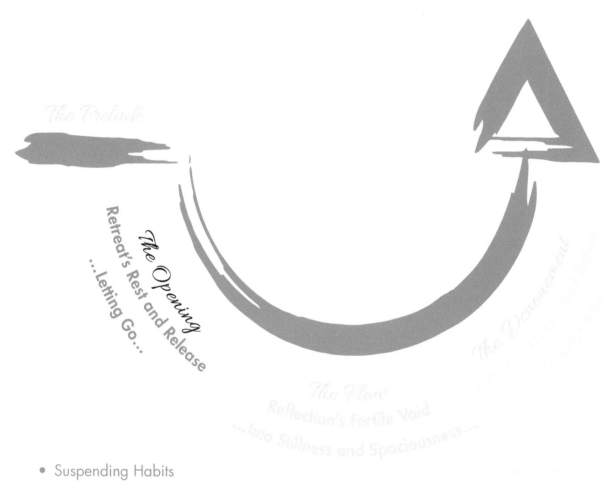

The Prelude

The Opening
Retreat's Rest and Release
...Letting Go...

The Flow
Reflection's Fertile Void
...Into Stillness and Spaciousness...

The Dénouement

- Suspending Habits
- **Seeing Anew**
- Relating to the Whole

- Initiating the Invitation
- Art of Listening
- Finding Freedom

Seeing anew is all about learning how to be fully present, awake and alive in the moment with 'what is'. The practices for Seeing Anew help us to wake up our senses to get in touch with what we are seeing, sensing and noticing. Seeing Anew helps us to fine-tune our whole-body powers of observation and to notice our noticing as we explore WHO we are in the world and HOW our world can support, inspire, resource and sustain us.

When we allow ourselves to gently notice the world within us and around us we start to sense a shift within us. Our busy minds are quieted for a fresher, more innocent intimacy with raw experience. This is the opening – or refinement – of our faculties for wonder, curiosity, grace and humility as we observe a broadening reality for ourselves in life, work and in the world. From here we start to redirect our attention from 'I in It' to 'Me and Us in This'. Seeing Anew helps us to see ourselves not as, in David Whyte's words, 'troubled guests in this world',[2] but as inheritors of a natural abundance which can help to inspire, guide and resource us as we navigate life's ebbs and flows. Seeing Anew helps redirect our attention away from our heads and into a more heart-based and soulful way of relating to life. In his poem 'Everything is Waiting for You', David reminds us that,[3] '(Our) great mistake is to act as if (we) are alone' and 'to feel abandoned is to deny the intimacy of your surroundings.'

For John Welwood:[4]

> Magic is a sudden opening of the mind to the wonder of existence. It is a sense that there is much more to life than we usually recognize; that we do not have to be confined by the limited views that our family, our society, or our own habitual thoughts impose on us; that life contains many dimensions, depths, textures, and meanings extending far beyond our familiar beliefs and concepts.

Alertness is the hidden discipline of familiarity and complacency. In the last verse of his poem 'For the Senses' John O'Donohue asks:[5]

> May your soul beautify
> The desire of your eyes
> That you might glimpse
> The infinity that hides
> In the simple sights
> That seem worn
> To your usual eyes.

Practices for Seeing Anew

The practices for Seeing Anew help us to see and experience the world from new and different sources and perspectives. Here are twenty which work for me and my practice.

Practice 38
Exercise: For Being Fully Present Now

John Welwood described Presence as[6] 'the capacity to meet experience fully and directly without filtering it through any conceptual or strategic agenda.' As he explains:

> At any moment, whatever we are experiencing, only one of two things is ever happening: either we are being with what is, or else we are resisting what is. Being with what is means letting ourselves have and feel our experience, just as it is right now. ... This is where genuine creativity, health, and communication, as well as spiritual power, arise from.

For Seneca the Younger, a Roman philosopher and statesman,[7] 'To be everywhere is to be nowhere.'

This practice helps us to cultivate the art of being. To quote again from John Welwood:[8]

> Forget about enlightenment. Sit down wherever you are and listen to the wind that is singing in your veins. Feel the love, the longing and the fear in your bones. Open your heart to who you are, right now, not who you would like to be. Not the saint you're striving to become. But the being right here before you, inside you, around you. All of you is holy. You're already more and less than whatever you can know. Breathe out, look in, let go.

This three-step exercise brings us into the present moment.

* Breathe deeply, ground and centre yourself

* Hold yourself with dignity

* First Step: 'Acknowledging What Is.'

  When you are ready ask yourself:

  'What is going with me in this present moment?'

  With loving kindness notice, acknowledge and welcome your experience in this moment at this time. Accept all that you are experiencing from your heart, body, mind and soul. Stay with whatever you are experiencing for a few moments.

* Second Step: 'Gathering In.'

Now gently focus all your attention on your breathing. Experience each in-breath and out-breath as they follow one after the other, helping you to anchor and still yourself. Feel a gentle body mind coherence and alignment sweep through your body.

- Third Step: 'Expanding Awareness.'

Now expand your awareness of your whole body breathing and tune into an awareness of the space around you.

An ancient Buddhist proverb invokes us: 'Don't just do something, sit there!'

Practice 39
Exercise: Listening to Our Felt Sense

The practice of Focusing was developed by the philosopher and psychologist Eugene Gendlin, in collaboration with his friend and colleague Carl Rogers.[9]

Eugene discovered that by learning to listen to our bodies we can tune into our innate wisdom – and thereby bypass our habitual ways of seeing. Eugene called this listening 'felt sense' or 'self-in-presence'. For Eugene:[10]

> Our bodies do our living... Our bodies don't lurk in isolation behind the five peepholes of perception... we act from the bodily sense of each situation. Without the bodily sense of the situation we would not know where we are, or what we are doing.

Here are the key stages for Focusing, which have been adapted from the work of Barbara McGavin and Ann Weiser Cornell:[11]

1. Breathe deeply, ground and centre yourself.

2. **Settling**

   Bring awareness into your body, moving from your periphery to settling at your centre.

3. **The Invitation**

   From your centre give yourself the time and space to notice what is wanting your awareness now. Possibly ask yourself 'I am wondering what is wanting my attention right now?' Or if you have a particular issue ask yourself 'I am wondering what is wanting my attention right now about this issue?'

4. **The Arrival**

   Now wait until something comes into your awareness.

5. **Shaping**

When something arrives, sense it in your body. Gently describe it using words, metaphors, images or gestures. Then check back in with how your body is feeling and ask it 'does this fit you well?'

6. **Befriending**

Take time to acknowledge it, befriend it and settle with it.

7. **Acknowledgement**

Now take time to sense how it is feeling – its mood, its emotion, how it feels itself. Let it know that you are listening and that you understand. Notice if it feels understood and if there is more to say. Stay here for as long as it and you need and then sense for a stopping place.

8. **Allowing**

Now receive and experience what has changed in your body.

9. **Appreciation**

Let it know you are willing to return.

Thank your body for what has come and return.

Practice 40
Inspiration: Your Artist Date

Julia Cameron in her bestselling book *The Artist's Way* coined the phrase 'the Artist Date'.[12] Julia describes the Artist Date as:[13]

A block of time, perhaps two hours weekly, especially set aside and committed to nurturing your creative consciousness, your inner artist ... Because in order to create we draw from our inner well ... and the Artist Date restocks that well...

For this practice adapt the concept of the Artist Date in a way which works for you. The root of the word 'inspire' is 'to breath in, to infuse'.[14] An Artist Date is an infusion of inspiration to counter the tyrannies of our daily to-do lists. Therefore:

- When you are quiet and still ask yourself 'What inspires me?' and 'Where are the places I would like to visit? Which activities I would like to do and/or people I would like to be with to feed my creative soul?'

- In your journal write down your own personal inspiration list. It can include anything, for example, music, arts, nature, exercise, films, theatre, holidays, pamper days, reading, any creative pursuit or other hobby, or group or community work.

- Schedule in at least two hours a week where you make time for you.

Practice 41
Exercise: Practising Gratitude

There is much that we take for granted. The practice of gratitude helps us to pay attention to the abundance in our lives – the joy and privilege of being alive right here right now: the kindness and generosity that we receive, the people we meet, the difference we can make to others, the pleasures that we enjoy and the beauty which surrounds us. Gratitude connects us to our own joys and the joys of others. For Eckhart Tolle,[15] 'Acknowledging the good that you already have in your life is the foundation for all abundance.'

To quote from John Welwood:[16]

> We already have so much abundance. We truly do. We need not search too far. It is within. The reason we fail to recognize this is because we haven't quite mastered the art of being. For abundance to prevail, we must have LOVE, gratitude, acceptance.

This practice is about noticing, appreciating, acknowledging and giving thanks.

- Make a vow to bring gratitude into everything you do.
- Tune into your senses. Wholeheartedly notice what you are noticing and take moments out of your daily life to express your thanks.
- Start a daily or weekly Gratitude Journal recording and giving thanks for all that you have received. Capture 5 things you are grateful for at each entry. Ask yourself, 'What have I received?' and 'What have I given to … ?'

Practice 42
Exercise: Waking Up the Senses!

In our busyness we forget to slow down and savour. Our senses are so important because, as Dejan Stojanovic reminds us,[17] 'Senses empower limitations, … senses expand vision within borders, … senses promote understanding through pleasure.'

- Choose an activity that you enjoy. This could be anything sensual like enjoying a view, drinking a glass of wine, cooking or eating a meal, gardening or walking.

- Breathe deeply and ground yourself.

- Now ask your eyes, 'What do you see?' Pay careful attention to your noticing.

- Now ask your ears, 'What do you hear?' Pay careful attention to your noticing.

- Now touch, 'What do you feel?' or 'What do you imagine this would feel like?' Pay careful attention to your noticing.

- Now ask your nose, 'What do you smell?' Pay careful attention to your noticing.

- Now move to your taste buds, 'What do you taste?' Pay careful attention to your noticing.

- Reflect on what you have discovered. Journal your findings.

Practice 43
Exercise: Noticing Our Noticing

Our vision can become blurred and myopic. This practice uses the metaphor of the aperture within a camera lens for us to practise what we are seeing and not seeing and can be applied to the workplace.

For example:

- What we are choosing to both focus in on and ignore?

- What we are choosing to zoom in and out of?

and

- What is in our foreground and background?

For this practice, next time you are out with your camera or are using your camera on your phone:

- Select a landscape, object, person or picture.

- Experiment with the different apertures and focus.

- Notice what you notice.

This is important because, as Arthur Schopenhauer wrote,[18] 'Every man or woman takes the limits of his own field of vision for the limits of the world.'

Practice 44
Exercise: Seeing Our Seeing

For Anais Nin,[19] 'We don't see things as they are, we see them as we are.'

Seeing our seeing is crucial to understanding how we learn. This practice was developed as part of the Coaching Supervision Academy's teaching on its Diploma course.[20] This practice helps us notice to where our attention goes and how we accept or judge what we see. This can either be done alone or in pairs. You will need a hand mirror each for this exercise.

- Make yourself comfortable on a chair. If you are working with a partner sit opposite each other.

- Firstly, look at yourself in your hand mirror. Move the mirror around so that you get a look at different angles and different perspectives of yourself.

- Notice what you notice. For example: 'What tone of voice are you using to yourself?', 'Are you at feeling at ease or feeling uncomfortable with the exercise?', or 'What bits of you do you like or want to turn away from?'

- If you are working with a partner turn your mirror to the other and show them different angles or perspectives of themselves.

- Reflect on your own or together if you are in pairs: 'What was the exercise like for you?', 'What did it bring up for you?', 'Where or what do you default to?' or 'What did you notice that was new for you?'

For Henry David Thoreau,[21] 'It's not what you look at that matters, it's what you see.'

Practice 45
Exercise: Seeing Our Listening

Zeno of Citium – the founder the Stoic School of Philosophy in Athens in 300 BC – reminds us that[22], 'We have two ears and one mouth, so we should listen more than we talk.'

This and the following practice are therefore best considered together. WHO we are is HOW we listen. This practice invites us to pay attention to WHO we are being as we listen to ourselves, others and what life is asking of us. This is because the quality of our listening will determine the quality of our seeing.

Otto Scharmer[23] has identified four fields of listening, which define the quality of the listening. I have adapted some of his terms to better suit the Reflect to *Create!* dance map whilst honouring his schema. The four fields or levels of listening are as follows and can apply whether we are listening to ourselves or to others:

1. **Field 1 Listening – Listening to Download**

   Here we listen from our closed minds and from an 'I in It' position to confirm what we think we already know. Field 1 is a connection to the past.

2. **Field 2 Listening – Listening to Differentiate**

   Here we listen from our opening minds and from an 'I in It' position to disconfirm what we thought we already knew. Field 2 is a connection to facts and evidence.

3. **Field 3 Listening – Listening to Empathize**

   Here we listen from our open hearts from an 'I in Thou' position to feel and see what another person might be feeling and seeing. Field 3 is a connection to people and relationships.

4. **Field 4 Listening – Listening to** *Create!*

   Here we listen from our souls and from a position of 'I in Now' and 'We and Us' to connect to the emerging field of possibility which is explored in the next chapter, 'Relating to the Whole'.

Fig 1: Fields of Listening

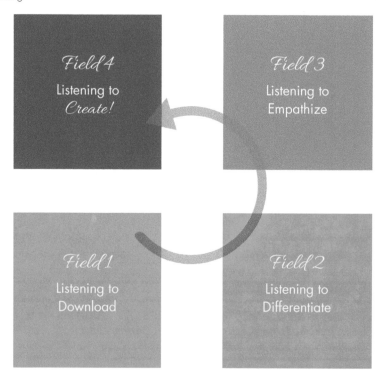

This practice invites you to inquire into the nature and quality of your listening.

The steps are:

- Ask yourself 'WHO am I being being as I listen?' from moment to moment, and from conversation to conversation.

- Ask yourself:

  o 'Which field or level of listening do I routinely operate from?'

  o 'What proportion of time do I spend listening from the different fields in a day?'

  and

  o 'What is making this so?'

Journal, draw or mind map what you are noticing.

- Ask yourself:

  o 'What am I noticing from my analysis?'

  o 'What impact is this having on me and on others around me?'

  and

  o 'What are my results from here?'

Journal, draw or mind map what you are noticing.

- Ask yourself 'What if anything do I want to change from this analysis?'

- Invite yourself to consider 'What disciplines or practices would help me to create the biggest shift in myself and for me here?'

For Alfred Benjamin:[24]

> Genuine listening is hard work; there is little about it that is mechanical… We hear with our ears, but we listen with our eyes and mind and heart and skin and guts as well.

Practice 46
Exercise: Seeing Ourselves in Conversation

Conversations are combinations of words, spaces and silences, which contain energy. Words, spaces and silences can either bring alive or deaden what we see.

Conversations contain the potential to move beyond the superficial everyday into the generative and transformative.

Therefore, seeing ourselves in our conversations – 'WHO we are being as we talk' – through our choice of words, tone, pace, delivery, connection and presence, will determine our capacity to create the relationships and the conversations which can bring forth the new.

Otto Sharmer has defined four fields of conversation which define the quality of the conversation. These also correlate to the four fields of listening from Practice 45. I have adapted some of Otto's terms to better suit the Reflect to *Create!* dance map whilst honouring his schema.[25]

Practices 45 and 46 are very closely linked because WHO you are being as you listen informs WHO you are being as you talk. The quality of our listening correlates with the quality of our conversations. All great conversations come from great listening.

The four fields of conversation are as follows and can apply whether we are conversing with ourselves or with others:

1. **Field 1 Conversations** – Conversing to Download and Maintain

   Here we converse from a collective autopilot. Niceness, politeness and routines are used to maintain the collective status quo. Listening is primarily from the head. The conversational stance is advocacy over inquiry. The silences can be awkward.

2. **Field 2 Conversations** – Conversing to Differentiate and Debate

   Here we converse to understand individual differences and defend individual positions. Listening is primarily from the head. The conversational stance is advocacy over inquiry. The silences can be tense.

3. **Field 3 Conversations** – Conversing to Inquire

   Here we converse to pursue individual curiosity, inquiry, learning and understanding. Listening is primarily from the heart. The conversational stance is inquiry over advocacy. The silences are contemplative and respectful.

4. **Field 4 Conversations** – Conversing to *Create!*

   Here we converse to collectively create and generate new insights and new wisdom. Listening is primarily from the soul or source. The conversational stance is inquiry over advocacy. Silences are profound.

Fig 2: Fields of Conversation

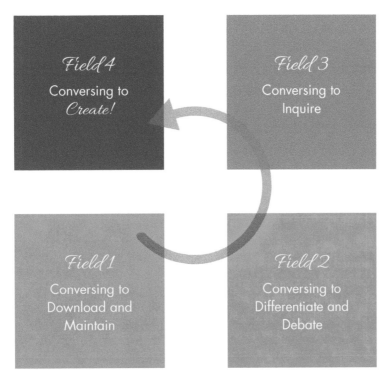

Practice 46 invites you to inquire into the nature and quality of your conversations. The steps are:

- Ask yourself, WHO am I being as I talk? from moment to moment, and from conversation to conversation.

- Ask yourself:

  ○ Which field of conversation do I routinely operate from?

  ○ What is the split of time spent listening from the different fields in a typical day for me?

and

  ○ What is making this so?

Journal, draw or mind map what you are noticing.

- Ask yourself:

- What am I noticing from my analysis?

- What impact is this having on me and on others around me?

and

- What are my results from here?

Journal, draw or mind map what you are noticing.

- Ask yourself, 'What if anything do I want to change from this analysis?'

- Invite yourself to consider 'What disciplines or practices would help me to create the biggest shift in me and for me here?'

Conversations as the crucible for change are further explored in the chapter on Supervision. Here is Stephen Hawking on why we need to learn how to hold generative conversations:[26]

> For millions of years, mankind lived just like the animals. Then something happened which unleashed the power of our imagination. We learned to talk and we learned to listen. Speech has allowed the communication of ideas, enabling human beings to work together to build the impossible. Mankind's greatest achievements have come about by talking, and its greatest failures by not talking. It doesn't have to be like this. Our greatest hopes could become reality in the future. With the technology at our disposal, the possibilities are unbounded. All we need to do is make sure we keep talking.

Practice 47
Reflection: Seeing the Power of Words to Shape Our Worlds

Words convey units of meaning and energy, which shape and create us. For Yehuda Berg[27]:

> Words are singularly the most powerful force available to humanity. We can choose to use this force constructively with words of encouragement, or destructively using words of despair. Words have energy and power with the ability to help, to heal, to hinder, to hurt, to harm, to humiliate and to humble.

The limits of our words and our language can limit our seeing. The words we use with and towards ourselves and also with others can imprison or free ourselves to see anew. Words like 'should' and 'must' imprison us. Words become sentences, which become thoughts that can close us down to other ways of seeing. David Whyte also cautions against naming what we see too early, lest we kill off our more subtle noticings. As he writes:[28]

> We can never know in the beginning, in giving ourselves to a person, to a work, to a marriage or to a

cause, exactly what kind of love we are involved in. Most of our heartbreak comes from attempting to name who or what we love and the way we love, too early in the vulnerable journey of discovery.

For this practice:

- Start to notice minute by minute the words or phrases you are using and the tone in which you are talking with yourself and with others. Even try recording yourself.

- Capture these in a journal or notebook.

- Notice what you are noticing. Ask yourself:

  - What are my patterns?

  - What are my triggers when I might move into my Voices of Judgement, Criticism, Comparison or Cynicism rather than my Voices of constructive Generosity, Abundance, and Creativity?

  - What impact are my patterns having on myself and on others?

- Invite yourself to find other words or phrases which might better match your intention.

As Gustave Flaubert wrote in Madame Bovary:[29]

Human speech is like a cracked kettle on which we tap crude rhythms for bears to dance to, while we long to make music that will melt the stars.

Practice 48
Reflection: Understanding Our Early Shapers

We are wired for relationship and connection. Seeing how we are being in our relationships – and what makes it so – is hugely helpful in developing ways of relating that support our creativity. There is a vast body of research and literature that supports these insights. I give below merely the key ones that have worked for me in my life and in my practice. Resources are signposted to help you find out more.

a. **Attachment Dynamics**
   John Bowlby's Attachment Theory[30] showed how our early experiences of feeling safe and being able to trust our primary care giver affect our ability to build relationships, promote relational wellbeing and risk ourselves.

   Mary Ainsworth went on to identify four attachment styles when a baby was left in what she called a 'Strange Situation'[31]. These were:

- Secure Attachment when a baby's needs a fully met by their primary carer;

- Avoidant Attachment when a baby does not notice either the arrival or departure of their primary carer;

- Ambivalent Attachment when the baby cannot be soothed;

or

- Disorganized Attachment where no pattern is discernable.

Insight into our own experiences of attachment can help us to understand ourselves and our clients as we risk ourselves so that we can learn to avoid re-enacting old patterns. Dan Siegel's pioneering work on interpersonal neurobiology is very insightful. His book, *The Developing Mind – How Relationships and the Brain Interact to Shape Who we Are*, is excellent.[32]

This practice invites you to consider:[33]

- Identifying your likely pattern. Headline questions to explore your attachment dynamics are:

  - Do you have a strong sense of who you are, and want close relationships and positive beliefs about yourself and others? If so you may have a Secure Attachment style.

  - Do you tend to be a loner, feel unable to express your feelings and prefer to distance yourself from conflict? If so you may have an Avoidant Attachment style.

  - Do you tend to be critical of yourself, find it hard to trust, fear rejection and tend to seek reassurance but never believe what other people say? If so you many have an Anxious or Ambivalent Attachment style?

  - Do you tend to seek relationships but when closeness is expected sabotage or run away? If so you may have a Disorganized Attachment style.

  - Or is there a mix?

- Create a secure base for yourself. Write or talk through with a trusted friend or colleague a 'story' of your life and the attachment styles you experienced.

- Identify the themes and underlying patterns. Try to make sense of how and why you act the way that you do.

- Seek help if you need it.

b. **Scripts and Stories We Tell Ourselves**

Transactional analysis focuses on how the early scripts and stories we tell ourselves can shape how we see ourselves.[34]

Seeing the scripts we are carrying helps us to see our seeing – and also our potential blind spots. Seeing our stories also helps us to re-parent ourselves and move into a more conscious adult-to-adult relationship with our lives and work. As Maya Angelou writes in her book *I Know Why the Caged Bird Sings*,[35] 'There is no greater agony than bearing an untold story inside you.'

This practice is a project, which helps you to develop your own Short Story Collection over a period of time:

- Ground yourself. Breathe deeply.

- Use a range of writing prompts, memorabilia and/or photographs to write freely about some of your most memorable days or events as you were growing up. You can also dictate these stories and get them transcribed or talk and record them with a trusted friend or colleague.

- Review your collection, asking yourself:

  - What are the emerging themes here? Find out what roles, assumptions and words might be repeating themselves for you?

  - What has served me and/or is true for me that I need to take forward?

  - What is no longer serving me and/or is no longer true for me and which I can now leave behind?

  - Invite yourself to write a new story for yourself based on what you have harvested.

As Patrick Rothfuss reminds us:[36]

It's like everyone tells a story about themselves inside their own head.
Always. All the time. That story makes you what you are. We build ourselves out of that story.

Practice 49
Reflection: Us in the Here and Now

Seeing ourselves in the here and now is critical to understanding what drives us, the energy we are transmitting, and our impact on others. Being alert to the transmission of energies as we talk can help us to spot when we might need to push the pause. In this way we can stop ourselves from getting caught up in old patterns.

This practice invites you to become aware of four unconscious relational dynamics, which can occur. In our noticing of these dynamics we can choose to shift to more conscious or adult to adult interactions.

A. Knowing the four processes

The four processes are:

a. Parallel Process

Parallel process is when we are working with another person and we become aware of an energy happening within ourselves which might resemble another similar energy or relationship in the other person's world.

b. Transference

Transference is when we are working with another person and we become aware of something from the other person's past which they unconsciously transfer or put onto us. This is often based on a relationship from the person's past.

c. Counter Transference

Counter Transference occurs when the person you are working with sees you as a person or in a role other than the one that is real.

and

d. Projection

Projection is when we see aspects within ourselves which we do not like, find difficult to accept or do not want to acknowledge and we unconsciously put these unowned aspects of ourselves onto others.

B. Identifying your triggers

○ Use journaling, drawing or talking with a trusted friend or colleague to identify situations where you have experienced each of the four processes.

○ Understand what happened before, during and after.

C. Developing

Develop your own strategies for managing your triggers and for returning to an adult-to-adult base for the work.

Practice 50
Reflection: Seeing the Ego State You Might be Operating from

Eric Berne[37] developed three observable ego states: Parent, Adult and Child. Each reflects an entire system of thought, feeling and behaviour, which shapes how we express ourselves, interact with each other and form relationships. Seeing which ego state we operate from moment by moment can support how we can learn from experience. All are helpful at the right moment and in the right context. The key is deciding which ego state to invite in and when.

The three ego states are:

- **Parent Ego State**

  The Parent Ego state is a set of thoughts, feelings and behaviours learnt from our parents and other key people in our lives. This part of our personality can be supportive and nurturing or boundary setting, critical and judgemental.

- **Adult Ego State**

  The Adult Ego state is a set of direct responses in the present. They are not influenced by our past narratives. This tends to be the most logical and rational part of our personality.

- **Child Ego State**

  The Child Ego state is a set of thoughts, feelings and behaviours learnt from our childhood. This part of our personality can be free, natural and spontaneous or can be strongly adapted to parental shapers.

This practice invites you to consider the following questions. Journal, draw or mind map your answers.

- What for you are the advantages and disadvantages of each ego state?

- Which ego state do you typically operate from?

- Which ego state do you typically trip into when you are triggered?

- Is there a pattern to your triggering?

- Use different scenarios to explore WHO and HOW you are being, moment to moment.

- How can awareness of your script and stories you tell yourself from Practice 48 and unconscious processes from Practice 49 help you to work from the optimum ego state needed moment by moment?

Practice 51
Inquiry: Seeing How we Prefer to Take in Information

Understanding how we prefer to perceive the world around us can help us to see our seeing and also our blind spots. These insights can help us to develop strategies to inquire from our less preferred modes of perceiving to gather in different perspectives or points of view. As Confucious reminds us,[38] 'Everything has beauty but not everyone sees it.'

For Marie von Ebner-Eschenbach[39] it is 'not what we experience, but how we perceive what we experience, [that] determines our fate'.

This practice invites you consider what might help. I have found Myers-Briggs Type Indicator™ and Honey and Mumford Learning Styles™ to be particularly helpful. However, there are many other psychometrics available to help us better understand our ways of perceiving. A range is listed in the Resources Section.

- **Myers-Briggs Type Indicator or MBTI**™

   MBTI™ was developed from Carl Jung's work by mother and daughter partnership Katherine and Isabel Briggs to identity and describe 16 distinctive personality types which relate to the different ways people prefer to use their perception and judgement.[40] Their MBTI Instrument is a self-assessment tool to help people identify their preferred type and what happens when they find themselves in the grip of working against their type.

   Katherine and Isabel identified four dichotomies, which make up the 16 personality types. There is no right or wrong – just the quest for deeper understanding.

For a quick self-assessment ask yourself the following:

✓ **Favourite World: Extraversion or Introversion?**

   Do you prefer to focus on the outer world of people and things (Extroversion) or on your own inner world of ideas and images (Introversion)?

✓ **Information Gathering: Sensing or Intuition?**

   Do you prefer to pay more attention to information that comes in through your five senses (Sensing), or do you pay more attention to the patterns and possibilities that you see in the information you receive (Intuition)?

✓ **Decision Making: Thinking or Feeling?**

   Do you like to put more weight on objective principles and impersonal facts (Thinking) or do you put more weight on personal concerns and the people involved (Feeling)?

✓ **Structure: Judging or Perceiving?**

Do you prefer a more structured and decided lifestyle (Judging) or a more flexible and adaptable lifestyle (Perceiving)? This preference may also be thought of as your orientation to the outer world.

When you decide on your preference in each category, you have your own personality type, which can be expressed as a code with four letters.

To find out more visit **www.myersbriggs.org**

• **Learning Styles**™

Seeing how we learn is foundational. Peter Honey and Alan Mumford identified four learning styles based on David Kolb's Learning Cycle[41]. From this they designed a 40-item and 80-item Learning Styles Questionnaire to help people identify their preferred learning styles and develop their least preferred styles, to become rounded learners. These four styles are Activitist, Pragmatist, Reflector and Theorist.

For a quick self-assessment, reflect on the balance within you, reflect on the impact and decide what action is needed.

○ **Activist**

An activist has a preference for doing and experiencing.

○ **Pragmatist**

A pragmatist has a preference for experimenting, having a go, and trying things out.

○ **Reflector**

A reflector has a preference for observing and reflecting.

○ **Theorist**

A theorist has a preference for understanding the underlying relationships, concepts and relationships.

Decide which style best describes and least describes you.

Understand the impact of your preferences and decide what action if any is needed.

To find out more visit: **www.talentlens.co.uk/develop/peter-honey-learning-style-series**

Practice 52
Reflection: Seeing Assumptions Using the Ladder of Inference

Chris Argyris's 'Ladder of Inference' – sometimes known as the 'Process of Abstraction' – can help us to bring into our awareness how we might be converting our experiences into action. This enables us to see the thinking which can force us into errors of judgement or wrong conclusions.[42] Potentially blindsided by our filters, the Ladder of Inference invites us to a more realistic or objective interpretation of our data.

The Ladder works from the bottom up but we can meet ourselves standing on any rung. As shown in Figure 9 the rungs are:

- Facts and Reality which become…

- Selected Reality which becomes…

- Interpreted Reality which becomes…

- Assumptions which become…

- Conclusions which become…

- Beliefs which become…

- Translated into Action.

This practice is for when we see ourselves perhaps moving too quickly to conclusions or judgment. It provides the steps for us to analyze our thinking by moving up and down the ladder rung by rung.

- Centre and ground yourself.

- Decide which rung of the ladder opposite you are now standing on.

- Here is the flow of questions for you to start from wherever you find yourself. The purpose is to trace the facts you are working with to find out what you are thinking and feeling and why.

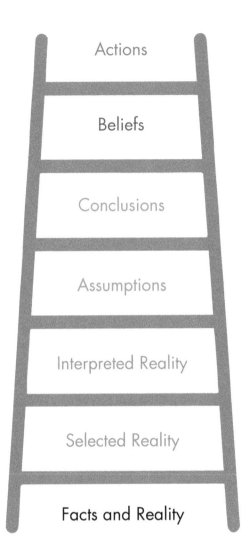

Fig 3: Ladder of Inference

Actions

Beliefs

Conclusions

Assumptions

Interpreted Reality

Selected Reality

Facts and Reality

- For Actions: Why have I chosen this course of action? Are there other actions I should have considered?
- For Beliefs: What belief lead to that action? Was it well founded?
- For Conclusions: Why did I draw that conclusion? Is the conclusion sound?
- For Assumptions: What am I assuming, and why? Are my assumptions valid?

- For Interpreted Reality: What am I seeing from the data?
- For Selected Reality: What data have I chosen to use and why?
- For Facts and Reality: What are the actual facts that I should be using here? What other data is needed here?

- From your new insights work back up the ladder opening up the possibility of a more balanced or a different course of action.

Practice 53
Exercise: Becoming a Wise Compassionate Observer

Here we begin to see the difference between ourselves as participants in and observers of our experience.

This frees us to notice and observe our internal experience whilst not fusing or identifying with it. Whatever we identify with we become the subject of its affects. Thoughts, feelings and sensations arise and subside in a wave-like motion within the quantum soup or implicit order. Experiencing the space between thoughts, feelings or sensations helps us to start to touch the Fertile Void.

This practice frees us to welcome all of our experience. Once we appreciate that we are not our thoughts or feelings, we can become our own wise compassionate observer who is always present within us and is always available to us. This is the permanent I, the I of compassionate witness. As Stephen Wolinsky writes:[43]

> As you notice that thoughts come and go, emotions come and go, sensations come and go, you realize that there is one common factor weaving throughout this huge mosaic of experience; You, the observer of all the comings and goings. Once You, as the observer, begin to appreciate that you are not your thoughts, feelings, and emotions, but rather a witnessing presence, a greater clarity emerges.

For the Sufi Master G. I. Gurdjieff:[44]

> A thing cannot observe itself. A thing identical with itself cannot see itself, because it is the same as itself, and a thing which is the same as itself cannot possibly have a standpoint apart from itself, from which to observe itself.

With this exercise you can tune into the quantum consciousness, to shift from experiencing experience from the 'ego-centric subjective lens' to the 'universal quantum lens' which is always present. Constant practice is required to finesse this way of relating to our experiences.

- Ground yourself, breathe deeply and centre yourself.

- When a thought, feeling or sensation arises ask yourself 'From where does this arise?'

- Notice how as the thought arises it also subsides. Ask yourself 'From where does this subside?'

- Notice then that there is a space between this and the next thought, feeling or sensation.

- Then ask yourself 'Who is it that who is always witnessing this in me?' with the realization that the answer is 'I am – the one who is always present.'

Practice 54
Exercise: The Difference between Shame and Guilt

Learning requires us to risk ourselves – to go out of our comfort zones.

We fear shame as we fear 'getting it wrong' or 'being wrong'. Shame is often muddled with guilt. Both can put the brakes on learning. However, the work of researchers into shame has highlighted the difference between shame and guilt.[45]

Brene Brown[46] is one of them. Brene argues that guilt is:

adaptive and helpful – it is holding something we have done or failed to do against our values [resulting in a] feeling [of] psychological discomfort. It is a potential springboard for taking action.

By contrast, Brene defines shame as:

unproductive and unhelpful … the intensely painful feeling or experience of believing that we are flawed and therefore unworthy of love and belonging – [that] something we've experienced, done, or failed to do makes us unworthy of connection.

Guilt can point to action needed. Shame can make us feel unworthy. The next time you feel you are getting it wrong, do the following:

- Journal what has happened.

- Draw a column down the middle of the page. Title the left-hand column 'Guilt' and the right-hand column 'Shame'.

- In the column titled 'Guilt' capture an analysis of what has happened, writing from a place of guilt or feeling guilty.

- In the column titled 'Shame' capture an analysis of what has happened, writing from a place of shame or shame feelings.

- Take a break.

- Step into the place of your wise compassionate observer.
- Compare and contrast the two columns.
- Journal what you notice and what you want to choose next time.

As Brene writes:[47]

> If we can share our story with someone who responds with empathy and understanding, shame can't survive.

Practice 55
Exercise: Seeing from Different Perspectives

For Henry Ford:[48]

> If there is any one secret of success, it lies in the ability to get the other person's point of view and see things from that person's angle as well as from your own.

For Atticus in *To Kill A Mockingbird*[49]

> if you can learn a simple trick you'll get along with all kinds of folk. You never understand a person until you consider things from his/her point of view...

This is the 'Chair Inquiry', useful where different perspectives on a particular issue need to be seen and appreciated.

Step 1:   Set up three empty chairs or positions on a table or draw three chairs or circles on a piece of paper. Place more chairs or circles depending on how many key players are involved in the issue.

Step 2:   Starting with the first chair state your perspective or position on an issue. Speak or journal freely from your position.

Step 3:   Now move to the second chair and step into the shoes of the other. Give yourself time to step into being them. Ask yourself 'What does it feel like to be here?', 'What does this person want to say from here?', and 'What does the situation look like from over here?' Journal what each would say from their position.

Step 4:   Repeat Step 3 for each of your key players.

Step 5:   When you have heard from everyone, return to your chair – the first chair. Ground and centre yourself.

Step 6:   Gather in and harvest all that you have heard.

Step 7:   Reflect on what you have learnt.

Everything depends on the perspective we take. For Alphonse Karr:[50] 'We can complain because rose bushes have thorns, or rejoice because thorns have roses.'

Practice 56
Journaling: Learning from Seeing Ourselves at Work

This is a journaling practice, which helps us to see ourselves at work. It is also very helpful for any in-depth analysis of any meeting, session or critical incident from which we need to learn.

Select an inquiry or an event which you want to study:

- Ground, centre and breathe.
- Journal in the following order:

   i.   Write the story of what happened.

   ii. Then ask yourself

      ★ What was I feeling?

      ★ What was I thinking?

      ★ How was I behaving?

   iii. Ask yourself: What am I learning from this?

   iv. Ask yourself: What is now needed? What – if any – are my action points?

Practice 57
More Inspiration: Inspiring You to See Anew

Here are some inspirational quotes and poems to support you in seeing anew.

For Johann Wolfgang von Goethe:[51]

> Man knows himself only to the extent that he knows the world; he becomes aware of himself only within the world, and aware of the world only within himself. Every object, well contemplated, opens up a new organ of perception within us.

Rabindranath Tagore wrote a beautiful blessing called 'The Senses':[52]

Deliverance is not for me in renunciation.
I feel the embrace of freedom in a thousand bonds of delight.

Thou ever pourest for me the fresh draught of thy wine of various
colours and fragrance, filling this earthen vessel to the brim.

My world will light its hundred different lamps with thy flame
and place them before the altar of thy temple.

No, I will never shut the doors of my senses.
The delights of sight and hearing and touch will bear thy delight.

Yes, all my illusions will burn into illumination of joy,
and all my desires ripen into fruits of love.

* * * * *

Reflective Questions

1. What are your reflections from reading this chapter?
2. Which of the nineteen practices are you most drawn to and why?
3. Which of the nineteen practices are you least drawn to and why?
4. What are you going to action now?

CHAPTER 7
Relating to the Whole

Only love expands intelligence. To live in love is to accept the other and the conditions of this existence as a source of richness, not as opposition, restriction or limitation.

Humberto Maturana[1]

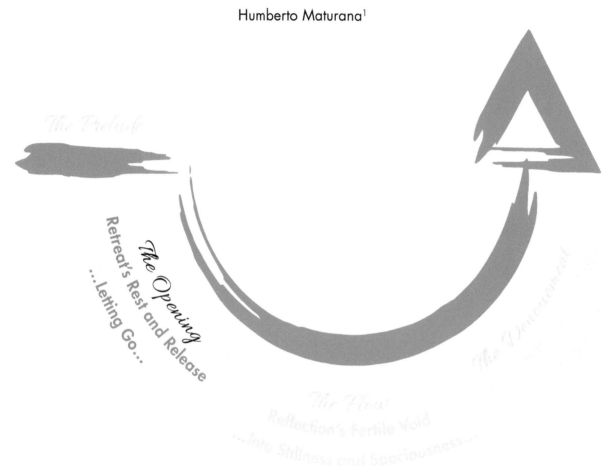

The Prelude

The Opening
Retreat's Rest and Release
...Letting Go...

The Flow
Reflection's Fertile Void
...Into Stillness and Spaciousness...

The Denouement

- Suspending Habits
- Seeing Anew
- Relating to the Whole

- Noticing the Nuance
- Art of Listening
- Finding Freedom

As Martin Luther King Jr. explains:[2]

> Whatever affects one directly, affects all indirectly.
> I can never be what I ought to be
> until you are what you ought to be.
> This is the interrelated structure of reality.

This chapter offers twenty-one practices to relate and sense from the whole. Working wholeheartedly means embracing our heart's natural intelligence and innate capacities for love, relationship, connection, and compassion. Our hearts see what our minds cannot. As Blaise Pascal wrote:[3]

> The heart has its reasons whereof Reason knows nothing.

For the Dalai Lama XIV[4]

> Love and compassion are necessities, not luxuries. Without them, humanity cannot survive.

This is the melting of the ego's artificial mind-made boundaries.

As Albert Einstein reminds us:[5]

> A human being is part of the whole, called by us the 'universe', a part limited in time and space. He experiences himself, his thoughts and his feelings, as something separated from the rest, a kind of optical illusion of his consciousness. This delusion is a kind of prison for us, restricting us to our personal desires and to affection for a few persons nearest to us. Our task must be to free to ourselves from this prison by widening our circle of compassion to embrace all living creatures and the whole of nature in its beauty.

For the Dalai Lama XIV:[6]

> Whether one is rich or poor, educated or illiterate, religious or nonbelieving, man or woman, black or white, we are all the same. Physically, emotionally and mentally we are all equal. We all share base needs for food, shelter, safety and love. We all aspire to happiness and we all shun suffering. Each of us has hopes, worries, fears and dreams. Each of us wants the best for our family and loved ones. We all experience pain when we suffer loss and joy when we achieve what we seek. On this fundamental level, religion, ethnicity, culture, and language make no difference.

This bigger perspective opens up our capacities to transcend ego and live and work from a place of unconditional love, compassion, acceptance and tolerance for another human being and all of life. This in its turn frees us from the fear of sharing our vulnerabilities, without which learning and creativity is stunted. As Honoré de Balzac reminds us:[7] 'The more one judges, the less one loves.'

Compassion is working from relational presence – the capacity to not just empathize, but to be truly with another. To be with all of WHO they are and what they bring – risking ourselves whilst staying grounded in ourselves. For Andrew Boyd:[8]

> This compassion hurts. When you feel connected to everything, you also feel responsible for everything. And you cannot turn away. Your destiny is bound with the destinies of others. You must either learn to carry the Universe or be crushed by it. You must grow strong enough to love the world, yet empty enough to sit down at the same table with its worst horrors.

As the Dalai Lama says:[9]

> This is my simple religion. There is no need for temples; no need for complicated philosophy. Our own brain, our own heart is our temple; the philosophy is kindness.

Practices for Relating to the Whole

There are many ways in which we can open ourselves up to our heart's intelligence. Here are twenty-one which work for me and my practice.

Practice 58
Exercise: For Relational Presence

This practice teaches us how to be with ourselves and with another, or with others in a group. It is done in pairs but with familiarity can be used at any time within ourselves to support our natural flow in any situation.

For this practice:

- In pairs sit facing each other, a comfortable distance apart.

- To start, each of you is gently invited to close your eyes.

- Privately, ground and centre yourself. Connect to your breathing. Go to the place inside yourself which is quiet and still and silent. There is nowhere to go, nothing to do and nobody is looking at you.

- Then after 10 to 15 seconds of silence, open your eyes and just be with each other without trying. Even though your eyes are available to each other you are not trying to connect through smiling, winking, or nodding. You are both just there for each other, steady and neutrally receptive.

- Allow any natural anxiety or discomfort to just drift way until you find your place of relational presence and connection.

- Open your heart to your partner.

- After 5 minutes of this come to a natural ending and thank your partner.

- Talk through with each other what you experienced.

This works because it is our gift of ourselves in the form of our personal presence and attention, which invites the other's soul to show up. As Parker Palmer writes:[10]

> Here's the deal. The human soul doesn't want to be advised or fixed or saved. It simply wants to be witnessed – to be seen, heard and companioned exactly as it is. When we make that kind of deep bow to the soul of a suffering person, our respect reinforces the soul's healing resources; our gift of self in the form of personal presence and attention, invites the other's soul to show up.

Practice 59
Exercise: Cultivating Heart Awareness
(1) Heart Breathing

This practice helps us to step into our hearts to work from our hearts.

- Find a quiet calm space or place to ground yourself and focus on your breath.

- As you breathe in and out feel your lungs gently expand and contract and your gut move in and out. Breathe into any areas of tension in your body.

- If the situation allows it place your hands over your heart area. If the situation does not allow it imagine your heart in your chest or imagine placing your hands on your heart.

- Now breathe in and out through your heart and feel your heart fill with loving calmness.

- Listen to what your heart wants to say.

As Milan Kundera writes in *The Unbearable Lightness of Being*:[11] 'When the heart speaks the mind finds it hard to object.'

Practice 60
Exercise: Cultivating Heart Awareness
(2) The Loving Heart

This practice helps us to experience feelings of love cascade through our bodies; and then to take the memory of that feeling into the rest of our day.

For this practice:

• Repeat Practice 59 so that you can feel yourself breathing calmly in and out through your heart.

• Then recall somebody, some experience, or some place that you love. Relive this loving feeling through your heart.

• Then invite this heart feeling to spread throughout your body, reaching out from your heart to your fingers, toes and head. Feel every cell being bathed in this love.

• Stay with this for about 5 minutes and then say to yourself or speak out whatever gratitude prayer, affirmation or forgiveness statement your heart needs to hear.

As Helen Keller says:[12] 'The best and most beautiful things in the world cannot be seen or touched but are felt in the heart.'

Practice 61
Reflection: 'When Did I Last Feel Truly Connected?'

Life's relentless pressures and preoccupations can mean that we forget to connect with the people, places and activities that we love. We can easily forget that as human beings rather than human doings we find energy and meaning in the connections we make.

This practice invites you to come home to yourself.

• Find a quiet space or place and go back to your most recent experience of feeling truly connected.

• Replay the setting and scenario. Write or draw it.

• Ask yourself:

   ○ 'How did this come about?'

   ○ 'What was I connecting to or with?'

   ○ 'What did I feel, think or notice about the experience?'

○ 'What have I learnt from this?'

○ Repeat the process to find the experience just before the one you have captured until you spot your own patterns.

Practice 62
Reflection: 'What Makes Your Heart Sing?'

For Kahlil Gibran:[13]

Work is love made visible. And if you can't work with love, but only with distaste, it is better that you should leave your work and sit at the gate of the temple and take alms of the people who work with joy.

This practice is a heart entrainment exercise to help you to discover what you most love and what make your heart sing.

• Clear a space.

• Ground and centre yourself. Breathe deeply.

• Swing your arms around your body.

• With your right hand start by gently tapping your left shoulder and move down the length of your left arm and then down the outside of your left leg to your foot. Then tap your way back to your left shoulder.

• Repeat with your left hand tapping your right shoulder and repeat, moving down your left arm and leg. Then tap back to your right shoulder.

• Now cross your arms and legs as is comfortable for you.

• Recall someone, some place or some intuition of what you love and let it enter your heart.

• End with an affirmation 'I love myself completely.'

• Come out of the pose. Sit down and journal, answering the questions:

○ 'What do I most love (in my work or life or in both)?'

○ 'What are my most profound gifts?'

○ 'What is my profound responsibility or contribution?'

This practice works because, as Antoine de Saint-Exupery wrote,[14] 'And now here is my secret, a very simple secret: It is only with the heart that one can see rightly; what is essential is invisible to the eye.'

Practice 63
Reflection: Love v. Fear and Choosing Love

Love may be defined as paying attention and being fully present to the pure existence of the other. Love is unconditional acceptance of the other. As Henry Miller said:[15] 'The moment one gives close attention to any thing, even a blade of grass, it becomes a mysterious, awesome, indescribably magnificent world in itself.'

When we are fully present we are connected to all of life. Loving ourselves, others and the world we live in can be blocked by our fears. Our fears disconnect us from being present.

Cultivating our capacity for love and compassion is both the work of the heart and a spiritual journey to appreciating the interconnectedness of all living things. As Brene Brown reminds us:[16]

> We cultivate love when we allow our most vulnerable and powerful selves to be deeply seen and known, and when we honor the spiritual connection that grows from that offering with trust, respect, kindness and affection. Love is not something we give or get; it is something that we nurture and grow, ... We can only love others as much as we love ourselves. Shame, blame, disrespect, betrayal, and the withholding of affection damage the roots from which love grows. Love can only survive these injuries if they are acknowledged, healed and rare.

This practice invites you to journal or talk through the following reflective questions – and also to continually return to them:

* 'What does "love" mean for you?'
* 'Who, what or where does your love reach out to?'
* 'How can you cultivate more love in your life'
* 'What would this mean for you?'
* 'What fears, attachments or beliefs are blocking you?'
* 'What needs to heal in you?'
* 'What might be possible?'

Practice 64
Exercise: Seeing Field Energy at Work

Everything is energy. We transmit and receive energy within every cell in every nanosecond of our lives. This can shed light or dark and all shades in-between in every aspect of our work and lives – and beyond.

Energy is invisible but felt. Practice 64 – which was developed by Miriam Orriss at the Coaching Supervision Academy – helps us make the invisible visible. This practice shows how we are co-creating our experiences through being in relational presence (or not).

For this practice you need to work in pairs and to have converted two coat hangers into energy rods. For each coat hanger, fashion a straight piece about 8cm long (which is the handle to be held in each hand) and at right angles fashion a straight wire about 25cm long.

- In pairs stand opposite each other about 8m apart.
- Person A holds the coat hanger and gently points it towards the Person B at right angles.
- Person B is invited to breathe normally.
- Person A then starts to take small steps towards Person B. At some stage the coat hangers will cross over and this will show Person B's electromagnetic field from their heart.
- Repeat the exercise with Person B experimenting with feeling happy and joyous and then feeling sad. See when the coat hangers cross over in each scenario. When we love or are happy we connect more with the zero point field and our radius becomes bigger. When we are sad or unhappy we disconnect more with the zero point field and the radius becomes smaller.
- Change roles and repeat.
- Debrief what was happening and what you noticed.

Practice 65
Exercise: Expanding Our Own Energy Field for Deeper Connection

We all have our own energy field, with a reach of between 30 and 60cm. We can either open up or close down our energy field – and thereby our physiology and body chemistry – depending on how we choose to react to whatever is happening at any point in time.[17]

This practice helps us to feel how we can expand our energy field and was designed by Wendy Palmer.[18]

Find a quiet space where you will not be interrupted.

- Start by standing upright.
- As you inhale imagine the air spiralling in an anti-clockwise direction.
- Exhale more slowly than you inhaled. Also exhale loudly, imagining that you are emptying a balloon and in a clockwise spiral moving through your body to your feet. Imagine that your

body is forming a root in the earth.

- Now ask yourself 'What would it be like if my energy at my back was equal and even to the energy on my front?' Take a moment to feel the balance.

- Now ask 'What would it be like if the energy at my left side was equal and even to the energy on my right side?' Take a moment to feel the balance.

- Now ask 'What would it be like if the energy above my head was equal and even to the energy below my feet where I am standing right now?' Take a moment to feel the balance.

- Notice what your body feels like now.

- Bring your attention to your jaw and shoulders and notice how the natural pressure of gravity draws your weight down. Breathe into your jaw and shoulders so that they relax.

- Now extend your energy field to include whatever it is you are working on. Energetically when you do this you are sending a message 'we are all in this together'.

- Notice the difference to your work or relationships over the rest of the day.

Practice 66
Exercise: Connecting through Holistic Therapies

Holistic therapies are different forms of healing which seek to restore alignment and balance to the whole body system. The holistic therapies belief is that if a part of our body system is not working properly then the whole of us will be affected.

The five therapies below give a feel for what is available. There are many others to choose from.

- **Aromatherapy**

  Aromatherapy is the practice of using the natural oils extracted from flowers, bark, stems, leaves, roots or other parts of a plant to enhance psychological and physical well-being and whole body healing. For more information visit the website of the International Association of Aromatherapists.[19]

- **Acupuncture**

  Acupuncture treatment is an ancient Chinese medicine which involves the insertion of very fine needles into specific points on the body to improve the flow of your body's qi, or vital energy. For more information visit the website of the British Acupuncture Council.[20]

- **Holistic Massage**

  Holistic massage aids lymphatic drainage, helps to release toxins and restores balance.

- **Reflexology**

  Reflexology works by seeing the whole body represented in different parts of our feet. Through gentle manipulation or pressing on certain parts of the foot relaxation and healing can be affected in the rest of the body. For more information visit the website of the British Society of Reflexologists.[21]

- **Reiki**

  'Reiki' (ray-key) is Japanese for 'universal life energy' and describes a system of natural healing which was founded by Mikao Usui in the early twentieth century. When this universal life energy flows there is balance and harmony within us and around us. Reiki is non-intrusive and seeks to connect us to our own healing energies. For more information visit the website of the Reiki Association.[22]

Practice 67
Reflection: 'We Are One World from Space'

We are one world. Viewed from space earth has no artificial boundaries or racial or cultural divisions.

This practice invites you to reflect on the insights of Dr. Ed Mitchell who was an astronaut on the Kittyhawk Apollo 14 mission, and to consider what this means for you.

- Consider this story...

  Returning home the earth was intermittently framed through the spaceship's window as a tiny crescent in a night of stars. It was from this window that Ed[23] 'experienced the strangest feeling he had ever had'.

  A feeling of connectedness ... instead all people and all planets in all of time are connected by some invisible thread ... there seemed to be one enormous force field, connecting all people, their intentions and thought and every animate and inanimate form of matter for all of time. Anything he did or thought would influence the rest of the cosmos and every occurrence in the cosmos would have a similar effect on him ... what the Eastern traditions call an ecstasy of unity...

- Take time out to pause and wonder.
- Imagine yourself in the Kittyhawk. Find a photograph of the earth from space.

- Ask yourself 'What am I seeing now?'

- Ask yourself 'What does this mean for me and my worldview?'

- Work with the image over time. Journal what is shifting in you.

Practice 68
Exercise: Weaving Together the Threads of Our Interconnections

With this Practice we can learn to honour the threads of our interconnections and interdependencies which have made our life and living possible. It helps us to see that we are not washed-up accidents, but belong to the world because of the history which has gone before us and the visible and invisible threads of support which we are fortunate to receive and which we also depend upon in our daily lives.

The practice can be repeated many times with many different scenarios and storylines. Here is the process and a few suggestions to get you started.

- Find a quiet space.

- Select a product, a piece of clothing, an object or a person. This may be, for example, a cup of coffee, a picture, a piece of equipment, or a tree.

- Start to tell yourself the story of how your choice got to be with you right here right now. In your imagination reach back to the sequence of events, people, activities, choices and decisions which might have been involved. Reach back in time and across space and locations.

- When you feel yourself getting stuck ask yourself 'who else?', and 'what else?' until you come to a natural ending.

- Draw, chart or write out the web of interconnections and interdependencies as you follow the threads of your thinking.

- Step back and reflect on what you have peeled back.

- Repeat the practice as often and as you like.

As Chief Seattle reminds us:[24]

> Humankind has not woven the web of life. We are but one thread within it. Whatever we do to the web, we do to ourselves. All things are bound together. All things connect.

Practice 69
Exercise: Sharing One Earth

Practice 69 helps us to see that whoever and wherever we are in the world we all share the same ground.

For this practice:

- Find some dry ground where you can lie down safely on your side.

- Centre yourself and breathe deeply.

- As you relax start to feel yourself as part of the earth.

- Choose a different place or a different country and imagine people putting their feet on the earth – the same earth that you share.

- Now choose another place or another country and repeat the exercise again and again.

- Feel your way into the connections which you are sharing with people you have never met.

- Reflect on what you are now feeling and experiencing.

Practice 70
A Parable: 'The Man Who Planted Trees' by Jean Giono

The parable 'The Man Who Planted Trees' was written by the Frenchman Jean Giono[25] after World War II for a short story competition. It is shared here as an invitation for you to consider your own legacy.

> This is a tale of a shepherd tending his sheep on a barren landscape somewhere in Europe between the two World Wars. His day job was to tend his sheep. His additional practice – which he gave himself – was to collect acorns during the day, to select the best 100 acorns he had collected by the fire at night and while walking his sheep the next morning to poke holes in the ground with his shepherd's crook and plant the 100 acorns from the day before. And then start all over again. After decades the shepherd had successfully reforested the landscape. The young trees held the soil which brought in other natural growth. The streams filled with water, birds, flora and fauna returned and young people came to build new homes.

- Reflect on this story.

- Ask yourself 'What seeds are you planting as part of your legacy for people who are coming after you?'

- Journal or draw what you discover.

Practice 71
Exercise: Opening to Nature's Wisdom

Nature is a huge source of inspiration, support, guidance and solace. Allowing ourselves the time and space to reconnect through mindful gardening, walking or sitting in nature opens us up to both a precious companionship and the wisdom of a bigger perspective. As Frank Lloyd Wright advises:[26] 'Study nature, love nature, stay close to nature. It will never fail you.'

There are many ways that we can bring this practice alive for ourselves. Here are just a few examples.

- Take time to notice the daily changes in plants, shrubs and flowers in your garden or a nearby park. Start a photo journal to capture the subtle and dramatic changes over the course of a year.

- Feeling the soil in your hands as you garden.

- Sit on a bench or picnic blanket admiring a view. Reflect on the geology and enduring presence of what you see as it also changes with the seasons, changing light and weather.

- Walk slowly and barefoot feeling the ground, grass or sand beneath your feet. Feel the different sensations in different parts of your feet as you walk.

My particular favourite practice for reconnecting with nature is Sitting with Trees. For this:

- Sit or stand with your back against a tree.

- Breathe deeply.

- Start to connect with the tree as a living being both with its roots beneath you and its branches up above you reaching into the sky.

- In your imagination start to trace the reach of the roots spreading widely and deeply into the soil, as they fetch water and nutrients essential for the tree's survival.

- Travel deep into the earth's crust imagining the different geological layers from the molten core, which support you and the tree today.

- Then travel back up to where your spine connects with the trunk.

- Breathe deeply.

- Now in your imagination travel up to the branches, twigs and leaves radiating out to the clouds and sky and then to the stars beyond.

- Then travel back to your body.

- Sit and enjoy this expanded and relaxed awareness of you in the world.

For Rainier Maria Rilke:[27]

If we surrendered to earth's intelligence we could rise up rooted, like trees.

Practice 72
Exercise: Connecting to Nature's Natural Rhythms and Seasons

Nature's natural rhythm can help us to locate ourselves within our own cycles of change. According to Russell Foster and Leon Kreitzman:[28]

We are reflexive creatures, and the seasons play a large part in human culture and in making our psychology and social behaviour what it is … The adaptations of our ancestors that enabled them to survive and reproduce by anticipating the seasonal vagaries of the climate still reside deep within our metabolism and life histories.

The cycle of conception, birth, blossoming, ageing and dying – the spring, summer, late summer, autumn and winter of our own lives – is also the shared experience of all living things through time. Accessing the wisdom of nature's seasons can both comfort and guide us as we journey through our own lives and join others in their own journeys.

Every life, issue or organization has its own season and seasonality. Working out what season we are in with whatever issue or question presents itself opens us up to new sources of insights; and also the exciting prospect that we can be youthful in any age and at any stage. Each of the five seasons listed below has a unique quality and brings its own questions for reflection and inquiry. As Albert Einstein encourages us:[29] 'Look deep into nature, and then you will understand everything better.'

For this practice:

- Select an issue or a question you are working on.
- Decide from the description of the five seasons which season you are in with this particular issue or question.

The five seasons are:

- **Spring**
  The season of seeding and blossoming

- **Summer**
  The season of relationships, fire and excitement

- **Late Summer**
  The season of harvesting the fruits

- **Autumn**
  The season of gratitude and letting go

- **Winter**
  The season for reflection, incubation and going deep

- Now ask yourself the questions relevant to the season you find yourself in and gently move through the seasons. Journal or draw what you discover. Get some fresh air. Go for a walking meditation as you work your way through these. Take regular breaks as needed.

  - If you are in Spring ask yourself 'What new beginning am I sowing and planting?'

  - If you are in Summer ask yourself 'What is now joyfully blossoming and flowering?'

  - If you are in Late Summer ask yourself 'What am I now harvesting?'

  - If you are in Autumn ask yourself 'What am I grateful for and what do I need to let go of?'

  - If you are in Winter ask yourself 'What is incubating and what do I need to reflect deeply upon?'

- Come full circle. Ask yourself 'What insights has travelling through nature's rhythms and cycles taught me here?'

For more information please read Karyn Prentice's book "Nature's Way: Designing the Life You Want through the Lens of Nature and the Five Seasons."[30]

Practice 73
Exercise: Shared Humanity (1) Loss and Death

We can often forget that 50% of life is actually about goodbyes and endings.

No one can escape the inevitability that either we have to say goodbye to someone who we love or they have to say goodbye to us. We can all connect through our shared experiences of heartbreak, loss, disappearance and death. This simple but profound realization cannot be erased or avoided as we also embrace the privileges of simply being human and being alive. This gives us an immediate vulnerability, a grounded humility and a wider context of our universal humanity within which we can choose to live our lives.

In an extract from her poem 'In Blackwater Woods', Mary Oliver tells us how we must learn to live in this world:[31]

> To live in this world
> you must be able to do three things:
> to love what is mortal;
> to hold it
> against your bones knowing
> your own life depends on it;
> and, when the time comes to let it go,
> to let it go.

David Whyte in his thought piece 'Vulnerability' puts our existence into a bigger context:[32]

> To have a temporary, isolated sense of power over all events and circumstances, is a lovely illusionary privilege and perhaps the prime and most beautifully constructed conceit of being human and especially of being youthfully human, but it is a privilege that must be surrendered with that same youth, with ill health, with accident, with the loss of loved ones who do not share our untouchable powers; powers eventually and most emphatically given up, as we approach our last breath.

> The only choice we have as we mature is how we inhabit our vulnerability, how we become larger and more courageous and more compassionate through our intimacy with disappearance, our choice is to inhabit vulnerability as generous citizens of loss, robustly and fully, or conversely, as misers and complainers, reluctant and fearful, always at the gates of existence, but never bravely and completely attempting to enter, never wanting to risk ourselves, never walking fully through the door.

For this practice:

- Breathe deeply and ground yourself. Have your journal close by.

- Reflect on the extract from Mary Oliver's poem. Ask yourself 'What does Mary's poem bring up for me?'

- Ask yourself 'How does an awareness that 50% of life is actually about loss and disappearance shift WHO I am, and how I want to be in my relationships and in my work?'

- Ask yourself 'What would it mean for me, my life and my work if I was able to become a generous citizen of loss?'

- Be ready to revisit this practice again and again as your conversation with loss and disappearance deepens.

Practice 74
Exercise: Shared Humanity (2) Five Longings

David Richo has identified five longings that as human beings we all share.[33]

Our five longings are Love, Meaning, Freedom, Happiness and Growth. We all want:

- To love and be loved
- To find meaning and to have a meaningful life
- To be free to be fully ourselves to fulfill our unique potential
- To find happiness, ease, peace and serenity
- To grow psychologically and spiritually

Paradoxically, what we long for in our daily lives already exists in our true natures. As David writes:[34]

> We notice that we have longings for the lasting in a world that is always changing. We can take that as a clue to the presence of something transcendent in us. With subconsciousness, we finally discover that all five longings reflect qualities in our true nature. We are seeking what we are. Our longings are never signs of neediness, only for our full humanity pressing for recognition. Each of these five reveals us to ourselves, showing us what we want, what our life is for, what keeps us going, what keeps us looking. Longings are mysterious. We often can't quite name them for ourselves or explain them. Nor can they ever be perfectly, fully, or finally gratified.

For this practice:

- Breathe deeply and ground yourself. Have your journal close by.
- Ask yourself 'Are these longings foundational for me?'
- Ask yourself 'How would I rank them for me?'
- Invite yourself to consider 'How could I embrace these longings whilst also knowing that complete fulfillment of all five at any point in time may be fleeting or may never happen for me?'
- Journal your reflections.

Practice 75
Exercise: Shared Humanity (3) Belonging and Exile

As human beings we all want to belong to something, someone and/or some place. We are creatures of belonging; although paradoxically we may only discover this through experiences of separation and aloneness.

As human beings we also have the capacity to be strangers to ourselves, to others and to our world. We are the only species that knows what it feels like to be in exile – distanced from ourselves, our work, or our contribution. Paradoxically once we are able to start to articulate our separation and lost-ness we can start to find our own way home. As David Whyte writes[35]:

> As human beings we have this immediate gateway – you've just to articulate exactly the way that you're exiled, exactly the way that you don't belong, exactly the way that you can't love, exactly the way that you can't move ... and you're on your way again. You're on your way home. If you can just say exactly the way that you're imprisoned – the door swings open.

For this practice:

* Breathe deeply and ground yourself. Have your journal close by.

* Ask yourself 'When have I felt that I most belonged to something, someone and/or some place?' and 'What did this experience show me?'

* Ask yourself 'When have I felt a stranger to myself, or in my work or in my relationships?' and 'What did it this experience show me?'

* Ask yourself 'How did I start to find my way home?'

* Reflect on your own experiences of belonging and exile, of found and lost or vice versa. Ask yourself 'Who am I, and how do I want to be in my relationships and in my work?'

* Be ready to revisit this practice again and again as your conversation with experiences of belonging and exile deepens.

A final thought from James Baldwin from his novel *Giovanni's Room*:[36] 'Perhaps home is not a place but simply an irrevocable condition.'

Practice 76
Exercise: Shared Humanity (4) Five Absences

Being absent is the opposite of being present. Being absent means that for whatever reason we have shrunk back inside our egos and lost our wider energetic connection, which creates a more wholehearted relational presence.

Absencing is a moving out of relational presence and a withdrawal of connection. In their book *WE: A Manifesto for Women Everywhere,* Gillian Anderson and Jennifer Nadel[37] have named five toxic Cs, which I see as blocking our relational presence. These are:

- Comparing
- Complaining
- Criticizing
- Controlling
- Competing

To these I add

- Closed

and

- Complacency

For this practice:

- Breathe deeply and ground yourself. Have your journal close by.
- Think back to a time when you felt disconnected from
    i.   Yourself
    ii. A key relationship
    iii. Events in your wider system

Give each scenario a working title.

- For each scenario reflect on which of the seven toxic Cs were in play. Comparison? Complaining? Criticizing? Controlling? Competing? Closed? Or Complacent?

    Add any others (which do not have to begin with C!) which may be relevant to you.

- Take a break. Breathe deeply. Be kind to yourself.

- Now for each scenario reflect on which of the seven Cs from "Our Humanity@Work" can bring you back into connection and relational presence.[38] Courage? Care? Curiosity? Compassion? Connection? Creativity? Contemplation?

- Journal what you have discovered.

Use this practice whenever you feel yourself losing your relational presence. As Marianne Williamson writes:[39]

> We are not held back by the love we didn't receive in the past, but by the love we're not extending in the present.

Practice 77
Meditation: Befriending Ourselves to Befriend Others

The Loving Kindness Meditation extends feelings of warm-hearted goodwill to befriend ourselves so that we can then befriend others. Loving kindness cultivates our innate capacities for generosity, kindness, connection and friendship.

For this practice:[40]

- Sit or stand with dignity. Focus on your breath.

- When you are ready say to yourself or out loud:

May I be safe and free from suffering.
May I be happy and healthy.
May I have ease of being.

- Breathe deeply. When you are ready bring to mind a loved one and say to yourself or out loud:

May they be safe and free from suffering.
May they be happy and healthy.
May they have ease of being.

- Breathe deeply. When you are ready now bring to mind a stranger who you have fleetingly met for whatever reason and say to yourself or out loud:

May they be safe and free from suffering.
May they be happy and healthy.
May they have ease of being.

- Breathe deeply. When you are ready now bring to mind someone who you are distant from or find difficult for whatever reason and say to yourself or out loud:

  May they be safe and free from suffering.
  May they be happy and healthy.
  May they have ease of being.

- Breathe deeply. When you are ready now widen your circle to include all living beings and say to yourself or out loud:

  May they be safe and free from suffering.
  May they be happy and healthy.
  May they have ease of being.

- Stay with where you are for as long as you can. Feel the waves of love, kindness, intention and connection wash through you.

For Sharon Salzberg:[41]

> For all of us, love can be the natural state of our own being; naturally at peace, naturally connected, because this becomes the reflection of who we simply are.

Practice 78
More Inspiration: Relating to the Whole

Here are some inspirational quotes and poems to support you in finding deeper connections which underpin life. For Martin Luther King Jnr[42] 'Whatever affects one directly, affects all indirectly. I can never be what I ought to be until you are what you ought to be. This is the interrelated structure of reality.'

As Yehuda Berg reminds us:[43] 'In truth, we are all part of the team of humanity. And as such, we are all obligated to share ourselves, and our talents, for the sake of the team.'

According to Nhat Hanh,[44] 'When we recognise the virtues, the talent, the beauty of Mother Earth, something is born in us, some kind of connection; love is born.'

Reflecting on kinship and our shared humanity, Albert Einstein writes:[45]

> To inquire after the meaning or object of one's own existence or that of all creatures has always seemed to me absurd from an objective point of view … The ideals which have lighted my way, and time after time have given me new courage to face life cheerfully, have been Kindness, Beauty, and Truth. Without the sense of kinship with men of like mind, without the occupation with the objective world, the eternally

unattainable in the field of art and scientific endeavors, life would have seemed to me empty.

We conclude with a poem from Judy Brown[46] called 'Retreat':

Each of us
holds a thread
of some vast tapestry
that we cannot
know alone.
It is in that awareness
that we gather,
laying down
our burdens
lifting up
the threads.

* * * * *

Reflective Questions

1. What are your reflections from reading this chapter?

2. Which of the twenty-one practices are you most drawn to and why?

3. Which of the twenty-one practices are you least drawn to and why?

4. What are you going to action now?

7 RELATING TO THE WHOLE

The Flow
Reflection's Fertile Void

The Flow

The Flow is the sequence designed to enable us to step into the stillness, and spaciousness, of Reflection's Fertile Void and to receive its universal, generative and creative potentiality.

The Flow sequence of three dance steps – which are described in the next three chapters and which should be considered together – shows how we can learn to listen and receive from this vast field of potential and possibility. The steps are designed to invite, support and resource us to notice and be with what is wanting to emerge from the field – to connect with possibility, potential and creativity.

The dance steps are

Step 4   Initiating the Invitation

Step 5   The Art of Listening

Step 6   Finding Freedom

The Flow sequence is a necessary and conscious preparation for *The Denouement* – Return's Harvest and Action, to actualize reflection's creativity and provide the practice steps for bringing the reshaped or new into the world.

The Flow

The Flow
Reflection's Fertile Void
...Into Stillness and Spaciousness...

- Initiating the Invitation
- Art of Listening
- Finding Freedom

The Mystery – Into Stillness, Silence and Spaciousness

To be creative means to be in love with life. You can be creative only if you love life enough that you want to enhance its beauty, you want to bring a little more music to it, a little more poetry to it, a little more dance to it.

Osho[1]

Reflection's Fertile Void is a mysterious, soulful, and universal space, which is available to us all at any time. It is also dynamic – full of life's universal, generative and creative energy and potentiality. The Fertile Void allows for not knowing, for returning to source, and to receive from source. Here we can be lost and found, and learn to listen to what life is asking of us.

It offers a vastness and spaciousness in which we can get in touch with life's energy and learn to both listen and receive – to get below and beyond the surface of our questions, issues or dilemmas. Here we learn to support ourselves, and our clients, to explore the core questions of any human life:

Who is my self?
Who am I becoming?
What is my work?
What is not me?
What is my 'why bother?'

For the team, organization or system these questions are:

Who are we?
Who are we becoming?
What is our work?
What is not our work?
What is our 'why bother?'

David Whyte writes:[2]

Reality met on its own terms demands absolute presence, and absolute giving away, an ability to live on equal terms with the fleeting and the eternal, the hardly touchable and the fully possible, a full bodily appearance and disappearance, a rested giving in and giving up: another identity braver and more generous and more here than the one looking hungrily for the easy, unearned answer.

This for Otto Scharmer is called Presencing[3] – the dance which enables us

to sense, tune into and act from our deepest source and highest future potential because the future depends on us to bring it forth and into being.

The Theory of Fritz Perls's 'Fertile Void'

The concept of the 'Fertile Void' was an integral part of Gestalt Therapy, which was developed by psychologists Fritz Perls, Laura Perls and Paul Goodman in the 1940s and 1950s.[4]

Fritz defined the 'Fertile Void' as an experience where 'meaning ceases and being begins'.[5] His definition emerged from the work of Salomo Friedlaender, who in 1918 had developed the concepts of 'polar differentiation' and 'creative indifference'. Salomo argued that as human beings we draw mental boundary lines by creating pairs of opposites and that we make decisions by positioning ourselves closer to one pole or the other (polar differentiation). As Ken Wilbur explained:[6]

> Every boundary line is a potential battle line ... Specifically the agonizing fight of life against death, pleasure against pain, good against evil – but in seeking to experience only the positive and eliminate the negative we forget that the positive is only defined by the negative. To destroy the negative is to destroy all possibility of enjoying the positive. The root of the whole difficulty is our tendency to view the opposites as irreconcilable, as totally set apart and divorced from one another.

However, as the pairs of opposites or polarities are actually extremes of the same continuum, the nearer we get to the midpoint of the continuum the harder it is to differentiate between one pole and the other. Friedlaender called this midpoint the point of 'creative indifference'. Fritz called this the 'fertile void' – where polar differentiation is set aside for a state of pure being, where all creative possibilities emerge. Arnold Biesser coined the phrase the 'Paradoxical Theory of Change' to describe this phenomenon. He said:[7]

> Change does not take place by trying coercion, or persuasion, or by insight, interpretation, or any other such means. Rather, change can occur when [we] abandon, at least for a moment, what [we] would like to become and attempt to be what [we] are.

This is learning to be present in the moment – from which anything might happen. For Lorraine Cohen:[8]

> The Fertile Void is a space of emergence and a rite of passage to live from a higher expression of your truest self and destiny. When you stop pushing and slow down you can ask those deeper questions (of yourself and your work) and connect to the core of your heart. The Fertile Void is not static. It is a place of transformation and creation ... a pathway to live from power, passion and purpose. Make your soul the guiding force in your life and use your mind for the practical functions of your life...

From Duality to Oneness

The ultimate merging and melting of the ego self into our higher self – and with this a Oneness with the universe – are experiences which we can learn to access at any time in the service of our life and work. Here the mind can let go, the heart can love and the soul can creatively dance with life's source to find its way home.

The journey from our dualist, defended, egocentric self to our higher self is also a profound spiritual journey, long explored by the world's philosophical, religious and contemplative traditions. This is the ultimate human journey: to find meaning, purpose, ease, grace and bliss.

CHAPTER 8
Initiating the Invitation

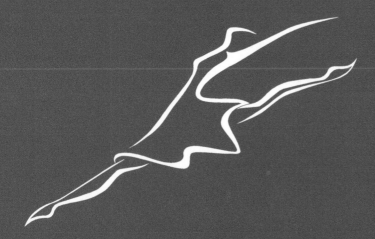

It is only in the intentional silence of the vigil and meditation, or in the quiet places of nature that we encounter the song of the universe. Like the wind through the telegraph wires, this song echoes along the pathways of the cosmic web: it includes the celestial spinning of the planets, as well as the hum of insects and the dancing song of the grass; it includes the song of all ancestors and spirits as well as the beating of our own hearts.

Caitlin Matthews[1]

The Flow
Reflection's Fertile Void
…Into Stillness and Spaciousness…

- Initiating the Invitation
  - Art of Listening
  - Finding Freedom

Reflection's Fertile Void returns us to our essence and to the source of life. Whilst always present and available it cannot be commanded to support and serve us. We need to create the invitation within ourselves – and in the others we work with – in order to step into the unknown and access its potentiality.

And creating the invitation takes both courage and compassion. As Lorraine Cohen cautions:[2] 'The Fertile Void is a place of preparation for something new to be birthed while living in the abyss.'

We need to develop the capability which the Romantic Poet John Keats called 'Negative Capability'.[3] This is the capability 'of being in uncertainties, mysteries, doubts, without any irritable reaching after fact and reason.'

The Romantic Poets also saw this as a return to what they called the 'central imagination' – our essence. Working with this uncertainty, complexity, ambiguity and paradox requires a different schooling. As philosopher and essayist Walter Benjamin writes:[4]

> Not to find one's way in a city may well be uninteresting and banal. It requires ignorance – nothing more. But to lose oneself in a city – as one loses oneself in a forest – that calls for a quite different schooling.

To artfully lose oneself is a conscious choice to be fully present to not knowing. As Rebecca Solnit observes of people being lost and found by Search and Rescue Teams in the Rockies:[5]

> The simplest answer nowadays for literal getting lost is that a lot of people who get lost aren't paying attention when they do so, don't know what to do when they realize they don't know how to return, or don't admit that they don't know.

Practices for Initiating the Invitation

Discovering that we are lost is the start of coming home. Here are thirteen practices which work for me. I choose from them depending on what I need at any point in time to help me to create the invitation to step into the space and spaciousness of the Fertile Void – that sacred space where revelation is possible.

Practice 79
Meditation: Stilling Ourselves

We are losing our ability to be comfortable with being still. Yet it is in the stillness that ideas, thoughts, and impressions can arrive and start to settle. In our stillness our hearts and souls start to feel safe to speak. Martha Beck in her book *The Joy Diet* recommends being still for at least 15 minutes a day.[6] The Quakers have a long-established practice which they call 'Sitting in Silent Waiting' or 'expectant waiting'. For the Quakers this 'centring down' is a time to become inwardly still in order to create an opportunity to experience God.

Practices 79, 80 and 81 (Stilling Ourselves, Embracing Silence and Embracing Solitude) are linked. Stillness can be a precursor to silence. As Franz Kafka writes:[7]

> Remain sitting at your table and listen. You need not even listen, simply wait, just learn to become quiet, and still and solitary. The world will freely offer itself to you unmasked. It has no choice: it will roll in ecstasy at your feet.

For Practice 79 (which can be done either on your own or with others):

- Ask yourself 'What is my relationship with stillness?' Journal your ideas.
- Ask yourself 'Can I make a friend of stillness?'
- Find a comfortable chair or space in a quiet place. Make sure you are warm.
- Switch off all electronic devices. Make sure you will not be interrupted.
- Sit or stand with your back straight.
- Breathe, ground and centre yourself. Relax your body. Quiet your mind. Breathe into your heart.
- When you are ready just be as still as you can.
- Hold the pose for as long as you can. You do not need to do anything or be anywhere.
- When you are ready reflect on your experience of being still.

For Lao Tzu:[8] 'To a mind that is still, the whole universe surrenders.'

Practice 80
Reflection: Embracing Silence

Silence enables us to tune into ourselves and into the world around us. As Mother Theresa invites us:[9]

> To see how nature – trees, flowers, grass – grows in silence; see the stars, the moon and the sun, how they move in silence … we need silence to be able to touch souls.

Music depends on silence: it allows the notes and rhythms to be heard. For Deepak Chopra, silence is the great teacher.[10]

> To learn its lessons you must pay attention to it. There is no substitute for the creative inspiration, knowledge, and stability that come from knowing how to contact your core of inner silence.

As Issac of Niniveh – a 7th-century Church of East Syriac Christian Bishop and Theologian – writes:[11]

> More than all things love silence: it brings you a fruit that the tongue cannot describe. In the beginning we have to force ourselves to be silent. But then from our very silence is born something that draws us into deeper silence. May God give you an experience of this 'something' that is born of silence. If you practice this, inexpressible light will dawn upon you.

The following is from Thomas Carlyle's 1831 translation of the *Sartor Resartus*:[12]

> Speech too is great, but not the greatest. As the Swiss Inscription says: '*Sprechen ist silber, Schweigen ist gold*' – Speech is silver, Silence is golden – or as I might rather express it: Speech is of Time, Silence is of Eternity.

As captured by the Simon and Garfunkel song 'The Sound of Silence', silence is not stasis but full of life:[13]

> Hello darkness, my old friend,
> I've come to talk with you again,
> Because a vision softly creeping,
> Left its seeds while I was sleeping,
> And the vision that was planted in my brain
> Still remains
> Within the sound of silence.

Practice 80 invites you to experiment with 'making silence' in your life. Here are a few suggestions for you to try:

- Ask yourself 'What is my relationship with silence?' Journal your ideas.

- Ask yourself 'Can I make a friend of silence?'

- Listen for the silences between speech or activity.

- Do not rush to fill empty spaces with noise or speaking.

- Sit in a wood or a field and listen to nature's own symphony.

- Listen to the noise of the weather around you.

- Sit for extended periods of time in pure silence.

- Sit in silence with another and feel the relational connection between you grow.

- Go on a Silent Retreat.

- Journal your experiments: 'What does silence feel like?', 'What worked for you?' and 'What did you discover?'

An extract from David Whyte's poem 'Coleman's Bed'[14] reminds us to hold ourselves in a 'corner of silence' until we discover what needs to be known to us:

> Above all, be alone with it all,
> a hiving off, a corner of silence
> amidst the noise, refuse to talk,
> even to yourself, and stay in this place
> until the current of the story
> is strong enough to float you out.

Practice 81
Reflection: Embracing Solitude

Solitude frees us to be ourselves without censorship. Solitude is a powerful resource: it gives us the space to discover the deepest sources of our intention, passions, joy and fulfilment and to return to share these gifts in our life and work.

Wendell Berry grants us this permission:[15]

> We enter solitude in which we also lose loneliness. True solitude is found in the wild places, where one is without human obligation. One's inner voices become audible ... In consequence, one responds more clearly to other lives.

Quoting Pythagoras, Ralph Waldo Emerson wrote:[16] 'In the morning, solitude; ... that nature may speak to the imagination, as she does never in company.'

Solitude is a difficult discipline. It feels alien in today's plugged-in world and can also be scary. As David Whyte writes:[17]

> A beautiful and difficult sense of being solitary is always the ground from which we step into a contemplative intimacy with the unknown ... but is often experienced as alienation, grief and abandonment. ... To be alone is to shed an outer skin ... Alone we live in our bodies as a question rather than a statement ... Being alone asks us to re-imagine ourselves, to become impatient with ourselves ... to start to tell the story in a different way ... to make a friend of silence ...

Consider your relationship with solitude.

- Ask yourself 'What is my relationship to solitude?' Journal your ideas.

- Ask yourself 'What is the difference for me between solitude and loneliness?' and 'How does this play out in my life?' Journal your ideas.

- Ask yourself 'Can I make a friend of solitude?'

- Ask yourself 'Can I put steps in place to reclaim my solitude?'

- Work out your own 'Solitude Ratio' – of time needed alone compared to time in the company of others.

- Can you, as Maya Angelou did, take at least one day out of life once a year to be on your own?

A final thought from Thoreau who writes:[18] 'I love to be alone. I never found a companion as companionable as solitude.'

Practice 82
Meditation: River Flow

Receptivity – our ability to receive – is key to working in Reflection's Fertile Void. We can achieve this by tuning out of the everyday.

Matthew Fox writes that creativity is an intimate place or space within us where the divine or universal powers of creativity meet the human power of imagination. He writes:[19]

> Imagination brings about not just intimacy but a **big intimacy**, a sense of unity with the cosmos, a sense of belonging and being at home, of our knowing we not only have a right to be here but a task to do while we are here ... Creativity as divine or universal intimacy flows through us and is bigger than we are, urging us to go to the edge and grow larger.

Here is a simple meditation to support our emptying.

- Sit or lie down comfortably. Ground, breathe and centre yourself.

- Close your eyes. Imagine yourself standing on the banks a beautiful river which you know. Imagine your mind as a river flowing gently to the sea and any thoughts or feelings that you have as small leaves or petals.

- If a thought or a feeling pops up simply and gently notice it, think about it for a moment if you need to and then release it into your river. Keep repeating this every time a thought or a feeling intrudes.

- Allow yourself to empty and feel a receptive spaciousness start to open up within you.

- Gently return to the room when you feel ready.

Practice 83
Meditation: Merging with Nature

This can work on its own or after the above practice to help step into the fertile void and expand our present-moment awareness.

For this practice:

- Choose something (preferably from nature) which is beautiful to you, to focus on.

- Ground and centre yourself.

- Gaze upon it and trace its shape, colour and contours with your eyes as if you are seeing it for the first time. Continue for as long as feels right for you.

- When you are ready, whilst continuing to gaze at your object start to gently and gradually expand your awareness to notice everything else which is around you.

- Using both your focused attention and peripheral vision immerse yourself fully and simultaneously in both. Start to feel yourself merge into a present-moment awareness and feel yourself step into the fertile void.

- Repeat this practice as often as you need as you go about your day.

As Henry David Thoreau wrote:[20] 'You learn that if you sit down in the woods and wait, something happens.'

Practice 84
Meditation: Gong Sound Bath

Sound was the first sign of life on our planet. A Sound Bath is a way of merging with the primordial womb and fertile void.

A Sound Bath is created by the practitioner playing eastern instruments like gongs, Himalayan singing bowls, chimes and tingsha bells at different rhythms, combinations, tempos and paces for deep connection, receptivity, and awakening.

For this practice:

- Find a practitioner or a recording of a Gong Sound Bath.

- Lie on a yoga mat and find a cushion for your head. Make yourself warm and comfortable.

- Close your eyes and relax. Slow down your mind and your body.

- The sound starts softly and increases in volume as the session progresses. The gong and other instruments are played in waves, which wash over your body, soothing you and opening you up to experiencing the fertile void.

- When the session is finished return gently to the room.

- Journal your experience and what emerged for you.

The Sound Bath can also work very powerfully if it is linked to a meditation, yoga or any other meditative practice and the effect can also be achieved using a piece of music that works for you.

Practice 85
Meditation: The Tree of Life Mudra Sequence

In Sanskrit 'mudras' are sacred and symbolic gestures which are used to access the higher states of consciousness beyond our everyday busy minds. Mudras offer us portals into the fertile void. Here is one which I love and which is demonstrated by Julia McCutchen on her website.[21]

For this practice:

- Find a quiet creative space for yourself, close to a chair.

- Set your intention for whatever inspiration, insight or motivation you need.

- **Clearing the Space**
  Stand up, and centre yourself. As you breathe in stretch your arms up to the sky above you, and as you breathe out, lightly sweep your fingers down your body whilst releasing a 'haaa' sound. Repeat this several times.

- **Grounding**
  Shake your body to loosen your muscles and to stimulate energy flows through your body. Drop your awareness into your body.

- **Calming**
  Now focus on your breathing. Feel your breath enter and leave your body. Breathe into your heart. Breathe in to the count of two and out to the count of four. Find your own balance and rhythm.

- **Imagining Yourself as a Tree**

  - Now imagine you have roots like a tree. Imagine that these roots emerge from the soles of your feet and reach deep into the earth you are standing on. In native traditions, the earth is Mother Earth the Divine Feminine. Send your awareness into your feet and feel your way in your connection with Mother Earth. At the same time, with arms hanging loosely by your side, turn your palms down so that they too are facing towards the earth.

  - Now when you are ready, bring your awareness back into your body and imagine that you have branches emerging from the top half of your body, which are reaching high up to the sky above you. In the native traditions, the sky is Father Sky, the Divine Masculine. Send your awareness into the upper part of your body and feel your way to your connection with Father Sky. At the same time turn your palms upwards towards the sky.

  - Now leave your left palm facing the sky and turn your right palm towards the earth. Feel both the masculine and feminine energies flow through you.

  - When you are ready, on your next in-breath bend your arms and bring your palms up to the level of your heart and have both palms facing towards the sky.

  - On the next in-breath raise your arms in a 'V' shape above your head. Look up into the 'V' shape you have created. Breathe and pause.

  - Now bring your palms together above your head and look forward or close your eyes. Breathe and pause.

  - On the next out-breath, draw both palms – and the energy with them – down to your face and feel the feminine and masculine energies dancing together. Breathe and pause.

  - When you are ready, bring your palms to touch your heart. Breathe and pause.

- **Sitting**
  Now sit comfortably on the edge of your chair with your feet a shoulder's width apart and flat on the floor with your spine straight. Place your palms facing down on your thighs. Breathe into your body and breathe into any tension you might be experiencing.

  - Now imagine your body as a hollow filled with warm liquid light that spreads from your feet through to your whole body. Feel your body filled with warmth and light.

  - Now place your hands on your heart, close your eyes and remember a moment when you felt wholeheartedly happy and joyful. Let the memory flood through your body.

- **Return**
  When you are ready, open your eyes, give thanks and return to your intention.

Practice 86
Visualization: Aligning Our Chakras

The word chakra derives from the Sanskrit word meaning 'wheel' or 'circle'. In the tantric traditions, the chakras are conceived as focal energy points or life force in the subtle body where the physical and the spiritual meet. When our chakras are blocked we can become stuck. When our chakras are aligned we are in balance.

There are seven main chakras:[22]

- The Muladhara, the base red sacral, is at the base of our spines and allows us to stay grounded and connected to the universal energies.

- The Svadhishthana, the orange solar plexus, is just above our navels and is linked to creativity, fertility and reproduction.

- The Manipura, the yellow solar plexus, is located in the stomach area and is linked to vitality and will.

- The Anahata, the green heart, is located in the centre of our chests and is the seat of love, empathy and compassion.

- The Vishuddha, the blue throat, is located in our throats and supports communication.

- The Ajna, the indigo 3rd eye, is located between our brows, and links us to universal consciousness and

- The Sahasrara, the violet Crown chakra, is located at the top of our heads and gives us access to pure thought and consciousness.

This is a guided visualization to help open, align and bring your chakras into balance:

- Sit comfortably. Place both of your feet on the ground. Allow your body to relax and let your arms rest loosely by your side. Breathe slowly and deeply.

- Now move your attention to the base of your spine. Imagine a red flower bud at the base of your spine. As the bud starts to gently open, see that it is vibrant and full of life energy. See the flower as joining you to the earth and her energy. Rest here.

- When you are ready, move your attention up your spine. Imagine an orange flower bud just below your navel. As the bud starts to gently open see the flowering also of your creativity. Rest here.

- When you are ready, move your attention up your spine and imagine a yellow flower bud just above your navel. As the bud starts to gently open see the flowering also of your agency and will. Rest here.

- When you are ready, move your attention up your spine and imagine a green flower bud in your chest. As the bud starts to gently open imagine the flowering also of your love. Rest here.

- When you are ready, move your attention up along your spine and imagine a blue flower bud at your throat. As the bud starts to gently open see the flowering also of your voice and your powers of communication. Rest here.

- When you are ready, move up your spine and imagine an indigo flower bud between your brows. As the bud starts to gently open see the flowering also of your intuition and connection to the universe and universal consciousness. Rest here.

- When you are ready, move up your spine and imagine a violet flower bud at the top of your head. As the bud starts to gently open see the flowering also of your oneness with pure consciousness. Rest here.

- Feel the flowering and the energy of your chakras within you. Bathe in the warm light and vibration within you. If you feel that the size of the flowers are different, just gently notice this and what is needed. Befriend the wisdom of each chakra centre.

- When you are ready, bring your palms together to give thanks.

- Journal any intuitions, thoughts or inspirations which might have emerged for you during the visualization.

A variation of this practice is to decide on a question or focus of inquiry before you start the visualization. Then as you travel up your spine, gently ask as each bud is unfolding if it has an offer or insight for you.

Practice 87
Exercise: The Joy of Wonder

Wonder is the art of remembering to see the magic in the everyday. It occurs when we take time and make space to be surprised and delighted by the small miracles that fill our lives. In this way the natural beauty of the world around us connects us to the mysterious abundance of the fertile void.

In her book *Thrive*, Arianna Huffington identifies wonder as one of the key elements in her metric for redefining a happy and successful life (the others are wellbeing, giving and wisdom).[23] As Walt Whitman writes:[24]

> After all, the great lesson is that no special natural sights – not Alps, Niagara, Yosemite or anything else – is more grand or more beautiful than the ordinary sunrise and sunset, earth and sky, the common trees and grass.

Albert Einstein thought of wonder as a precondition for life. He wrote:[25]

> The most beautiful thing we can experience is the mysterious. It is the source of all true art and science … Whoever is devoid of wonder remains unmoved, whoever cannot contemplate or know the deep shudder of the soul in enchantment, might as well be dead for he has already closed his eyes upon life.

Practice 87 is about making Wonder a daily practice for you. Here are some suggestions:

- Find the magic in the ordinary. Examples might include:
  - Pausing to be delighted or surprised by something you are seeing, hearing or doing
  - Pausing to see the beauty of nature and the changing of the seasons around you
  - Admiring a piece of art, photography, writing or music
  - Surrounding yourself with objects of beauty
  - Noticing miracles
- Journal what you notice. Notice what shifts in you as you engage with this practice.
- If you feel yourself getting irritated or closing down in any way, reconnect with your memories of feeling wonder.

As Mary Oliver reminds us:[26]

> Every day I walk out into the world
> to be dazzled, then to be reflective.

It suffices, it is all comfort –
along with human love,
dog love, water love, little-serpent love,
sunburst love, or love for that smallest of birds
flying among the scarlet flowers.

'Wisdom,' says Socrates,[27] 'begins in wonder.'

Practice 88
Exercise: The Joy of Wandering

We have learnt with our SatNavs, devices and productivity measures a fear of getting lost. Meandering and wandering off piste gives us the freedom to lose ourselves for a while. Wandering without knowing the route or having a fixed destination awakens our dulled senses and makes us alive and alert to new experiences.

As D. H. Lawrence wrote in *Women in Love*[28]

> That's the place to get to – nowhere. One wants to wander away from the world's somewheres, into our own nowhere.

For this practice try something new without the need for a purpose or a destination. For example:

* Make a meal without following the recipe

* Go for a walk without a map

* Switch off the computer

* Get lost in a book

* Put aside the 'to do ' list for a day

* Day dream

* Play with the word 'Nowhere': 'Now where', 'no where', 'now here'.

* Imagine. Follow your thoughts. Ask 'What if?'

For J. K. Rowling,[29]

> the idea of just wandering off to a cafe with a notebook and writing and seeing where that takes me for a while is just bliss.

Practice 89
Exercise: Creating Sacred Spaces

Sacred means 'holy'. Creating the spaces and finding the places for ourselves where we can retreat from the everyday to connect with the fertile void is crucial to supporting our creativity. This is a space for uninterrupted reflection and unrushed creative work. We tend to reduce touching the sacred to holy buildings but we can also easily create sacred spaces to support our work closer to home. Our environments can either support or drain us. This practice and the next are linked in this way.

As Joseph Campbell writes:[30] 'Our sacred space is where you can find yourself again and again.'

A range of suggestions are offered showing ways that you can create your own sanctuary for yourself depending on your circumstances and what works for you:

- Convert a place in your home into your sanctuary. Empty or fill it with comfortable furnishings, inspirational books, images, pictures, icons, flowers, plants and candles.

- Design your own altar.

- Find places in Mother Nature which you can use as your private sanctuary.

- De-clutter and surround yourself more generally with items which inspire you and which help you to touch the sacred in the everyday.

- Choose your rituals or how you want to be in your sacred space.

As Joseph further writes:[31]

> Sacred space is an absolute necessity for anybody today. You must have a room, or a certain hour or so a day, where you don't know what was in the newspapers that morning, you don't know who your friends are, you don't know what you owe anybody, you don't know what anybody owes to you. This is a place where you can simply experience and bring forth what you are and what you might be. This is the place of creative incubation. At first you may find that nothing happens there. But if you have a sacred place and use it, something eventually will happen. Our life has become so economic and practical in its orientation that, as you get older, the claims of the moment upon you are so great, you hardly know where the hell you are, or what it is you intended. You are always doing something that is required of you. Where is your bliss station? You have to try to find it.

Practice 90
Exercise: Creating Sacred Rituals

Creating rituals both for your sacred space and for your other workspaces can calm the mind, open the heart and anchor your work.

Below are a number of possible ways to create rituals for yourself depending on your circumstances and what works for you:

- Setting time aside to journal
- Setting time aside to be in your sacred space
- Setting time aside to meditate, exercise or relax
- Lighting a candle
- Putting flowers or plants on your desk
- Placing crystals, icons or inspirational quotes close to your computer or workstation

Practice 91
More Inspiration: Initiating the Invitation

Poems and quotes may support you in Initiating the Invitation into the Fertile Void. Below are some of my favourites.

> The creative process might be simplified if we stopped searching for ideas and simply made room for them to visit.
>
> Robert Grudin[32]

For William Blake, in his 'Auguries of Innocence', touching the Fertile Void was:[33]

> To see a World in a Grain of Sand
> And a Heaven in a Wild Flower,
> Hold Infinity in the palm of your hand
> And Eternity in an hour

In her poem 'Sands' Judy Brown shares the secret of how to write poetry, which can be applied to any act of creativity:[34]

....Writing poetry
is the practice
of seeing in stillness
listening for silence
that has wonder beneath it.

In her poem 'Fire' Judy Brown reminds us that it is the spaces in between that allow us to create:[35]

What makes a fire burn
is the space between the logs,
a breathing space.
Too much of a good thing,
too many logs
packing in too tight
can douse the flames
almost as surely
as a pail of water would.

So building fires
requires attention
to the spaces in-between,
as much as the wood.

When we are able to build
open spaces
in the same way
we have learned
to pile on the logs,
then we can come to see how
it is the fuel, and the absence of fuel
together, that make fire possible.

* * * * *

Reflective Questions

1. Which of the thirteen practices are you most drawn to and why?

2. Which of the thirteen practices are you least drawn to and why?

3. What are you going to action now?

CHAPTER 9
The Art of Listening

The Flow

Inner guidance is heard like soft music in the night by those who have learned to listen.

Vernon Howard[1]

The Flow
Reflection's Fertile Void
...Into Stillness and Spaciousness...

- Initiating the Invitation
- ## Art of Listening
- Finding Freedom

Profound listening comes from developing profound presence. Learning to listen to ourselves and others with curiosity, and with a willingness to be changed by it, is an act of deep respect and humility. As the pianist Alfred Brendel writes:[2] 'The word "listen" contains the same letters as the word "silent".'

Listening then becomes a way of hearing to understand – rather than a pause before we impose our already pre-scripted reply. For the Greek Philosopher Epictetus:[3] 'We have two ears and one mouth so that we can listen twice as much as we speak.'

As Peter Senge reminds us:[4]

Ears operate at the speed of sound, which is far slower than the speed of light the eyes take in. Generative listening is the art of developing deeper silences in yourself, so you can slow your mind's hearing to your ear's natural speed, and hear beneath the words their deeper meaning.

How we choose to listen is how we choose to create our reality. For theoretical physicist Werner Heisenberg, reality is observer created. Listening with an open mind and open heart for what is wanting to unfold from within the pre-verbal fertile void is the key to unlocking hidden potential and creativity.

Many people have already described the different levels of listening, which we can all access. I have adapted Otto Scharmer's four levels[5] and I define and describe them in Practice 45. The levels range from 1: Listening to Download, to 4: Listening to *Create!*, and they are all qualitatively different.

As Otto Scharmer writes:[6]

Level 4 listening differs in texture and outcomes from the others. ... You have connected to a deeper source – a source of who you really are and to a sense of why you are here – a connection that links you with a profound field of coming into being with your emerging authentic self.

I also see deep listening as a profound act of intimacy, of being heard, of being seen and of belonging, which we can extend to ourselves and to others. Level 4 listening is where we listen to connect with our own source (and what we intend) and to the Source of Life. As Epictetus writes in 'Caretake This Moment'.[7]

When your doors are shut and your room is dark you are not alone.
The will of nature is within you as your natural genius is within.
Listen to its importunings.
Follow its directives.

For some this is a place of profound communion and grace. In this extract of his poem 'The Opening of Eyes', David Whyte speaks of the power of listening to our hearts.[8]

> That day I saw beneath dark clouds
> the passing light over the water
> and I heard the voice of the world speak out,
> I knew then, as I had before
> life is no passing memory of what has been
> nor the remaining pages in a great book waiting to be read.
>
> It is the opening of eyes long closed.
> It is the vision of far off things
> seen for the silence they hold.
> It is the heart after years
> of secret conversing
> speaking out loud in the clear air.

Practices for the Art of Listening

There are many ways in which we can enhance our listening. Here are twenty-one practices which work for me. I choose from the list depending on what I need at any point in time.

Practice 92
Exercise: Listening Minute by Minute

Ernest Hemingway wrote:[9] 'When people talk, listen completely. Most people never listen.'

Often we tune out. When we tune out we are absent and the person talking can sense this shift.

This practice reminds us to cultivate our minute-by-minute listening skills so we tune into our own internal voice and the dialogue of others. For this practice:

- Tune into your own listening patterns. Notice when you tune out and switch off. Notice when you tune in. Journal what you notice and how you feel.

- Notice the impact on you when other people tune out and switch off from you. Journal what you notice and how you feel.

- Carry a notebook so that when you notice stray thoughts write them down so you can return to being fully present to the issue in hand.

As M. Scott Peck wrote:[10] 'You cannot truly listen to anyone and do anything else at the same time.'

Practice 93
Exercise: Listening to Each Other

As Roy T. Bennett writes:[11]

> Sometimes all a person wants is an empathetic ear; all he or she needs is to talk it out. Just offering a listening ear and an understanding heart for his or her suffering can be a big comfort.

This practice is for deep listening to each other.

- Work as a pair.

- Sit opposite to each other (with knees almost touching)

- Decide who is A and who is B in your pair. Each decide privately on the topic you want to explore.

- Ground and centre yourselves.

- Start to connect heart to heart.

- When you are ready look warmly into each others' eyes.

- B then creates an invitation for A to speak. B sits still and listens gently and wholeheartedly to A for 5 minutes without interruption or expression.

- After 5 minutes pause.

- Swap over. A then creates an invitation for B to speak. A sits still and listens gently and whole heartedly to B for 5 minutes again without interruption or expression.

This practice can also be extended to working in threes and fours.

For Karl A. Menniger,[12]

> Listening is a magnetic and strange thing, a creative force. The friends who listen to us are the ones we move toward. When we are listened to, it creates us, makes us unfold and expand.

Practice 94
Visualization: The Magic Gift Shop

Our answers are often quietly hidden within ourselves. All we have to do is listen to ourselves. For H. Jackson Brown Jnr,[13] 'Sometimes the heart sees what is invisible to the eye.'

This visualization exercise can help us to hear and see what we already know but which the strategic mind might prefer to shut out. This practice needs quiet, paper and coloured crayons or pens. You will need to arrange for the visualization exercise to be recorded on audio or read out to you by a facilitator:[14]

For this practice:

- Decide on the focus of your inquiry or your question to yourself.

- Draw what your current reality looks and feels like to you.

- Now sit or lie comfortably. Ground and centre yourself.

- When you are ready, listen to the visualization exercise.

Imagine yourself on a street in a town anywhere in the world ... (pause).

Follow this road through your curiosity until you come to a little street that is very narrow ... (pause). Walk down this street and see many shops and cafes in different colours ... (pause).

Explore this street taking in all the sights and sounds, colours and smells as you explore ... (pause).

You come to a gift shop and you are very interested in entering it. It is full to the top with so many different things from many places! Take time to walk through this shop and look at all the wonderful things inside. You can pick up and touch anything in the shop. Notice the things that you are drawn to ... (pause).

When you have explored the whole shop the owner says that you may choose one gift to take away with you ... Take some time in selecting just the right gift to take with you ... (pause).

When you have chosen, thank the shop owner and leave the shop ... Make your way down the little street ... (pause). Turn into the road where you began your exploration and with your gift return to the present moment here in this room.

- Now draw your gift. Capture its essence and its meaning for you.

- Journal what you have discovered.

Practice 95
Visualization: The Rose

This is another visualization helping us to hear what our strategic mind might prefer to shut out. This visualization allows you to not be necessarily working on a question but to allow impressions or images to just arise and arrive within you. You will need to arrange for the visualization exercise to be recorded on audio or read out to you by a facilitator:[15]

- Sit or lie comfortably. Ground and centre yourself.

- When you are ready, listen to the visualization exercise.

Imagine a rosebush: roots, stems, leaves and on top a rosebud. The rosebud is closed, and enveloped by its green sepals. Take your time in visualizing all the details closely.

Now imagine that the sepals are about to start to open. As they do so, you become aware of a blossoming also occurring in the depth of your being. You feel that something in you is opening and coming to light (pause)…

As you keep visualizing the rose you feel that its rhythm is your rhythm, its opening is your opening. You keep watching the rose as it opens up to the light and the air, as it reveals itself in all of its beauty (pause)…

You smell its beauty and absorb it into your being.

Now gaze into the centre of the rose, where life is most intense. Let an image emerge from there. This image will represent what is most beautiful, most meaningful, most creative that wants to come to light in your life right now. It can be an image of absolutely anything. Just let it emerge spontaneously, without forcing or thinking (pause) …

Now stay with this image for sometime, and absorb its quality (pause) …

This image may have a message for you – a verbal or a non-verbal message. Be receptive to it (pause) …

When you are ready and in your own time, return to the present moment.

- Journal what you have discovered.

Practice 96
Exercise: Walking a Labyrinth

The sacred geometry of the Labyrinth is a meditation to help us access our inner wisdom and the Divine within us.

A labyrinth is not a maze. It is often said that we enter a maze to lose ourselves, and a labyrinth to find ourselves. Labyrinths have only one path to the centre and back out again. The choice is whether we want to trust the process to enter it. Perhaps the most famous labyrinth is at Chartres Cathedral in Paris. We can either physically walk a labyrinth or, using the image below, trace our fingers or write our way in and out of the labyrinth.

For the practice:

- Frame your question or inquiry for contemplation.

- Ground and centre yourself.

- When you are ready enter the Labyrinth calmly and slowly. Open your senses.

- Gently, tune into your feet walking, your fingers tracing or your pen flowing on the paper. Listen to what is coming up for you.

- Gently follow the path until you reach the centre.

- Stay in the centre for as long as you need. Keep listening to what is coming up for you.

- When you are ready begin your return journey. Keep listening to what is coming up for you.

- When you have exited the Labyrinth reflect or journal to capture your experience.

Fig 1: Paper Labyrinth

Practice 97
Exercise: Listening for Your Word of the Year

For this practice, which was designed by Susannah Conway:[16]

- Set aside 5 days.

- **Day 1: Dreaming**

  - Ask yourself 'What would my ideal day look and feel like in the next 3, 6, or 12 months?' Chose the timescale which works best for you.

  - Journal your thoughts.

  - Rest this for 24 hours.

- **Day 2: Harvesting**

  - Re-read your journal from Day 1. Circle or highlight any words which feel important.

  - On a new page write down the words you have captured. Are there any other words you want to add to your list?

  - Give yourself a break.

  - When you are ready return to your list and circle up to five words that speak to you most.

  - On another new page list the five words. For each word write down the dictionary definition and your definition; ask yourself for any other supporting words which surround your word for you; ask yourself if there might be an even deeper meaning for you to your word; and finally ask yourself how does your word now feel?

  - Rest this for 24 hours.

- **Day 3: Noticing**

  - Add anything which has emerged for you overnight.

  - Now ask yourself what quality of word do you need going forward. For example, do you need an active or a passive word or do you need an inward or an outward word?

  - Notice your emotional and bodily reactions to your five words as you ponder what you need going forward.

  - Select the one or two words from your list of five which you love.

  - Rest this for 24 hours.

- **Day 4: Reflecting**
  - As you reflect on your one or two words from Day 3, relax. Go for a walk, colour in a mandala, paint or draw.
  - Listen to what else emerges for you.
  - Now select or confirm the word which you feel you will carry you forward.
  - Rest this for 24 hours.

- **Day 5: Honouring**
  - Now create ways for you to keep your word alive every day. Create a list of actions or checklists which you want to honour.

As Ossie Davies writes:[17]

> We can't float through life. We can't be incidental or accidental. We must fix our gaze on a guiding star as soon as one comes upon the horizon and once we have attached ourselves to that star we must keep our eyes on it and our hands upon the plough. It is the consistency of the pursuit of the highest possible vision that you can find in front of you that gives you the constancy, that gives you the encouragement, that gives you the way to understand where you are and why it's important for you to do what you can do.

Practice 98
Exercise: Listening to Your Intuition

For Flannery O'Connor:[18] 'I write because I don't know what I think until I read what I say.'

This practice helps us to listen to our intuition by writing in four short bursts of seven minutes.

For this practice:

- Frame your question or inquiry.
- Ground and centre yourself.
- Silence your inner critic; and do not stop to edit or correct your writing.

- **Part 1: Finding your 1st Three Words**
  - Set your timer for seven minutes.
  - When you are ready write as fast as you can for the full seven minutes.
  - When the timer goes off, go over your writing and circle the three words that most stand out for you.

- **Part 2: Finding your 2nd Three Words**

  o Set your timer for another seven minutes.

  o When you are ready write as fast as you can using the three words you have circled from Part 1 for inspiration for the full seven minutes.

  o When the timer goes off go over your writing and circle three different words that most stand out for you.

- **Part 3: Finding your 3rd Three Words**

  o Set your timer for another seven minutes.

  o When you are ready write as fast as you can using the three words you have circled from Part 2 for inspiration for the full seven minutes.

  o When the timer goes off go over your writing and circle three different words that most stand out for you.

- **Part 4: Writing Your Poem**

  o List the 9 words you have circled.

  o Set your timer for another seven minutes.

  o Now write a poem or a piece of prose using the nine words you have gathered.

  o If you are in a group, sharing your poem or prose is optional.

Practice 99
Exercise: Using Metaphor and Rune Cards

We do not know what we do not know. Using cards can help us to unlock our intuition. The cards are a way into helping us to explore our world through the world and language of metaphors, symbols and archetypes.

There are many metaphor and rune cards available.[19] You can also collect your own from postcards or magazines. There are also a wide variety of ways of using the cards. Here are just a few suggestions.

For this practice:

- Frame your question or inquiry.

- Ground and centre yourself.

- Create a sacred space with the cards. Only the practitioner may touch the cards once the practice has started.

- Here are a number of ways that you can use the cards:

- **Exercise 1: Magnetic Attraction!**
  - Shuffle the cards.
  - Spread the cards face up.
  - Choose the card you are intuitively drawn to.
  - Study the card and read what it means to you.

- **Exercise 2: Intuitive Choice!**
  - Shuffle the cards.
  - Spread the cards face down.
  - Select a card.
  - Turn it face up.
  - Study the card and what it means to you.

- **Exercise 3: Past, Present and Future!**
  - Shuffle the cards.
  - Place the cards either face up or face down.
  - Now select three cards and place them in the order you chose them from left to right in front of you.
  - Your 1st card on your left represents your Past.
  - Your 2nd card in the middle represents your Present.
  - Your 3rd card to your right represents your Future.
  - Study each card and read what it means to you.
  - Stand back and see the interconnections.

Other variations are to use your 1st card as your *Overview*, the 2nd card as your *Challenge*, and the 3rd card as your *Course of Action*.

Another alternative is to use your 1st card as *The Voice of Instinct;* your 2nd card as the *Voice of*

Reason; and your 3rd card as the *Voice of Humanity* to act with wisdom.

- **Exercise 4: North, South, East and West.**

  - Shuffle the cards.

  - Place the cards either face up or face down.

  - Now select four cards and place the 1st card to your North, the 2nd card to your South, the 3rd card to your West and the fourth card to your East.

  - Your 1st card represents the *Positives* of your situation: your qualities, your strengths and the possibilities in the situation.

  - Your 2nd card represents the *Negatives* of your situation: your internal and external obstacles, your difficulties and the points of clarification needed.

  - Your 3rd card represents your *Advice* from the universe or Oracle: what direction is needed?

  - Your 4th card represents the *Outcome*: what you may be able to expect from the development of events and how you may prepare yourself for what is to come.

Practice 100
Exercise: Listening to the Magic Box

'The Magic Box' is another way of exploring the world and language of metaphors, symbols and archetypes. The Magic Box enables us to listen as we create a visual representation or constellation of our relationships.[20]

For this practice you need to work in pairs. You need a cloth to create the stage and a collection of objects. Only the practitioner can touch the cloth or the objects.

- Ask the practitioner to spread the cloth on a table. This creates the sacred space and boundaries to contain the work. Open up the Magic Box of objects close by.

- Ask the practitioner to frame their question or inquiry and then to centre and ground themselves.

- Start by asking the practitioner to select an object which stands out for them in relation to their question and place it on the cloth. Invite the practitioner to say a little about why they have chosen the object and placed it where they have.

- Then go on to ask them to add and place other objects which speak to their issue until they feel complete.

- As the stage unfolds simply ask open questions about what the different objects may be thinking, feeling, seeing and hearing from their various positions. When this is complete ask 'What is now needed?' or 'What would help now?'

- When no more insights or connections are available ask the practitioners to put away the objects and fold up the cloth to signal the end of the inquiry.

Practice 101
Meditation: Listening to All of Ourselves

All too often we find that we fall into the trap of only listening to our head brain. This cuts us off from the vital wisdom we all have within us. Listening from the whole of ourselves is a rare gift to ourselves and to our clients.

For this simple but profound practice you ideally need some space to move around but it can also be done sitting on a chair.

- Frame your question or inquiry.

- Stand up. Ground and centre yourself.

- Now put your hand on your gut and ask 'What would my gut say?' Stay here for 3 to 5 minutes. When you are ready move or walk somewhere else.

- When you are ready put your hand on your heart and ask 'What would my heart say?' Stay here for 3 to 5 minutes. When you are ready move or walk somewhere else.

- Now put your hand to your soul/wiser self, perhaps in a prayer position or by opening your arms, and ask 'What would my soul or spirit say?'

- Now put your hand on your head and ask 'What would my head say?' Stay here for 3 to 5 minutes. When you are ready move or walk somewhere else.

- When you are ready come out of the reflection and capture what has emerged for you in your journal.

As the writer Anthony J. D'Angelo reminds us:[21] 'Listen to your intuition. It will tell you everything you need to know.'

Practice 102
Inquiry: 'What is it that remains?'

The 13th-century mystic Meister Eckhart posed the question 'What is it that remains?'

His answer was: 'That which is inborn in me remains.'

This practice is a simple and profound meditation as you listen in Reflection's Fertile Void to find your meaning and your legacy: 'Who am I?' and 'What is my work?'

- Sit with the question. 'What is it that remains?' and 'What is it that remains for me and of me?'

- Write your own obituary.

- Meditate. Reflect. Listen. Dwell.

- Journal, paint, draw or design what emerges for you.

Practice 103
Inquiry: 'How will you go about finding that thing which is totally unknown to you?'

The pre-Socratic philosopher Meno asked of a person and of a life: 'How will you go about finding that thing which is totally unknown to you?'

However, as Rebecca Solnit writes:[22]

> The things we want are transformative, and we don't know or only think we know what is on the other side of transformation. Love, wisdom, grace, inspiration – how do you go about finding these things which are in some ways about extending the boundaries of self into unknown territory, about becoming somebody else?

This practice is another simple and profound meditation as you listen in Reflection's Fertile Void to 'that thing or things which are totally unknown you'.

- Sit with the question. 'What is totally unknown to me?' and ask yourself 'Do I want to find it?'

- Meditate. Reflect. Listen. Dwell.

- Journal, paint, draw or design what emerges for you.

Practice 104
Exercise: Listening to Dance!

Reflection's Fertile Void is full of life: of listening for the natural receptivity, response and reciprocity – and for the spaces in between – which is life.

A fun way to directly experience this is through co-creating an improvised dance (or an improvised piece of music).

- Find a partner. Choose your music.
- Decide who will lead and who will follow.
- Stand together touching hands.
- The leader initiates the moves and the follower follows.
- As you both attune to your natural flow and rhythm the leader will follow the follower and both the leader and follower will merge.
- Enjoy your co-created dance!
- Journal what it felt like to let go, and to tune in to each other.

As Gabrielle Roth, the founder of the 5Rhythms movements, wrote:[23]

> In the rhythm of the body, we can trace our holiness, roots that go all the way back to zero ... states of being where all identities dissolve into an eternal flow of energy. Energy moves in waves. Waves move in patterns. Patterns move in rhythms. A human being is just that, energy, waves, patterns, rhythms. Nothing more. Nothing less. A dance.

There are many ways to dance any number of dances – on your own, with a partner, in a class and/or in a community. This practice invites you to find your way to dance with life.

Practice 105
Exercise: 'The Future is Already Here!'

The future is already present. The seeds of the future are already sown in the fertile void. However, we can often be too busy being busy to listen.

This practice invites us to listen for the apparently random clues and hints of the future in our everyday.

- Create your own Treasure Chest! Be curious! Have fun!

- Jot down, draw or photograph anything which is unusual or delights, surprises or worries you over, say, a month (it could be longer or shorter depending on what you need). This could be anything from quotes, magazine cuttings, comments, images, ideas or impressions. Refrain from analyzing or judging what you are noticing.

- At intervals – or at the end of your chosen period – revisit your treasure chest. Gently, look for any patterns which may be emerging.

- Reflect and journal the possible invitations from the patterning.

- Ask yourself 'Which seeds are yours and which are not yours?' and 'Which seeds are asking for your attention, planting and nurturing?'

- Continue your quest as needed.

- Do not force the story or the evidence!

As Rumi wrote:[24] 'The inspiration you seek is already inside you. Be silent and listen.'

Practice 106
Exercise: Hosting a Listening Temenos

This practice teaches us to create a listening environment where we can hear ourselves – and others – think as we explore the edges of our not knowing and potentiality. We cannot instruct ourselves – or each other – to listen wholeheartedly with respect, openness, encouragement and appreciation but we can create, through the Art of Hosting, the conditions to encourage it. This is further explored in Chapter 14 on supervision.

This practice has been inspired by a traditional greeting, which is shared by the Zulu people in South Africa.[25] The greeting is an invocation, spoken in two parts. The first part is 'Sikhona', which means 'I am here to be seen.' The second part is 'Sawubona', which means 'I see you.'

Hosting creates the safety for us to invoke the Zulu greeting and to listen from the whole of us. The safety comes from HOW we chose to listen and WHAT we contract with and/or between ourselves for our wholehearted listening: for carefully creating the conditions and the processes for the dance.

Human qualities create the humane conditions for hosting a Listening Environment. These are the qualities of the 7Cs of Care, Courage, Curiosity, Compassion, Connection, Creativity and Contemplation. Listening to ourselves – and others – with these qualities creates vibrations of warmth, equality, respect, acceptance and safety within us, which are necessary for deep dives into Reflection's Fertile Void.

In order for you to create the conditions for hosting a Listening Environment:

- Complete the 7Cs Self Assessment Map and re-assess how you extend these qualities to yourself and others for listening. You can download a PDF of the Map from my website or copy the illustration below.

- Explore how you can build these qualities into your contracting with yourself and others when you work – and how you can blend these with the Ethical Guidelines and Codes of Conduct from your own professional body.

- Explore and journal what the term 'hosting' means to you.

- Explore and journal what 'being a host' means for you. Consider how you would host a dinner party or a celebration and map how you feel and what you do into your work context.

- Consider how you need to prepare yourself to host with ease, grace, inclusivity and generosity.

As the *temenos* or container for the work is created, attention should also be paid to what needs to emerge. This welcoming includes the responsibilities of the Host to themselves (if they are working on their own) or others if they are working in pairs or in groups to *Arrive,* to *Work* and to then *Depart.*

a. The Arrival

- Hosting the space.

- Extending a Welcome.

- Offering a Grounding or Centring practice.

- Checking in with self – and with each other if you are working in a group.

- Extending the Zulu greeting of 'Sikhona' and 'Sawubona' to each other.

- Contracting for the session. What is needed and how to BE in the work.

b. The Work

- Using the Reflect to *Create!* dance map to host the inquiry.

c. The Departure

- Harvesting insights, learning and actions from the work.

- Appreciating self or others if you are working in a group.

- Inviting a closing word to capture feelings at the end of the session.

Practice 107
Exercise: The Talking Stick

This Practice builds on the previous practice for facilitating pair work or for working in groups.

As the Dalai Lama has said:[26] 'When you talk you only repeat what you already know. When you listen you may learn something new.'

Often we can talk over each other. The 'Talking Stick' – real or metaphorical – is a useful tool to encourage everyone to really listen to each other. Using it does not follow the pattern of our everyday conversations when we typically speak when we want to.

The Talking Stick is borrowed from the native traditions. Everyone has their turn to speak without the fear of being interrupted. When one person speaks everyone else is required to listen with their full attention.

PattersonPrenticeDesigns have designed the 'Basket and Harvest' process for group supervision, which incorporates the Talking Stick and which can be applied in any setting. Listening in this way is a radical act of respect to the other.

The format for this practice is in three parts as follows:

1. The Presentation

- The Presenter raises their question or issue.

- The Host asks any clarifying questions to hone the question for the group to work on.

- The Presenter then sits back holding a metaphorical basket in their lap as they listen to what now emerges from the group.

2. The Offerings

- ○ The Host then invites each person in the group to have the Talking Stick. In turn each person offers – without giving criticism, advice or judgment – what they are noticing in themselves, what they are curious about, or what they are wondering about from the Practitioner's presentation. Everyone listens to the holder of the Talking Stick without interruption or discussion.

3. The Harvesting

- ○ The Host then invites the Presenter to gather all the offerings within their basket and reflect on what has been useful or enlightening. It is also OK for them to say that nothing has been useful. No discussion with the group is entered into.

- ○ The Host then offers any last comments that may be helpful.

- ○ The Host then invites each member of the group to reflect on their learning from working on the Presenter's issue, as something that they want to apply to their life or work.

A variation on this might be in The Offerings Sequence for the Host to host 3 rounds. In the first round, each person offers a word which comes to mind, in the second a bodily sensation and in the third an image. In the Harvesting Sequence, each person offers a question for the Presenter to consider as they reflect on the contents of the Basket.

For this practice

- • Consider how you might apply this approach to your team or group conversations.

- • Consider how you might apply this approach to hear and resolve differences.

- • Journal your experiences.

Practice 108
Exercise: The Power of Day Dreaming

'I have a dream ....' said Martin Luther King in his public speech on 28th August 1963 during the march on Washington for jobs and freedom.[27] Dreams have the power to inspire and invent the future.

Allowing ourselves to listen to our day dreams is a powerful way of inhabiting the Fertile Void.

For this practice

- Ask yourself 'I wonder....' , 'What is possible....?' And 'What if ....?' questions.

- Allow yourself to ponder, to doodle, muse, draw, meander.

- Allow your dreams to germinate and surface.

- Stay open and inquiring. Do not rush to judge.

- Journal what you are dreaming.

Practice 109
Exercise: Dynamic Inquiry

Dynamic Inquiry is a style of conversation designed to discover the feelings and dreams of a system's key players and stakeholders in order to create different futures.

For this practice:

- Frame your question.

- Invite your interviewees to a focused conversational inquiry. This could be either 1:1 or in smaller groups. Practice 107 may also be adapted here.

- Co-create a safe and confidential Listening Environment. Practice 107 may also be used here.

- Take notes or record and transcribe your conversations.

- Using stickers complete a thematic analysis of the core themes and patterns which emerge. Test to see if there is a consensus or a shared language and where there are outliers.

- Play with your findings to see if new possibilities or potential are revealed for testing in Reflect to *Create's!* Denouement – Return's Harvest and Action.

As Janine Benyus writes:[28] 'The answers to questions are everywhere: we just need to change the lens with which we see the world.'

Practice 110
Exercise: World Cafés' Deep Democracy

A World Café is a structured process whereby groups of people discuss a topic at several tables, and individuals switch tables periodically. World Cafés are a form of deep democracy. They engage key stakeholders to reveal different perspectives and tap into a collective wisdom to access potential and possibility. The specifics of purpose, context, numbers, and location can be factors in each Café's unique invitation, question choice and design.

The core principles for hosting conversations that matter are:[29]

1. **Context Setting**
   Create the invitation and clarify the purpose and boundaries within which the conversation will be hosted.

2. **Design the Welcome**
   Extend a warm welcome by creating a café-style layout with, say, 4 to 5 chairs per table, decorated with flowers, writing materials, and resources.

3. **Explore Questions that Matter**
   Design questions which matter to the participants.

4. **Encourage Everyone's Contribution**
   Use the talking stick to invite and create the space for everyone's best thinking. See Practice 107.

5. **Cross Pollination**
   Invite each table to name a table host who stays to provide continuity and as café participants periodically swap tables to build, diversify and cross-pollinate insights.

6. **Listen Together for Deeper Patterns and Connections**
   Practice focused relational presence to speak one's own truth whilst listening together to what is wanting to emerge at both the personal and collective level.

7. **Harvest and Share Collective Discoveries**
   At a plenary table hosts share the collective wisdom which has surfaced from their table. Build shared wisdom and collective insights for next steps.

As Margaret Wheatley writes:[30]

> As separate ideas or entities become connected together, life surprises us with emergence – the sudden appearance of new capacity and intelligence ... The magic in the middle ... the Voice in the centre of the room.

Practice 111
Inquiry: Finding the Language for Listening

Rainer Maria Rilke reminds us to embrace love, and live our questions, and not to rush at answers, which are not yet formed or ready to emerge. As he wrote:[31]

> Try to love the questions themselves as if they were locked rooms or books written in a very foreign language. Don't search for the answers, which could not be given to you now, because you would not be able to live them. And the point is, to live everything. Live the questions now. Perhaps then, someday far in the future, you will gradually, without even noticing it, live your way into the answer.

Listening is a radical act of trust and patience as we explore the questions that life asks of us. Our early intuition inhabits a different landscape, inviting us to listen in different ways to our everyday speech. Poetry, art, music, nature and literature can help us tune into new and different base notes and timbres which can help support us in our listening. This is because, as John O'Donohue wrote,[32]

> There is an unseen life that dreams us; it knows our true direction and destiny. We can trust ourselves more than we realize, and we need have no fear of change.

For this practice ask yourself:

- 'What is life inviting me into?' and 'What does life want of me?'
- Which poets, writers, musicians, artists or places can help support me to listen with a different ear?
- How can I learn to trust my listening?
- How can I learn to listen in the Fertile Void with ease and grace?

For Paul Goodman:[33]

> Confusion is the state of promise
> The Fertile Void where surprise is possible again.

Practice 112
More Inspiration: The Art of Listening

Here are some poems and quotes to support your listening into the Fertile Void.

Rumi wrote:[34] 'In Silence there is eloquence. Stop weaving, (start listening) and see how the pattern improves.'

The poet Dean Jackson reminds us:[35] 'Listening is an art that requires attention over talent, spirit over ego, others over self.'

For Parker J. Palmer:[36]

> Before you tell your life what you intend to do with it, listen for what it intends to do with you. Before you tell your life truths and values you have decided to live up to, let your life tell you what truths you embody, what values you represent.

Judy Brown's poem 'Why the Journal?' reminds us why listening and journaling is so important and also provides a segue into the next chapter, Finding Freedom.[37] My journal is the most powerful listening device I have.

> Why the Journal?
> To sit with something of yourself,
> As you would sit in church,
> Or with a tearful child.
>
> Why the Journal now?
> To notice (and listen for) questions
> That are threads
> In webs of life
> We are often too fast to see.
>
> Why the journal?
> To be whole.

* * * * *

Reflective Questions

1. Which of the twenty-one practices are you most drawn to and why?

2. Which of the twenty-one practices are you least drawn to and why?

3. What are you going to action now?

CHAPTER 10
Finding Freedom

And the world cannot be discovered by a journey of miles,
no matter how long,
but only by a spiritual journey,
a journey of one inch,
very arduous and humbling and joyful,
by which we arrive at the ground at our feet,
and learn to be at home.

From 'A Spiritual Journey' by Wendell Berry[1]

The Flow

Reflection's Fertile Void

...Into Stillness and Spaciousness...

- Initiating the Invitation
- Art of Listening
- Finding Freedom

Freedom comes when we learn to listen to our intuition and allow our inner wisdom to guide us home to ourselves.

Finding Freedom is both appreciating the work of the everyday self to keep us operational, functioning and safe <u>and</u> embracing the journey of our soul which uniquely defines us and which frees us to connect with others through our shared humanity. For Eckhart Tolle:[2]

> There is a vast realm of intelligence beyond thought, that thought is only a tiny aspect of that intelligence. You also realize that all things that truly matter – beauty, love, creativity, joy, inner peace – arise beyond the mind. You begin to awaken.

A person's vocation comes from the inside out and is the marriage of soul and role; of self and service. For Frederick Buechner vocation is 'the place where your deep gladness meets the world's deep need.'[3]

This is a spiritual journey to discovering the ground on which we stand <u>and</u> the horizons that we see and want to create. My love of Nordic walking is all about appreciating the earth beneath my feet and the horizons where I am headed. Balance, focus and perspective are all lost if I try to look at both at the same time. As David Whyte writes:[4]

> The (daily) dance of distraction makes more real, and more necessary, our ability to return to essential ground, .. or to an essential work … to renew our (own) primary essential invitation again … And is a radically courageous act of freedom. We withdraw not to disappear, but to find another ground from which to see; a solid ground from which to step, and from which to speak again, in a different way, a clear, rested, embodied voice we begin to remember again as our own.

For Parker J. Palmer good work comes from practitioners who have penetrated their own inner darkness and dividedness and have arrived at their own place of 'hidden wholeness' where they are at one with themselves.[5] Life is a process of becoming. As Parker writes:[6]

> Our souls have no race, ethnicity or role: our souls are at the core of our shared humanity as well as our individual uniqueness. When we create spaces where the soul feels safe, it will help us deal with the most divisive issues.

For Marianne Williamson:[7]

> Love is what we are born with. Fear is what we learn. The spiritual journey is the unlearning of fear and prejudices and the acceptance of love back in our hearts. Love is the essential reality and our purpose on earth. To be consciously aware of it, to experience love in ourselves and others, is the meaning of life. Meaning does not lie in things. Meaning lies in us.

For Rumi,[8] 'Our task is not to seek for love, but merely to seek and find all the barriers within yourself that you have built against it.'

Reflect to *Create!* is the process of alchemy where we have the opportunity to turn the base metal of our experiences into gold.

The French philosopher Pierre Teilhard de Chardin argued that we are spiritual beings having a human experience. Not being ourselves or living a life which is not our own is exhausting. The poet May Sarton wrote of the relief on coming home to herself:[9]

> Now I become myself.
> It's taken time, many years and places.
> I have been dissolved and shaken.
> Worn other people's faces.

This is freedom to know yourself and to love your life. This is our birthright freedom to find our own place in the world, to choose what we do and do it well, to find our own note which can hold our song. To find our heart song, which is so hard for the penguin Mumble in the film *Happy Feet*.[10] In that film, the heart song is the individual's unique song which helps every penguin find their mate. Mumble could not sing but he could dance. The film tells the story of how he falls in love. This is Derek Walcott's 'Love After Love':[11]

> The time will come
> when, with elation
> you will greet yourself arriving
> at your own door, in your own mirror
> and each will smile at the other's welcome,
> and say, sit here. Eat.
> You will love again the stranger who was your self.
> Give wine. Give bread. Give back your heart
> to itself, to the stranger who has loved you
> all your life, whom you ignored
> for another, who knows you by heart.
> Take down the love letters from the bookshelf,
> the photographs, the desperate notes,
> peel your own image from the mirror.
> Sit. Feast on your life.

Practices for Finding Freedom

There are many ways in which we can find freedom. Here are the twenty-one which work for me.

Practice 113
Inquiry: Befriending Our Soul's Wisdom

The *Concise Oxford Dictionary* defines our soul as[12] 'the spiritual or immaterial part of a human being, held to survive death'.

For the Buddhists, the soul is called our Original Nature. For the Hasidic Jews it is called a Spark of the Divine, for the Quakers it is our Inner Teacher or Inner Light and for the Humanists it is our Identity and Integrity. As Parker J. Palmer writes:[13]

> What we call it matters little, since its origins, nature and destiny… are forever hidden from us. But that we name it matters … as it is the ontological reality of selfhood that keeps us from reducing ourselves to biological mechanisms, psychological projection, sociological constructs or raw material to be manufactured into whatever society needs – diminishments of our humanity that constantly threaten the quality of our lives.

For Parker:[14]

> We are born with a seed of selfhood that contains the spiritual DNA of our uniqueness – an encoded birthright knowledge of who we are, why we are here, and how we are related to others. We may abandon that knowledge over the years but it never abandons us.

Our souls bring us home to ourselves. Our souls want to tell us the truth about ourselves and our world. Our souls give us the language to connect with others though the gift of life and through our shared humanity.

For Mary Oliver:[15]

Nobody knows what the soul is,
it comes and goes like,
wind on the water.

As Mary says,[16] 'This is the first, wildest and wisest thing I know … that the soul exists and it is built entirely out of attentiveness.'

Practice 113 is a deeply reflective and meditative practice. Ask yourself:

- 'When did I last feel my soul?' Try to capture the experience through journaling, writing or drawing or through sharing it with another person. What happened? How did it happen?

- 'When did I last hear the whisperings of my soul?' Again try to capture the experience. What did your soul whisper to you? How did you react?

- 'How can I befriend my soul more?'

- 'How does my soul like to be treated by me?'

Practice 114
Exercise: The Lost Art of Remembering to Remember

Coming home to ourselves is remembering to remember who we are. Homecoming is remembering our birthright and making life choices which support us rather than distort us or throw us off track. We can often find ourselves suffocated by temptations, demands and requirements which may superficially please but in which we can also lose ourselves. As Laura Riding writes:[17]

> To be nobody but yourself in a world which is doing its best, night and day, to make you everybody else means to fight the hardest battle which any human being can fight; and never stop fighting.

As David Whyte writes in 'What to Remember When Waking', there is a small opening into the day which closes the moment you start your plans, because:[18]

> What you can plan
> is too small for you to live by.

> What you can live by
> wholeheartedly
> will make plans enough
> for the vitality hidden in your sleep.

> To be human

is to become visible
while carrying
what is hidden
as a gift to others.

This practice invites you to return to what your soul carries for you. Ask yourself:

- 'What does my soul want me to remember?'

- 'What is my soul asking of me today/right now/or in this?'

- 'What are the costs to me of not remembering?'

- Journal, draw or paint what you owe to yourself to remember.

- Choose an inspirational object, quote or image to remind you to remember.

Practice 115
Inquiry: Belonging to Ourselves

Maya Angelou once said,[19] 'You are only free when you realize you belong no place – you belong every place – no place at all. The price is high. The reward is great.'

True freedom and true belonging is belonging to ourselves so we can then gift ourselves to others. True belonging is making our home and being at home with who we are. As Brene Brown writes:[20]

> True belonging is the spiritual practice of believing in and belonging to yourself so deeply that you can share your most authentic self with the world and find sacredness in both being a part of something and standing alone in the wilderness. True belonging doesn't require you to change who you are; it requires you to be who you are.

In this extract from the poem 'Invictus', William Ernest Henley writes:[21]

> Out of the night that covers me,
> Black as the Pit from pole to pole,
> I thank whatever gods may be
> For my unconquerable soul.
>
> .....

It matters not how strait the gate,
How charged with punishments the scroll.
I am the master of my fate:
I am the captain of my soul.

For this practice ask yourself:

- 'What does the word "home" mean for me?'

- 'Where do I feel my home is in this world?'

- 'When and where am I free to be myself and belong to me?'

- 'Do I feel myself to be the captain of my own soul?'

- 'To what extent do I belong to myself rather than others?'

- Journal your reflections.

Practice 116
Meditation: Following Our Soul's Path

Finding our own ground to stand on **and** the horizon which invites and beckons us is a frontier conversation with our souls which is at the essence of who we are and who we are becoming. Standing on our own solid ground and seeing where we are headed provides us with our own bigger context.

As Mary Oliver invites us in her poem 'The Summer Day'[22]:

Tell me what is it you plan
to do with your one wild and precious life?

We make our path though the terrain of our lives step by step. As Antonio Machado wrote:[23]

Wanderer, your footsteps are the road, and nothing more; wanderer, there is no
road, the road is made by walking. By walking one makes the road, and upon glancing behind one sees
the path that never will be trod again. Wanderer, there is no road.

For this Walking or Running Meditation Practice:

- As you step forward, periodically switch your attention between the ground beneath your feet and the horizon.

- Feel into what happens within your body as you pay careful attention to both.

- Try doing both at once and see what happens.

- Ask yourself 'What does being able to stand on solid ground mean for me?', 'What does this look like?' and 'What does it gift me both now in nature and in my life and work?'

- Then ask yourself 'What new horizons are revealing themselves to me?'

- Photo journal or journal your reflections.

As Nobel-winning poet Seamus Heaney said in a Commencement Address,[24] 'The true and durable path into and through experience involves being true to your own solitude, true to your own secret knowledge.'

Practice 117
Meditation: On the Poem 'The Woodcarver' and the Inner Work Before the Work

Who we are is how we work. As Parker J. Palmer writes:[25]

I want my inner truth to be the plumbline for the choices I make about my life – about the work that I do and how I do it, about the relationships I enter into and how I conduct them.

This practice is a meditation on a poem called 'The Woodcarver' by Chuang Tzu which speaks of the beauty which can be created once the inner work is done.[26]

Khing, the master carver, made a bell stand
Of precious wood. When it was finished,
All who saw it were astounded. They said it must be
The work of spirits.
The Prince of Lu said to the master carver:
'What is your secret?'

Khing replied: 'I am only a workman:
I have no secret…'

When I began to think about the work you commanded
I guarded my spirit, did not expend it
On trifles, that were not to the point.
I fasted in order to set
My heart at rest.
After three days of fasting
I had forgotten gain and success.

After five days
I had forgotten praise and criticism.
After seven days
I had forgotten my body
With all of its limbs.

By this time all thought of your Highness
And the court had fallen away.
All that might distract me from the work
Had vanished.
I was collected in the single thought
Of the bell stand.

Then I went to the forest
To see the trees in their own natural state.
When the right tree appeared before my eyes,
The bell stand also appeared in it, clearly, beyond doubt.
All I had to do was put forth my hand
And begin.

For this practice:

- As you read and reread the lines reflect what they mean and what they mean for you.

- Ask yourself 'How and when do I do my own inner work before the work?'

- Ask yourself 'What am I noticing for me and for my work as a result?'

- Ask yourself 'How could I bring more of the spirit of Khing the Woodcarver into my life and work?'

- Journal, paint, model or draw your discoveries.

Practice 118
Exercise: Life on the Mobius Strip

Our souls invite us to work from the inside out. We are born whole with no separation between our inner and outer lives. We learn dividedness.

A möbius strip, which is also called the twisted cylinder, is a one-sided surface with no boundaries and looks like an infinite loop. This practice is therefore an activity which shows how we can become divided and what returning to wholeness looks like. It also beautifully shows how reality is co-created by a conversation between our interior selves and the outside world. We shape who we are becoming by the choices we make.

- Cut a half-inch strip from a sheet of A4 paper.

- Let one side represent your outer on stage life – your image, impact and influence. Let the other side represent your inner or off stage life – your mind, heart, and soul. Or what we can describe as the outer world and our inner truth.

- **Step 1:**
  Now, holding the strip of paper at each end see how the strip has become a separating wall dividing our outer world and inner truth; our onstage and backstage lives.

- **Step 2:**
  Then join the two ends of the strip together with sellotape. Here our inner truth becomes the radar for our choices but can then create a barrier to anything or anybody that we might find inconvenient, challenging, uncomfortable or disruptive.

- **Step 3:**
  Now take your circle and pull the two ends apart, give one end a half twist and then rejoin the two ends. Holding the strip in one hand use the index finger on your other hand to trace what seems to be the outside of the strip which then seamlessly guides you to the inside of the strip. The message of Step 3 is, as Parker J. Palmer writes:[27] 'Whatever is inside us continually flows outward to help form, or deform, the world – and whatever is outside us continually flows inwards to form, or deform our lives.'

- Notice how you felt as you completed each Step. Journal what was coming up for you and how the 'wall' plays itself out in your life and work.

- Ask yourself 'What am I sending from within myself out into the world, and what impact is this having?' and 'What is the world sending back to me, and what is the impact it is having inside me?'

- Then ask yourself 'How I am choosing between what gives light and life and what gives dark and death moment by moment?'

Practice 119
Inquiry: Freeing our Inner Quantum Creativity

Dr. Amit Goswami in his book *Quantum Creativity: Think Quantum, Be Creative*[28] describes 'quantum thinking' as a conversation between our quantum selves who dwell in possibility and our ego selves who dwell in practicalities to bring the new into the world.

In his book he identifies two categories of creativity where inner creativity seeks deeper truth and spiritual growth and outer creativity seeks to problem-solve. He writes:[29]

> Both inner and outer creativity are about freedom … outer creativity should become the expression of your inner freedom in the outer world… We become most creative when we recognize that the cosmos is trying to act through us.

In this way creativity is the dance to freedom: to free ourselves to become uniquely ourselves which is then expressed uniquely by us through our life and work.

For this practice ask yourself:

• 'How do I feel this creative tension between my quantum self and my ego self?'

• 'What does this look like for me?' and 'What metaphor is evoked as I reflect on this?'

• 'To what extent do I feel that the cosmos is trying to act through me?'

• Journal or draw your reflections.

Practice 120
Exercise: Freedom in the Eternal NOW

Alan Watts writes that real freedom exists in the eternal NOW[30]. Alan explains that the root of all of our anxieties and frustrations lies in our powers of memory and prediction which seek to impose control on life but which deny how life is. The past and future take us out of connection with life's source, which is created, moment by moment, in the present. Alan writes:[31]

> This moving vital NOW is the mysterious real world which words and ideas can never pin down. Almost every spiritual tradition recognizes that a point comes when two things must happen: a person must surrender their separate feeling 'I' and face the fact that they cannot define the ultimate. This vision is the unclouded awareness of this something we call life – an awareness without the sense of separation from it.

Freedom comes from appreciating that there is no security, no permanence, no continuity and no reality except what you are aware of and what you can co-create in the present moment. This means that every experience is new, and at every moment in our lives we are in the midst of the new and unknown.

For this practice:

- Ask yourself 'What is my relationship with the Past, Present and Future?'

- Ask yourself 'How do my memories of the past or my predictions for the future interfere with my present?'

- Ask yourself 'How do I experience the eternal NOW and freedom to be in the moment?'

- Ask yourself 'How can I learn to anchor myself more fully in the present?'

- Ask yourself 'How can I fall in love with where I am?'

- Journal your discoveries.

As Omid Safi writes:[32]

> So much of our lives are spent in a fractured state of heart. We are, too often, scattered. We speak about being scatterbrained. The truth of the matter is that the scatteredness is much more systematic. We are scattered at every level: body, soul, mind, spirit. We do this to ourselves. We throw ourselves to the past, often clinging to a past pain and trauma. Or, we hurl ourselves towards the future, attaching ourselves to a hope for the future, or fear of losing something. We are in the past, or in the future, everywhere but here. To pray with the heart, to have presence in the heart, is a remedy. It is a healing, an un-scattering. Presence is simply to have our heart be where our feet are.

Practice 121
Exercise: Choosing Choice!

Creativity is born from freedom; born from our inner choice to give birth to something new and not to struggle or strive. We are free to co-create with life in every living moment. This means that at any and every moment we can choose either creativity or destruction, or the light or the dark. What we choose second by second, minute by minute, shapes WHO we are and WHO we are becoming. As Bryant McGill reminds us:[33] 'You are creating through your choices, even now. Choose wisely.'

For this practice ask yourself:

- 'What am I choosing second by second?'

- 'What is my default when I feel under pressure?'

- 'How aware am I of the choice I am making?'

- 'How free do I feel as I choose choice?'
- Journal your reflections.

Practice 122
Inquiry: Catching Up with Ourselves

We live on the frontiers of our own becoming. Life constantly presents frontier conversations for us to choose 'WHO and WHAT is me?' and 'WHO and WHAT is not me?' We are fortunate in that where we live we have an incredible freedom to create our lives through the choices we make. We are also free to drift. Therefore catching up with ourselves is a constant practice to ensure that we stay true to ourselves. In his poem 'The Journey' David Whyte reminds us that:[34]

Sometimes everything
   has to be
      inscribed across
         the heavens

so you can find
   the one line
      already written
         inside you.

Sometimes it takes
   a great sky
      to find that

first bright
   and indescribable
      wedge of freedom
         in your own heart.

You are not leaving
Even as the light
   fades quickly now,
      you are arriving

For this practice:

- Reflect on how you catch up with yourself.

- How do you take stock of how you are being in the moment?

- How do you live the creative tension between 'What is me?' and 'What is not me?' in the moment?

- Write your own Eulogy reflecting what others might say about you.

Practice 123
Exercise: Welcoming All of Ourselves

Moving to wholeness invites us to welcome all aspects and sides of ourselves. This is a visualization exercise designed to invite ourselves or our clients into a wholehearted loving acceptance of ourselves. It helps support the journey from dividedness into integration.

You can do this exercise either sitting or lying down and with a blanket to stay warm. It can be recorded or read out loud depending on your situation and context. It is a slow-paced exercise, so take your time. Place paper and pens close by.

- Close your eyes. Relaxing and breathing gently you find yourself in a field in the summer time. A house is standing nearby. This house does not need to be a place you know. Spend a few minutes breathing into the sights, sounds and scents of the field.

- Then slowly, by degrees, become aware of the house. Begin to see what it looks like.

- Now you move towards the house. This is the house of your sub-personalities. Step into it. Spend a few minutes looking around, sensing the colours and atmosphere. This is the house of you.

- Take one last look around the house. When you are ready leave the house and return to the field. Turn round to face the house.

- Now invite three or four of your sub-personalities to come out of the house. These are the ones you know best. If you can, give each one a name. Welcome and greet them as they come out of the house.

- Next expect some less well-known or unfamiliar sub-personalities to emerge from the house. Welcome and greet them, attempt to get a feel for them, and name them if you can.

- When you are ready take the two sub-personalities who get on least well together and take them away to the centre of the field. Discuss with them their problem with each other. Listen to what they need from each other. Perceive what can be done for and with them.

- Now begin to draw the conversation to a close and see if you can help them resolve or reconcile what is needed. Then return these two sub-personalities to the others. Take time to see them all return to the house and close the door behind them.

- Now you can return to the room. Curl up if necessary but in returning hold your memories of the field.

- Now draw your Self in the centre of the paper. Now draw a general character sketch of each of your sub-personalities radiating out from you like spokes on a wheel.

- When you have completed your drawing ask yourself and journal:
  - 'What are the strengths and weaknesses of each?'
  - 'What is the centrality and prominence of each of them in my life?'
  - 'As the Self (yourself) – the wise, compassionate, non-judgemental observer in the centre – how can I create harmony, peace and wholeness?'

Practice 124
Exercise: Being your Own Mandala

A mandala in Hinduism and Buddhism is a spiritual symbol used to represent an awakened universe. Mandalas can be both geometric and organic. They typically have a centre point from which an array of symbols, shapes and forms radiate. In essence mandalas represent our connection between our inner and outer worlds.

For this practice you need pens, paints, rulers, pencils and rubbers.

- Choose an already printed mandala, which can either be from a book or downloaded from the internet.

- Colour in and or pattern your mandala as the inspiration hits you.

- Journal what comes to you as you design your mandala.

Practice 125
Meditation: Bliss is Doing and Being What We Love

When our soul meets our role we act from the authentic truth within us. When we are free to act from our souls we are more likely to achieve what we intend. Doing and being what we love creates an electromagnetic field which puts us in alignment with our true nature, as we connect with others. These vibrations and this resonance enable us to make our unique contribution because of the source from which we are choosing to operate.

As Rumi wrote:[35] 'Let yourself be silently drawn by the strange pull of what you really love. It will not lead you astray.'

For Joseph Campbell:[36]

> If you follow your bliss, you put yourself on a kind of track that has been there all the while, waiting for you, and the life that you ought to be living is the one you are living. Wherever you are — if you are following your bliss, you are enjoying that refreshment, that life within you, all the time.

For this practice meditate and ask yourself:

- 'What makes my heart sing?'
- 'What is my bliss?'
- 'How do I support others to help them to find their bliss?'
- Journal what you notice.

Practice 126
Exercise: Passion and Obligation Choices

Life's demands and events can sometimes send us off our own track. This practice helps us to remember our own why and who we are.

For this practice:

- Ground and centre yourself.
- Draw a line down the centre of a page in your journal.
- Title the left-hand column 'Passions'. Title the right-hand column 'Obligations'.
- Now list or draw your passions or loves and then your obligations and duties. Use ratios or percentages to allocate the amount of time or energy you feel that you typically allocate to each over a week or a month.
- Now ask yourself 'how might I shift the balance to do more of what I love?'
- Journal your action plan.

Here is Steve Jobs's permission for your edit:[37]

> I have looked in the mirror every morning and asked myself: 'If today were the last day of my life, would I want to do what I am about to do today?' And whenever the answer has been 'No' for too many days in a row, I know I need to change something.

Practice 127
Reflection: To Break a Promise

Promises are loaded with passion, meaning, commitment, duty and obligation. However, there can be times when we have to face into the reality that some promises which were made in another time no longer serve and also that new promises to self, others and life, are needed. David Whyte has written a beautiful poem, 'To Break a Promise'.[38]

> Make a place of prayer, no fuss,
> just lean into the white brilliance
> and say what you needed to say
> all along, nothing too much, words
> as simple and as yours and as heard
> as the bird-song above your head
> or the river running gently beside you.
>
> Let your words join
> one to another
> the way stone nestles on stone,
> the way water just leaves
> and goes to the sea,
> the way your promise
> breathes and belongs
> with every other promise
> the world has ever made.
>
> Now, leave them to go on,
> let your words
> carry their own life
> without you, let the promise
> go with the river.
>
> Have faith. Walk away.

For this practice:

- Read the poem.

- Sit with it.

- Reflect on times in your life when you had to break a promise. Ask yourself:

- ○ 'How did I feel?'
- ○ 'What happened?'
- ○ 'What followed?'
- Now reflect on times in your life when you made a promise. Ask yourself:
  - ○ 'How did I feel?'
  - ○ 'What happened?'
  - ○ 'What followed?'
- Journal how you set yourself free by the promises you both break and make?

Practice 128
Exercise: Vision Quests

An ancient ceremony called the 'Vision Quest' (or 'Vision Fast') is a sacred journey for the completion of an old life, the movement through a threshold and the return to the world reborn. Typically vision quests are organized trips in the wilds in community. However, you can also create your own vision quest and create your own community of support around you.

You need to build in five key elements in designing your own Vision Quest:

- Preparation
- Solitude
- Immersion in Nature
- Fasting (or light eating)
- Return

For this practice:

- Book 3 to 5 days out of your diary
- Find a place where you can be alone. Take yourself off the grid. Switch off your devices.
- Plan in as much simplicity as you can. Fast or eat as lightly as is right for you.
- Immerse yourself in nature and in the weather. Watch the dawn, sunset and night sky.
- Sit and be with whatever is emerging for you.
- Return gently and get the support you need to help you to process your experiences. Arrange to share your insights with a group of fellow pilgrims or with your Supervisor.

Practice 129
Reflection: Letter to Self!

A powerful way to stay connected to our why and who we are is through writing letters to ourselves for some future date.

For this practice:

- Gift yourself some quiet time and meditate.

- Write to yourself as a loving friend to your future self or as your older self to your present self.

- Use writing prompts like 'Say YES!', 'What NOW?', or 'WHO am I ?'

- Either file away the letter and diary a date when you will re-read it or ask a friend to post it to you at some future date. Linking this to an Equinox as the earth tilts on its axis is a powerful way of also staying connected with nature's natural rhythms and cycles of change.

Practice 130
Reflection: With Freedom Comes Responsibility

Freedom also needs us to honour our interconnectedness. We cannot be free if our freedom diminishes or removes the freedom of others. We learn and work best when we are free to give and with freedom comes responsibility.

Different Codes of Ethics and Practice have been created by different professional bodies. These have all been designed to ensure robust professional responsibility, integrity and accountability in our work.[39] A checklist has been offered by Brene Brown using the acronym 'BRAVING'[40] for balancing our individual freedoms with our shared responsibility to the collective.

The acronym 'BRAVING' means:

- 'B' is for 'Boundaries': for a mutual respecting of boundaries

- 'R' is for 'Reliability': for a mutual honouring of promises, commitments and follow through

- 'A' is for 'Accountability': for owning our own errors and mistakes and resolving as appropriate

- 'V' is for 'Vault': for the protection of privacy and confidentiality

- 'I' is for 'Integrity': for choosing to honour our values and what is right or best possible

- 'N' is for 'Non-judgement': for choosing acceptance

and

- 'G' is for 'Generosity:' for choosing generosity and abundance over scarcity.

For this practice:

- Reflect on how you balance your own freedom with responsibility.

- Ask yourself 'Do I sacrifice my own freedom on the anvil of responsibility to others?' or vice versa?

- Ask yourself 'How do I calibrate this balance in my life and work?' and 'When does it come out of balance?' and 'What are the impacts of when this happens for me, my clients and my work?'

- Journal your reflections.

Practice 131
Inquiry: Voluntary Simplicity

Simplicity is a choice. Choosing simplicity gives us back our freedom to remember the essentials and return to our essence. As Oliver Wendell Holmes writes:[41] 'For the simplicity that lies this side of complexity, I would not give a fig, but for the simplicity that lies on the other side of complexity, I would give my life.'

For this practice:

- Notice your impulse to choose busyness. Notice how you might be choosing distraction and overload. Chart this if you can over a day or a couple of days. Study your patterns. Ask yourself over a typical day what is your ratio between doing and being.

- Now ask yourself 'Why?', 'Who or what does this serve?' and 'What are the costs to me?'

- Now explore how you can choose more moments of voluntary simplicity – of slowing down, of doing one thing at a time, or finding joy in the beauty of the present moment.

- Journal and plan what is possible for you here.

As Mary Oliver writes in an extract from her poem 'When I am Among the Trees':[42]

> When I am among the trees,
> …
> …
> they give off such hints of gladness.
> I would almost say that they save me, and daily.
>
> Around me the trees stir in their leaves
> and call out, 'Stay awhile.'
> The light flows from their branches.

And they call again, 'It's simple,' they say,
'and you too have come
into the world to do this, to go easy, to be filled
with light, and to shine.'

Practice 132
Inquiry: Extreme Self-Care

As we become more fully awake and alive we also need to practice extreme or radical self-care. As we awaken into ever deepening consciousness and at the same time realize our highest potential we need to also find ways to nurture and protect ourselves. Fragile roots and saplings need nourishment and support. Practising Extreme Self-Care is both a duty to ourselves and to others for living a conscious and authentic life. Charles Handy defined this as 'proper selfishness'. As he says:[43]

> It is proper to be concerned with ourselves and a search for WHO we truly are, because that search leads us to self-respect which in the end only comes from responsibility, responsibility for other people and other things.

For this practice:

- Test your own reactions to the notion of Extreme or Radical Self-Care.

- Ask yourself 'How might I be creating an aura scarcity and deprivation by not attending to my own self-care?'

- Ask yourself 'Where is this showing up in my life and work and what does it feel like?' Examples might include: being deprived of sleep, help, support, companionship, fun, peace, touch, space or recognition.

- Ask yourself 'What would taking Extreme Self-Care mean for me?' – 'How would I create a soul nourishing environment for myself and what would it look like?'

- Journal your insights, choices and actions.

As Cheryl Richardson writes:[44]

> Enjoying a life of Extreme Self Care means living and working in a soul nurturing environment: developing a greater appreciation for, and connection with nature; doing work that provides an opportunity to express your greatest gifts and talents; and caring for your emotional, physical and mental health in a way that is aligned with WHO you are and WHAT you most need. When you allow yourself to want this and then have it, you can't help but want it for others as well.

Practice 133
More Inspiration: Finding Freedom

Here are some inspirational poems and quotes to support you in finding freedom.

As John O'Donohue writes in an extract from his poem 'For Freedom':[45]

> As a bird soars high
> In the free holding of the wind,
> …
> May your life awaken
> To the call of its freedom.

As we enter the future with freedom, possibility comes to meet us. John invites us to trust the wisdom of our souls:[46]

> Your soul knows the geography of your destiny. Your soul alone has the map of your future, therefore you can trust this indirect, oblique side of yourself. If you do, it will take you where you need to go, but more important it will teach you a kindness of rhythm in your journey.

Writes David Whyte in his poem 'Self Portrait':[47]

> I want to know
> if you know
> how to melt into that fierce heat of living
> falling toward
> the center of your longing.

Judy Brown invites us to 'Trust the Tug of Yearning':[48]

> Trust the tug of yearning.
> Let your heart follow what it most loves.
> Longing is a powerful compass.
> It will always bring you home,
> although the road may sometimes be a rough one.

* * * * *

Reflective Questions

1. Which of the twenty-one practices are you most drawn to and why?

2. Which of the twenty-one practices are you least drawn to and why?

3. What are you going to action now?

The Denouement
Return's Harvest and Action

The Denouement is the sequence designed to enable us to return to harvest, test and apply the discoveries and riches from *Flow* to reshape what already exists or bring the new into the world.

The Denouement sequence of three dance steps – which are described in the next three chapters and which should be considered together – is where choices, options and decisions are designed, formulated, tested and applied. The invisible is made visible. The implicit is made explicit. Feedback is given and received.

The dance steps are

Step 7: Crafting Focus

Step 8: Working Wisely

Step 9: FeedingForward

Moving up the right-hand side of the U curve involves building the practices and disciplines for designing, testing, and experimenting.

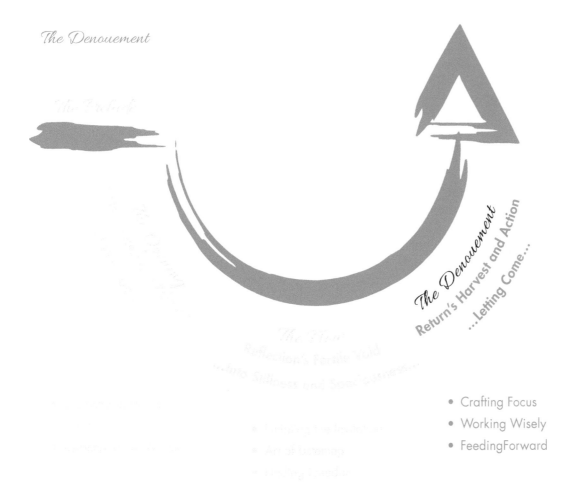

The Prelude

The Float
Reflection's Fertile Void

The Denouement
Return's Harvest and Action
...Letting Come...

- Crafting Focus
- Working Wisely
- FeedingForward

Vision is not enough, it must be combined with venture.
It is not enough to stare up the steps, we must step up the stairs.

Vaclav Havel[1]

This sequence bridges the gap between the reflective or contemplative life and the active life. As Parker J. Palmer writes[2]:

> Our drive for aliveness expresses itself in two elemental and inseparable ways: action and contemplation. We may think of the two as contrary modes but they are of one source and the both seek to celebrate the gift of life. When we fail to hold contemplation-and-action together we abandon

the creative tension between the two and both ends fly apart in madness. Action flies off in a frenzy – a frantic and even violent effort to impose one's will on the world, or at least to survive against all odds. Contemplation flies off into escapism – a flight from the world into a realm of false bliss.

Action and contemplation co-exist at source, which is our drive to be fully alive. Parker J. Palmer continues:[3]

Action and contemplation are not high skills or specialties for the virtuoso few. They are warp and weft of human life, the interwoven threads that form the fabric of WHO we are and WHO we are becoming.

To act is to be fully alive. Work is love in action. When we act we not only express what is in us and help give shape to the world, we also receive what is outside us and we reshape our inner selves. In the archetypal Hero's Journey, which was popularized by Joseph Campbell, the hero returns from the 'special world' with gifts and treasure.[4] Returning from our own journeys to sensitively and appropriately test our insights and findings requires great skill, integrity and judgement.

As an ancient Chinese proverb reminds us:[5]

I hear and I forget.
I see and I remember.
I do and I understand.

CHAPTER 11
Crafting Focus

The *Concise Oxford Dictionary* defines 'focus' as[1]:

The point at which rays or waves meet after reflection or refraction ... the point at which rays appear to proceed ... converge or make convergence to a focus ... the adjustment of the eye or lens to give a clear image.

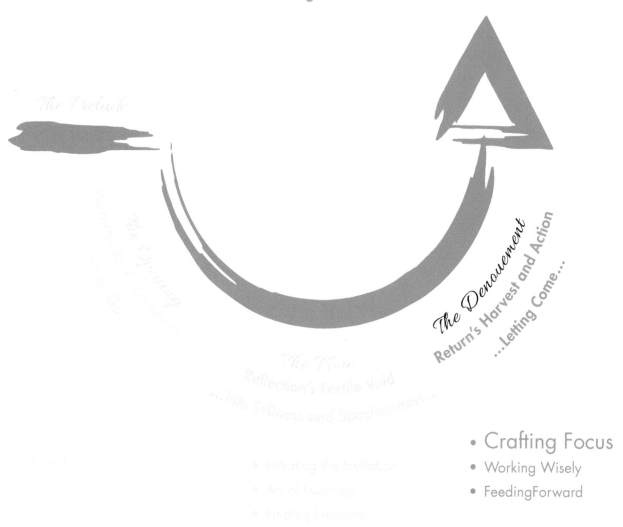

The Prelude

The Opening

The Flow
Reflection's Fertile Void
...Into Stillness and Spaciousness...

The Denouement
Return's Harvest and Action
...Letting Come...

- Crafting Focus
- Working Wisely
- FeedingForward

Focus is not usually something we can just arrive at. Rather is it crafted, honed and refined as we step closer to realizing what is needed. Focus is the search for clarity in a blurred world. Focus is also about leadership: stepping forth, becoming visible and defining action. Focus is the bridge between who we are and how we express our deepest sense of ourselves in our work through the choices we make.

The discipline of Focus ensures what Buddhists call 'Right Action'. 'Right Action' is determined by 'Right View' and 'Right Conduct'.[2] 'Right View' is ensuring that every action is based on the tests of right intention and right motivation. This will ensure that the action is what we intend – and is beneficial to the individual, to others and to society. It also takes into account the three fundamental aspects of reality: everything changes; nothing exists independently; and nothing exists without a cause.

'Right Conduct' is the quality of the actions taken from the 'Right View' which are healthy and generative (and where harm can only be justified if it prevents a much greater harm).

As Daniel Goleman writes, there are three types of focus.[3] He describes our 'Inner Focus' which attunes us to WHO we are, our 'Other' focus which attunes us to people, and our 'Outer Focus' which attunes us to the navigation of our world. We need to be attuned to all three types of focus whilst also holding the three types in alignment for 'Right Action'. 'Focused Focus' creates the clarity to make this attunement and alignment possible.

This dance step also enables us to decide on what needs to be created and when. Focus is a masculine energy for action, which creates responsibility and accountability. Focus is also a call for action. Focus is an invitation to experiment – to take small steps to test ideas without risking over-commitment or disappearing down blind alleys. As Lao Tzu said:[4] 'An ant on the move does more than a dozing ox.'

Practices for Crafting Focus

There are many ways in which we can craft focus. Here are twenty three practices which work for me.

Practice 134
Exercise: Sorting the Wheat from the Chaff

Finding the gems in our insights – and how they need to be offered, placed and paced in the world – is the key to wise action. Whittling can be seen as a process of focussing – a process of delicate shaping and refining of your insights into gifts and actions to test in the world.

For this practice:

- Decide on your question and put aside some time to review your insights and discoveries which you have captured in your journal or sketchbook from dancing through Moves 1 and 2 (The Opening and The Flow). These are your raw pieces of wood.

- Now metaphorically take these pieces of wood, sort your wheat from your chaff, and see what beautiful shapes emerge to signal or represent what now needs your action or focus. You can try this with wood or clay or from sketching as you shift to making ever bolder outlines on the page.

- Draw, design or find images or photographs of what you have found to remind and inspire you.

For Ann Voskamp:[5] 'Simplicity is ultimately a matter of focus.'

Practice 135
Exercise: Mind Mapping

A variation on Practice 134 is to create a colourful mind map to the many divergent possibilities, which will have been generated from dancing in Reflection's Fertile Void. The branches (and sub-branches) – which will naturally emerge from your question at the centre of your mind map – will help you to create clarity and coherence.

As part of this process you may also want to pause and take yourself on a meditative walk. Research by Professor Barbara Oakley has shown that walking in green spaces helps us with both divergent and convergent thinking to arrive at what is needed.[6] As Zig Ziglar wrote:[7] 'Lack of direction, not lack of time, is the problem.'

Practice 136
Exercise: Designing your Vision Board

Cutting out pictures from magazines, or finding images from the internet to represent what you have discovered, helps to make the implicit both material and explicit. These visuals give us clarity and focus. As Gary Keller writes:[8]

> You need to be doing fewer things for more effect instead of doing more things with side effects. Make sure every day you do what matters most. When you know what matters most, everything makes sense. When you don't know what matters most, nothing makes sense.

As Steve Jobs said:[9]

People think focus means saying yes to the thing you've got to focus on. But that's not what it means at all. It means saying 'No' to the hundred other good ideas that there are.

Practice 137
Inquiry: Remembering to Tune into Ourselves

Constantly tuning – and re-tuning – into what our heads, hearts, bodies and souls are telling us as we craft our focus tells us if we are on track. Without a grounded and embodied alignment within ourselves, our focus – and our energy – become blunted and stunted. Crafting focus is a constant process of iteration and reiteration to try to avoid diversion and unintended consequences from our actions.

If ever you are losing your connection with yourself simply:

- Pause and ground yourself.

- Place your right hand on your gut and your left hand on your heart and breathe deeply.

- Stay in this position until you feel yourself calm and settle.

As Alan Seale writes:[10] 'The more we extend ourselves ... the more rooted or grounded we must become.'

Practice 138
Exercise: Committing to 'Yes!'

Focus comes alive and is made real when we make a commitment. This means that we need to cross a threshold from ideas to action. Saying 'yes' to an action means finding the courage to risk ourselves. Making a commitment often does not require us to risk ourselves entirely but to test and then correct as we go.

As Martin Luther King said:[11] 'Take the first step in faith. You don't have to see the whole staircase, just take the first step.'

As Theodore Roosevelt reminds us:[12] 'Do not wait until the conditions are perfect to begin. Beginning makes the conditions perfect. Do what you can, with what you have, where you are.'

This practice is aimed at taking out some of the very natural fear we all face when we want to say 'Yes!'

- Brainstorm a list of options for the different ways in which your idea can be made real.

- Create list of criteria against which to assess each one for feasibility and achievability.

- Once a preferred option has emerged develop a 'what if' risk management around it.

- Give yourself the permission to get it less than perfect or wrong so that you can move closer to getting it right.

- Value yourself and celebrate your courage in taking these first steps. As you test and receive feedback on your ideas return to Chapter 4 to give yourself the gifts of self-compassion.

Remember that for Mark Twain:[13]

> The secret to getting started is to get started. The secret of getting started is breaking down complex overwhelming tasks into small manageable tasks and starting on the first one.

Practice 139
Inquiry: Walking the Chaordic Path

The Chaordic Path was developed by the Chaordic Alliance. The stepping stones on a Chaordic path show how we can stay true to our original intention when making changes. They provide just enough form to test ideas without stifling creativity.

For this practice imagine or draw nine Stepping Stones:[14]

- **1st Stepping Stone: What is the Need?**
  Explored via questions like: 'What need am I/are we facing here?' or 'What is needed right now?'

- **2nd Stepping Stone: What is my/our Purpose?**
  Flows from need. Purpose Statements are established via questions like: 'What could this work do, inspire and/or create?' or 'What is our vision and mission here?'

- **3rd Stepping Stone: What are my/our Principles?**
  How the work will be done. Explored via questions like: 'How do I/we want to work on this?' and 'How do I/we want to behave as we work?'

- **4th Stepping Stone: Who?**
  Explored through asking questions like: 'Who cares about this?', 'Who do we need to include?' and 'What relationships need to be nurtured or created for our work here?'

- **5th Stepping Stone: What is my/our Concept?**
  Explored through asking questions like: 'What organizational forms are needed for the work to happen?', 'What options are present?' and 'What vehicles are needed for the work?'

- **6th Stepping Stone: What are my/our Limiting Beliefs?**
  Limiting beliefs explore what might be holding us back. Explored via questions like: 'What do

I/we fear?', 'What am I/are we assuming which no longer serves?' or 'What do I/we need when I/we start to feel anxious?'

- **7th Stepping Stone: What is my/our Structure?**
Structure defines the way that decisions and actions will be taken. Structure is explored via questions like: 'What is the lightest structure needed to serve our need and purpose here?' and 'What role(s) are needed here?'

- **8th Stepping Stone: What is my/our Practice?**
Practice is working in alignment with what has been created. Practice is explored through asking questions like: 'How do I/we stay true?', 'What happens when I/we step out of alignment with what we intend?' and 'How can I/we reconnect or correct what is no longer working?'

- **9th Stepping Stone: What is the Harvest?**
Harvest means gathering in what has been achieved. Harvest is explored through questions like: 'What feedback and feedforward loops are needed so that I/we can understand the difference we are making/have made?' and 'How do we know when we have met the need?'

Practice 140
Leading: Embodying Intention for Wise Action

Owning our Intention – how and what we want to reshape or create – is a whole body commitment. Intention needs to be embodied in us for it to survive the knocks and challenges of our everyday pressures. Where Intention goes, Attention follows and Energy flows. We change the field of Intention when we change how and where we place our Attention. Practice 140 is an exercise which helps us to experience how we can embody our Intention – and what happens when we do not.

Working with a partner if possible for this practice:

- Take time to revisit – and if necessary refine – your intention. Ask yourself 'What brings potency and purpose to my work?' One way to explore this is to invite your head, gut, heart and soul to answer this question separately. Journal each response or ask a partner to capture your responses.

- Step 1: Standing opposite your partner, place your right hand on your left shoulder. Now ask your partner to give you a small push when you are not expecting it.

- Step 2: Return to position, with your right hand on your left shoulder, but now rest your left hand on your stomach. Again invite your partner to give you a small push when you are not expecting it.

- Step 3: Return to position. Now with your right hand on your left shoulder and your left hand resting on your stomach. Bring to mind a difficult question or piece of case work and receive your partner's pressure again.

- Step 4: Take time to reconnect to your higher Intention and repeat, but this time walking through the push.

- Reflect on what felt different, what changed and its messages for you. Journal what you notice.

As Brenna Yovanoff writes[15]: 'Intention is one of the most powerful forces there is. What you mean when you do a thing will always determine the outcome. The law creates the world.'

Practice 141
Exercise: Decisive Action

Crafting focus may be thought of as bringing the Circle, which represents wholeness, integration and emergence, within the Triangle, which represents intention, direction and action. The Circle is round and the Triangle is pointed, incisive and efficient. This visual helps us to understand that when it is time to take action everything comes to a focal point. This can be illustrated using a real or imaginary sword or a calligraphy brush to show authentic presence in action and to illustrate how to make a clean decisive cut without ego or aggression.

For this practice:

- Start with an embodied centring and grounding. Feel the connection between heaven and earth.

- Now connect with your Intention. Gather yourself and everything together for a moment of decisive action. Lift an imaginary sword high and bring it down swiftly in front or point it horizontally whilst also stepping forward. This is a cutting through of doubts, worries, hesitations or fears; with this there is a letting go and an opening up of space.

- Another option is to repeat the first two steps using a calligraphy brush. Here the stroke or mark, which is left on the paper, is the gathering in of intention into a moment of decisive action.

Practice 142
Exercise: Working with Yin and Yang

In the Chinese tradition, focus and balance come from the harmonization of the two fundamental energies in the universe – the complementary opposites of Yin and Yang. In the Hindu and Tantric traditions these are known as Shakti and Shiva.

Yin is the feminine gentle energy, which flows, attends and receives. Yang is the masculine active energy which sets intention and direction. Yin opens our hearts and minds to receive and Yang provides focus and discipline.

Together they are the constantly flowing dance of creation. In the *Taijitu* Yin is black and Yang is white. The world is depicted as one indivisible and unchanging whole through the interplay of these complementary opposites. Crafting focus requires us to find the intersection between both Yin and Yang energies where flow meets focus.

Fig 1: The Taijitu

For this practice:

- Reflect on the balance of your own masculine and feminine energies. Ask yourself 'How do they show up and when in me?' and 'What impact does this have for me?'

- Now identify one action you could take to restore more balance. If you have too much Yin energy (and not enough Yang energy) develop strategies to give you more clarity and focus such as scheduling, timetabling and project planning. If you have too much Yang energy (and not enough Yin energy) develop strategies to nurture your creativity and intuition – like going on an Artist Date (see Practice 40).

- Check in with yourself in a week's time to notice any differences. Journal what you are noticing.

Practice 143
Exercise: Flow in Motion

Another way of experiencing flow in motion is to get mindfully involved in, for example, Tai Chi, Aikido, Judo, Yoga, Pilates or dance. All of these teach bodily awareness.

Taking any of the above exercises:

- Notice the ebb and flow of your movements.

- Notice how particular moves require different focus.

- Notice the oscillations between action and rest.

- Consider how you could apply the lessons learnt to the projects that you want to bring into the world.

Practice 144
Reflection: Calibrating the Lightest Touch

Busyness is often prized. Obvious movement can be valued over subtle but significant shifts. However, when ideas move into alignment, a tipping point is reached which often needs just the lightest touch to achieve real progress.

Preparation, focus and readiness to act are important but timing is key. Perfect conditions are not always possible but, like taking a yacht out of a harbour, some conditions are better than others. As Lailah Gifty Akita writes:[16] 'All my dreams will be fulfilled at the proper time.'

For this practice:

- Bring to mind two initiatives or projects which you have worked on. Choose one which worked well and one which worked less well or failed in some way.

- Examine each with specific reference to:

  a. Your personal readiness

  b. Timing

  and

  c. Favourable conditions

- Reflect on what you noticed.

- Consider how you could become a better mariner.

Practice 145
Inquiry: Welcoming Interference

Focus requires us to stay open – rather than closed – to all that is emerging. When we are on a track we can sometimes see interference as an irritation or a nuisance. When we welcome interference and challenge we shift our energy towards it. Instead of seeing interference as a mean or deliberate block we need to gently explore what its message for us is. We need to learn to hold our project with the right attention, as we would a glass ball. When we hold a glass ball too tight it breaks! When we hold a glass ball too loose it falls!

This practice invites you to consider your relationship with challenge or interference.

- Ask yourself 'How do I define challenge or interference?' and 'Do I differentiate between what I might see as a bad or a good challenge?'

- Ask yourself 'How do I relate to challenge or interference when I want to achieve something?'

- Ask yourself 'How can I shift my energy from irritation or annoyance into a welcome when interference presents?'

- Ask yourself 'What is the message from the interference for me here?' and 'What do I now need to pay attention to and learn about?'

- Reflect on how you can welcome interference whilst finding ways to stay true to your intention. Take time to consider if your Intention needs to be refined or amended in any way.

As Steve Maraboli writes:[17] 'Don't give up! It's not over. The universe is balanced. Every setback bears with it the seeds of a comeback.'

Practice 146
Exercise: Dream v. Reality

Creative tension always exists between the dream and the reality of getting there. Focus is about committing to the dream and translating it into the real world. Crafting focus is the conversation between where you want to be and how you are going to get there.

The dream is always tempered by what is pragmatic, achievable and realistic at any point in time. For this practice:

- Imagine a tightrope.

- As you start to turn your dream into reality ask yourself 'What or where are my non-negotiables?', 'Where can I trade or compromise?', 'What can I let go of completely?', ' Is this still the right course?' and 'When or how will I know when now is not the time for this?'

- Journal your answers. Revisit regularly and also when you find you have a critical choice to make.

As Peter Senge writes:[18]

> Vision without systems thinking ends up painting lovely pictures of the future with no deep understanding of the forces that must be mastered to move from here to there.

Practice 147
Exercise: Invoking the Spirit of the Warrior

Chogynam Trunga defines 'warriorship' as:[19]

> The path or a thread that runs through your entire life. It is not just a technique to apply when an obstacle arises or when you are unhappy or depressed. Warriorship is a continual journey: To be a warrior is to learn to be genuine in every moment of your life.

Warriorship is not about aggression or war, but instead invites us to engage with our world – in all of its messiness – from the inside out. The warrior spirit is gentle and intelligent whilst also being committed, focused, firm and brave in the pursuit of positive change. The warrior's weapons, writes Meg Wheatley, are compassion and insight.[20]

For this practice:

* Consider how you might be embodying the warrior spirit by being the change you want to see in the world.

* Ask yourself 'How can I keep coming back to my own authenticity moment by moment?'

* Ask yourself 'Who or what do I choose to be in the service of now.?'

Practice 148
Inquiry: Wicked Problems and the Doughnut of Influence

The term 'Wicked Problems' was first coined by Charles West Churchman in 1967. The term is used to describe problems which are difficult to solve because of incomplete, contradictory or changing contexts and requirements – and where solving one aspect of a wicked problem can lead to unintended consequences elsewhere.

Wicked problems therefore need to be solved using a different consciousness from that which created them. Wicked problems contrast with tame problems, which can be solved by what is already known. Many of those problems we encounter in the VUCA world may be described as Wicked, where we need to innovate our way out. As Robert Flood et al write:[21]

Most…problems in organizations [and elsewhere] are 'wicked problems'… but most [problem solving] methods are suitable for simple, well-structured problems. The usual approaches do not, therefore, help organizations [or people] deal with their most important problems.

Holding this definition can be helpful when crafting focus. For this practice:

- Review your to do lists. Draw three columns in your Journal. Label the left-hand column 'Tame Problems', the middle column 'Complex Problems' and the right-hand column 'Wicked Problems'.

- Now divide your projects between the three columns.

- Ask yourself 'What is my split between all three?', 'What differences in approaches, resources and timetabling are needed from me (and from the people I work with) to respond to each?' and 'What areas and in what ways can I make progress in each?'

- Draw a doughnut shape for each project. In the centre describe and place those tasks and activities over which you have direct control and can action. In the middle ring describe and place those activities over which you have some control but where you need others to help you. Develop your strategies for influencing and asking for help. In the outer ring describe and place those tasks and activities over which you have no control at the moment. Watch and notice emerging trends and patterns. Be clear what is yours and what is not yours. Review your doughnut every month and see what is shifting and has shifted.

- Revisit the Practices 11–17 for Self-Compassion and Practice 152 for Patience as you address your issues.

Practice 149
Inquiry: Focus in Complexity

Ralph Stacey's Complexity Model offers another lens on how to craft focus in Complexity.[22] His matrix places problems into the four categories of 'Simple', 'Complicated', 'Complex' and 'Chaos', based on how close or far participants are to both agreement and certainty about how to move forward.

The working definitions are as follows:

- **Simple:** which is close to both certainty and agreement based on technical rational decision-making, and using data from the past to predict the future.

- **Complicated:** which is close to certainty but further from agreement where there is disagreement about which outcomes are desirable. Or which is close to agreement but further from certainty where the path is unclear and the link between cause and effect is unknown.

- **Complex:** which is a creative but boundaried tension between certainty and agreement which frees innovative thinking.

- **Chaos:** which is very high levels of both uncertainty and disagreement and where traditional methods of planning, visioning and negotiation are insufficient.

For this practice:

- Review your to-do lists. Draw four columns in your journal. Label the left-hand column 'Simple Problems', the next column 'Complicated Problems', the next column 'Complex Problems' and the right-hand column 'Chaos'.

- Now divide your projects between the four columns.

- Follow your inquiry as per the practice above.

Practice 150
Inquiry: Asking for Help

Our fatal mistake is to think that we are alone. Appreciating how and when to ask for help is key to happiness and success. Crafting the invitation for help is key to our creativity.

For this practice reflect on this passage from David Whyte:[23]

> Help is strangely something we want to do without, as if the very idea disturbs and blurs the boundaries, as if we cannot face how much we need in order to go on. We are born with the absolute need for help, grow only with a continuous succession of extended hands, and as adults depend upon others for our further success and possibilities in life even as competent individuals. It may be that the ability to know the necessity of help and how to ask for it, is one of the transformative dynamics that allows us to emancipate ourselves into each new epoch of our lives. Without the understanding that we need a particular form of aid at every crucial threshold in our lives and without the robust vulnerability in asking for help we cannot pass through the door that bars us from the next dispensation of our lives: we cannot birth ourselves.

Now ask yourself:

- 'How do I feel about asking for help?'

- 'How do I feel about receiving help?'

- 'How and when do I ask for help – and when don't I ask for help when I need it?'

- Journal your reflections.

Practice 151
Exercise: Honouring 10 Simple Rules for Change

Remembering simple – although not necessarily easy – rules for change can help us to craft and maintain our focus. The wisdom of each helps us to stay steady in the face of overwhelm and complexity. I have found that the 10 simple rules that work for me are:

1. Respectfully honour that everyone and everything has a right to a unique and different place in the system.

2. Ensure that a dynamic balance between giving and receiving is enabled over time.

3. Appreciate that what has come first has a natural precedence over what follows.

4. Attend to the part, the whole and the greater whole together.

5. Learn from every interaction.

6. Play to – and reinforce – the strengths in self and others, and trust that people want to do their best.

7. Search for what resonates, feels true and is useful.

8. Put yourself in the shoes of the other.

9. Welcome apparent resistance as FeedForward as well as illuminating blind spots.

10. Trust that the answer is somewhere in the system.

For this practice:

• Reflect on the 10 Simple Rules.

• Ask yourself 'Do I agree?', and then 'What would I add, change or amend and why?'

• Ask yourself 'Which ones do I find easiest to embody and why?' and 'Which ones do I find hardest to embody and why?' Journal your responses.

• Decide on your areas of focus and development.

As Pablo Picasso wrote:[24] 'Learn the rules like a pro, so you can break them like an artist.'

Practice 152
Exercise: Practicing Patience

Work has its own natural pace and rhythm. When we work outside these natural processes we often find that we struggle. As the Polish proverb reminds us:[25] 'Do not push the river, it will flow by itself.'

Patience is an underrated quality. Finding the right note, tone, or action takes careful observation over time to achieve the intended impact with grace and elegance.

Patience is needed to edit and redraft as we learn from feedback. We work like aeroplane pilots, correcting our course with small touches until we can literally land our ideas or our project with maximum impact. Too soon and we – and it – are not ready. Too late and the window of opportunity has gone.

For this practice:

- Consider your attitude towards and relationship to patience.

- Ask yourself 'Where does patience show up in my life?' and 'Do I see patience as a sign of weakness or a sign of wisdom?'

- Ask yourself 'How can I learn to trust the process of correcting, editing and redrafting?' and 'When do I know it is the time to stop what I am doing because time and place are not supportive right now?'

As Fulton Sheen writes:[26] 'Patience is power. Patience is not an absence of action; rather it is "timing", it waits on the right time to act, for the right principles and in the right way.'

Practice 153
Inquiry: Taking Risks and Risk-Taking

Taking risks is an inevitable part of bringing the new into the world. This is because what we are trying – by definition – has not been tried in this way before. Fear of taking risks or making mistakes can hold us back. Acknowledging and welcoming risk as an inevitable part of our work can embolden us if we also learn to take care of ourselves whilst we risk ourselves.

For this practice:

- Consider your attitude towards and relationship to risk.

- Ask yourself 'What am I assuming about risk?' and 'What scripts have I absorbed and do I now need to question?'

- Ask yourself 'What are the costs and benefits to me of my current stance?'

- Now design and plan your own risk management strategy, which identifies your risks and charts how you can protect yourself and your project as you move forward.

As the Zulu proverb reminds us:[27] 'You cannot cross a river without getting wet.' But you can prepare and take protective clothing and equipment!

Practice 154
Exercise: Finding the Win-Win

Understanding our negotiating style and approach to conflict can be very helpful to avoid unconscious bias as we try to build consensus, commitment and momentum with others.

Therefore in our negotiations with others it is always worth examining our scripts, our intentions and our natural preferences to avoid sabotaging ourselves, our relationships or our projects.

This practice can be explored either through the Win-Win or Tough Love Matrix.

- **Using the Win-Win Matrix**

  o Ask yourself 'What do I intend and what am I aiming for?' through four different positions.

  o The four positions are achieving a Win-Win for everyone; a Win-Lose or a Lose-Win for one party; or a Lose-Lose for everyone.

- **Using the Tough Love Matrix**

  o Ask yourself 'How do I want to balance achieving my goals with maintaining (and even improving) my relationships with others?' through four possible positions.

  o The four different positions are: Detachment and Disinterest where you do not care about either the outcome or the relationship; Accommodation and Appeasement where you care more about the relationship than your goals; Goal Centred where you care more about your goals than the relationship; and Tough Love where you care equally for the relationship and your goals.

- For each matrix, ask yourself 'What am I prepared to trade, amend or hang onto in this?' and 'What would this mean for my intended outcome?'

- Journal your reflections and design your approach.

Practice 155
Exercise: Learning by Doing

We make the path by walking. We learn by and through our doing. Life is messy and unpredictable, and we also learn through our action what works and what does not. Our built-in fear of failure, our desire to be 'right', and our need to be perfect can prevent us from showing up, having a go, and turning our dreams into reality. Small-scale prototyping, testing and experimenting are the secrets to making change happen.

This practice is an invitation to trust that we have both the courage to experiment and the humility to know when to adjust, improve or stop based on the feedback that we receive.

In Chinese 'Tao' means 'the way things are'. Tao encourages us to see all events – whether we interpret them as good or bad or something in between – as being in harmony with the way of things.

For this practice:

- Ask yourself 'How readily do I make my path by doing?'

- Ask yourself 'What makes me linger at the start line?' and 'What am I assuming and what am I fearing as I hover over the start line?'

- Ask yourself 'If I knew there was no right or wrong way but that the key is finding my way what would I do?'

- Reflect on times when initially you got stuck in overthinking but you broke out of the cycle so, to adapt the Nike advert, you could say, 'Just Did It'.

- Journal your insights.

- Give yourself a Permission Slip to start!

Remember the invocation found on a bench at Syon Park in Middlesex, England: 'I am glad I did rather than wished I had.'

Practice 156
More Inspiration: Crafting Focus

Here are some inspirational poems and quotes to support you in Crafting your Focus. John O'Donohue in his poem 'For a New Beginning' reflects on the excitement of crafting focus:[28]

> Though your destination is not yet clear
> You can trust the promise of this new opening;
> Unfurl yourself into the grace of beginning
> That is at one with your life's desire.
>
> Awaken your spirit of adventure;
> Hold nothing back, learn to find ease in risk;
> Soon you will be home to a new rhythm,
> For your soul senses the world that awaits you

Mary Oliver's poem 'When Death Comes' cautions against regret:[29]

> When it is over, I don't want to wonder
> if I have made of my life something particular, and real.
> I don't want to find myself sighing and frightened, or full of argument.
> I don't want to end up simply having visited this world.

As Yehuda Berg writes:[30] 'It is enough to make a small shift within and a small action in the world. Collectively these have a huge effect.'

Or as Anita Roddick said:[31] 'If you think you're too small to have an impact, try going to bed with a mosquito in the room.'

Johann Wolfgang von Goethe reflects on our responsibility to focus when he wrote:[32]

> Knowing is not enough; we must apply.
> Willing is not enough; we must do.

For Richelle E. Goodrich:[33] 'If I must start somewhere, right here and now is the best place imaginable.'

Mary Wollstonecraft reminded us:[34] 'The beginning is always today!'

* * * * *

Reflective Questions

1. Which of the twenty-three practices are you most drawn to and why?

2. Which of the twenty-three practices are you least drawn to and why?

3. What are you going to action now?

CHAPTER 12
Working Wisely

The Denouement

How you do one thing is how you do everything.

Zen saying[1]

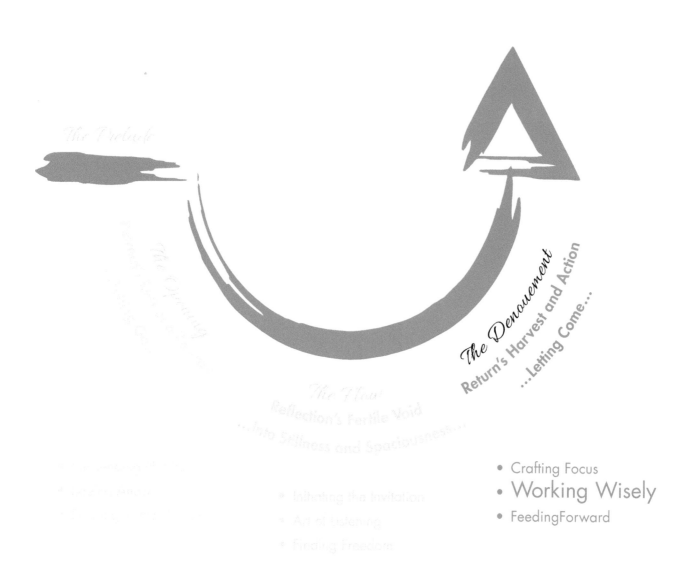

The Prelude

The Denouement
Return's Harvest and Action
...Letting Come...

The Flow
Reflection's Fertile Void
...Into Stillness and Spaciousness...

- Crafting Focus
- **Working Wisely**
- FeedingForward

- Inhabiting the Invitation
- Art of Listening
- Finding Freedom

Work is love in action. Working Wisely means making wise choices – and being held responsible and accountable for those choices – in service of you, your clients and your life.

Working Wisely means paying attention to the 'what' and the 'how' of making change happen. Working Wisely is a balancing act, which requires holding the system in mind as you move forward to test your ideas. As the prophet Kahlil Gibran writes:[2]

> Work is love made visible. And if you cannot work with love but only with distaste, it is better that you should leave your work and sit at the gate of the temple and take alms of those who work with joy.

Wisdom is an underused word and an underrated quality. *The Oxford English Dictionary* defines it as:[3]

> Being wise; (possession of) experience and knowledge together with the power of applying them critically or practically; sagacity, prudence, common sense…'
> 'A course of action, speech or opinion dictated by or in harmony with or showing experience and knowledge judiciously applied.

As Hermann Hesse cautioned:[4]

> Wisdom cannot be imparted. Wisdom that a wise man attempts to impart always sounds like foolishness to someone else … Knowledge can be communicated, but not wisdom. One can find it, live it, do wonders through it, but one cannot communicate and teach it.

Working Wisely means working with the whole. At the heart of Working Wisely is our personal relationship with the whole, with nature, with the universe and with our shared humanity. As Matthew Fox writes:[5]

> Wisdom is finding the balance between head and heart, upper and lower chakras, earth and sky, masculine and feminine, joy and sorrow, yin and yang, energy and rest, human and divine, and the cosmos and the psyche.

Reflection's Fertile Void focused on how we can tune into our intuition and inner knowing. Working Wisely is what we choose to do and how we choose to act from our inner knowing. This is when a generous criticality is required for responsible decision-making. There will be times when we assess that it is not appropriate to act or disclose, because either the timing is not right, the environment is not receptive or sharing is not required. As Stanley Baldwin said when he lambasted the press in 1931:[6] 'Power without responsibility – is the prerogative of the harlot throughout the ages.'

In the Hebrew Bible Sophia or Wisdom was present at the creation of the world. In Proverbs Sophia sees herself as the 'artisan' or master worker at the right hand of God the Creator.

Creativity and Wisdom co-exist and complement each other. Creativity without wisdom can lead to chaos: creativity with wisdom innovates, balances and heals.

Working Wisely also means working with humility. As Socrates so powerfully reminds us:[7] 'The only true wisdom is in knowing you know nothing.'

We do not know what we do not know. We can only deepen our capacities for paying attention and learning from experience, whilst also attempting to do no harm.

Learning to work in this way is a journey and an aspiration – we can never fully arrive as we are human and we are fallible. Wisdom helps us to navigate the inevitable tension between what we want and what the world wants from us with ease, grace and generosity. As Lao Tzu wrote:[8]

Knowing others is intelligence;
knowing yourself is true wisdom.
Mastering others is strength;
mastering yourself is true power.

This is echoed by Rumi when he writes:[9] 'Yesterday I was clever, so I wanted to change the world. Today I am wise, so I am changing myself.'

Practices for Working Wisely

There are many ways in which you can discover wiser working, to help you navigate the creative tension between what you want and what the world wants from you. Here are twenty which work for me.

Practice 157
Inquiry: Redefining Work as Service and Love in Action

Dr. Martin Luther King debunked the exclusivity of leadership when he said:[10]

Everyone can lead and be great because everyone can serve.

Robert K. Greenleaf popularized the phrase 'servant leadership' when he wrote:[11]

The servant-leader is servant first… It begins with the natural feeling that one wants to serve, to serve first. Then conscious choice brings one to aspire to lead. That person is sharply different from one who is leader first, perhaps because of the need to assuage an unusual power drive or to acquire material possessions…The leader-first and the servant-first are two extreme types. Between them there are shadings and blends that are part of the infinite variety of human nature.

I would like to extend the term to 'servant worker', in order to capture all work. As Greenleaf continues:

The difference manifests itself in the care taken by the servant-first to make sure that other people's highest priority needs are being served. The best test, and difficult to administer, is: Do those served grow as persons? Do they, while being served, become healthier, wiser, freer, more autonomous, more likely themselves to become servants? And, what is the effect on the least privileged in society? Will they benefit or at least not be further deprived?

Service is an innate human capacity. Service is love in action. As Viktor Frankl wrote:[12]

Being human always points and is directed to something or someone, other than oneself – be it a meaning to fulfill or another human being to encounter. The more one forgets himself – by giving himself to a cause to serve to another person to love – the more human he is.

For this practice:

- Ask yourself:
  - 'Do I see work as service and as love in action?'
  - 'How comfortable am I with this concept and why?'
  - 'How am I serving?' and 'How do I know if I am working in service of another?'
  - 'How do I attend to serving the needs of myself, my clients and their systems at any point in time?'
  - 'How do I serve without also sacrificing myself?'
- Journal your answers.
- Observe yourself in action over the next month. What we you noticing?
- Ask yourself how you might role model this for others.

As M. Scott Peck writes:[13]

Love is the will to extend one's self for the purpose of nurturing one's own or another's spiritual growth... Love is as love does. Love is an act of will – namely, both an intention and an action. Will also implies choice. We do not have to love. We choose to love.

Practice 158
Exercise: Radical Acceptance

Jeff Foster coined the phrase 'falling in love with where you are'.[14] The phrase captures a radical acceptance of embracing reality in the present where everything is welcome.

Everything happens in the present now. A past remembering happens in the present. A future vision happens in the present. Allowing thoughts to be like waves or clouds without clinging or attachment gives us the heart space within ourselves to hold everything and to be fully present. Working Wisely is working with the insight that all there is is now, which is our true home from which we can step forward.

As Jeff writes:[15]

> As we open to life, love and healing, we awaken from our dream of separateness, we meet not just the bliss but also its pain ... and the meeting can get messy ... But eventually we come to trust the process of no process at all ... that our deepest sorrows are an intelligent movement of life (not a threat to life). We remember that we are vast enough to hold it all.

For this practice:

- Ask yourself 'What is it like for me to be here now?'

- Reconnect with a time when you have been able to say 'I felt so spacious that I felt able to hold it all?' Then ask yourself 'When, how and why did this happen?' and 'How can you invite more of this quality into your life?'

- Ask yourself 'How can I detach myself from attachment/my attachments to respond to what is needed when I work?'

- Decide on a scale of 0 to 10 your radical acceptance of where you are now and how you would strengthen your practice.

- Ask yourself how you might role model this for others.

Practice 159
Inquiry: Working in the Now

Presence is our natural state. Working from a state of presence with an open mind and an open heart enables us to trust ourselves to know what is needed from us at any point in time. This is called our Relational Field and it can be as small or as vast as we choose to make it. Presence is available to us anywhere and at any time when first we connect and become present with ourselves to then energetically connect heart-to-heart with another. This connection makes love in its broadest sense the eternal organizing (and unifying) principle of life, work and relationships. As E. M. Forster wrote in *A Room with a View*:[16]

> You can transmute love, ignore it, muddle it, but you can never pull it out of you. I know by experience that the poets are right: love is eternal.

For this practice:

- Connect back to a time when you felt you were working from a state of Presence with a client. Ask yourself 'Why?' 'What did it feel like?' and 'What happened?'

- Now connect back to a time when you felt disconnected as you worked with a client. Again ask yourself 'Why?', 'What did it feel like?' and 'What happened?'

- Consider what helps you to connect and what stops you. You might want to review some of the practices from Move 1's *The Opening* as you consider this.

- Journal your reflections and design ways that you can facilitate your capacity to connect.

- Ask yourself how you might role model this for others.

Practice 160
Inquiry: You Are Enough

Caught up in a scarcity mentality we forget that life is innately generous. Habitual striving, seeking, comparison and competitiveness mean that we can forget that we are already enough and already have what we need both within ourselves and between us. As Wendell Berry wrote in his poem 'What We Need is Here':[17]

> Geese appear high over us,
> pass, and the sky closes. Abandon,
> as in love or sleep, holds
> them to their way, clear
> in the ancient faith: what we need
> is here. And we pray, not
> for new earth or heaven, but to be
> quiet in heart, and in eye,
> clear. What we need is here.

Working from an abundance – rather than a deficit – mindset changes how help is defined and sought.

For this practice:

- Ask yourself:
  - 'What is my relationship to scarcity and abundance?'
  - 'How have my scripts influenced me in this?'
  - 'Do I/can I believe that who I am and what I have is enough?' and 'If not what else is needed?'
  - 'How could I move from a scarcity to an "I am enough" mindset?'
- Journal your reflections.
- Ask yourself how you might role model this for others.

Accepting the simple gifts of right here right now in this place gives us a great launch pad. As William Stafford writes in his poem 'You Reading This, Be Ready':[18]

Starting here, what do you want to remember?
How sunlight creeps along a shining floor?
What scent of old wood hovers, what softened
sound from outside fills the air?
Will you ever bring a better gift for the world
than the breathing respect that you carry
wherever you go right now? Are you waiting
for time to show you some better thoughts?

When you turn around, starting here, lift this
new glimpse that you found; carry into evening
all that you want from this day. The interval you spent
reading or hearing this, keep it for life –

What can anyone give you greater than now,
starting here, right in this room, when you turn around?

Practice 161
Inquiry: Unfolding, Reshaping and Never Arriving

Everything is moving and shifting. We can never fully arrive, as we have already changed in the process of seeking to arrive. What makes us real is our struggling conversation with a desired horizon rather than any possibility of arrival. We are shaped by our journeying.

Working wisely is working with the central dynamic of a constant shaping, reshaping and unfolding in response to what is emerging as we journey. This truth is beautifully captured in David Whyte's poem 'Santiago':[19]

The road seen, then not seen, the hillside
hiding then revealing the way you should take,
the road dropping away from you as if leaving you
to walk on thin air, then catching you, holding you up,
when you thought you would fall,
and the way forward always in the end
the way that you followed, the way that carried you
into your future, that brought you to this place,
no matter that it sometimes took your promise from you,
no matter that it had to break your heart along the way:
the sense of having walked from far inside yourself
out into the revelation, to have risked yourself
for something that seemed to stand both inside you
and far beyond you, that called you back
to the only road in the end you could follow, walking
as you did, in your rags of love and speaking in the voice
that by night became a prayer for safe arrival,
so that one day you realized that what you wanted
had already happened long ago and in the dwelling place
you had lived in before you began,
and that every step along the way, you had carried
the heart and the mind and the promise
that first set you off and drew you on and that you were
more marvellous in your simple wish to find a way
than the gilded roofs of any destination you could reach:
as if, all along, you had thought the end point might be a city
with golden towers, and cheering crowds,
and turning the corner at what you thought was at the end
of the road, you found just a simple reflection,
and a clear revelation beneath the face looking back
and beneath it another invitation, all in one glimpse:
like a person and a place you had sought forever,
like a broad field of freedom that beckoned you beyond;
like another life, and the road still stretching on.

For this practice:

- How do you feel you are 'more marvellous in your simple wish to find a way'?

- Journal your reflections.

Practice 162
Exercise: Working with Self-Awareness and Humility

Perfect self-awareness is not possible because we are human. Working with humility – opening ourselves up to what we do not know, our vulnerabilities and our fallibilities – frees us to tread wisely.

For this practice:

- Reflect on the following from David Whyte[20]:

  Self knowledge is not clarity or transparency... it is an understanding of self in confluence... and not a set commodity to be unearthed and knocked into shape.

  Self knowledge is a fiercely attentive form of humility and thankfulness ... A coming to know the way we hold the conversation of life ... it is the humble demeanor of the apprentice, someone paying extreme attention, to themselves, to others, to life, to the next step ... someone who does not have all the answers but who is attempting to learn what they can about themselves and those with whom they share the journey ...The real foundation of self knowledge is the self forgetfulness that occurs when we meet something other that we wish to know.

- Journal your reactions and reflections. Be curious about yourself as you read and re-read the piece.

- Ask yourself 'What kind of apprentice am I?'

Practice 163
Visualization: Being Your Own Compass Rose

The Compass Rose is a reflective walking map, which I have developed with my colleague Karyn Prentice[21]. For this practice you are invited to see yourself as the central meeting and balancing point between the cardinal points on the north/south, and east/west axis – of where our souls meet our roles and between different ways of doing and ways of being. The compass points of the northwest, northeast, southwest and southeast provide valuable data to inform the central axis. We hold it all within us as we work. Working Wisely is seeking a balance over time within and between the different compass points to support wholeness and health.

Fig 1: The Compass Rose

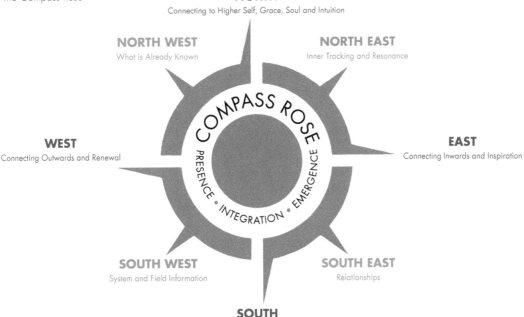

NORTH
Connecting to Higher Self, Grace, Soul and Intuition

NORTH WEST
What is Already Known

NORTH EAST
Inner Tracking and Resonance

WEST
Connecting Outwards and Renewal

EAST
Connecting Inwards and Inspiration

SOUTH WEST
System and Field Information

SOUTH EAST
Relationships

SOUTH
Connecting to Role, Roots, Psychological Understanding and Rites of Passage

COMPASS ROSE
PRESENCE • INTEGRATION • EMERGENCE

For this practice:

- Imagine yourself as your own Compass Rose.
- Now inquire. Ask yourself:
  - 'How do the different elements meet in me?'
  - 'How do they relate to each other in me?'
  - 'If they each had a voice what would they want to say to each other and to me?'
  - 'How do they co-exist – or not – in me?'
  - 'Where is the harmony and where is the conflict?'
- Journal your insights.
- Ask yourself if more balance is needed and if so how this can be achieved over time.

For Thomas Merton,[22] 'Happiness is not a matter of intensity but of balance, of order, rhythm and harmony.'

As Jana Kingsford reminds us:[23] 'Balance is not something you find, it is something that you create.'

Practice 164
Exercise: Greeting Resistance

Resisting resistance creates an 'either/or' rather than an 'and' mentality. Resistance is some form of feedback from the system, which is trying to tell us something. Working Wisely is accepting that this something is often some piece of data which we need to attend to and work with in some way.

When we encounter resistance we can either ignore, fight or greet it. Martial arts traditions teach how we can lean into an oncoming threat, join its energy and soften, work with it or redirect it.

In Aikido, attacks are not resisted but embraced. The person being attacked (or *Nage* – pronounced 'nah-gay') does not defend in the usual sense by blocking and striking back against the person offering the attack (*Uke*, pronounced 'ooh-kay'). Instead, Nage receives the attack as a gift of energy. Nage moves into Uke's space, blending with the attack energy to soften its power to harm. These moves can be illustrated by the experience of a rider jumping on a runaway horse. The rider rides the horse until the rider is at one with the horse energy, which then enables the rider to redirect that energy.

For this practice:

• Consider what Aikido could teach you.

• Reflect on three actual scenarios where you ignored, fought and greeted resistance. What happened? How counter-intuitive is this for you?

• Journal your insights and reflections.

Practice 165
Reflection: Working in Flow

'Flow' is a theory of optimal experience, which has been developed by Mihaly Csikszentmihalyi.[24] Mihaly defines flow as:

> The state in which people are so involved in an activity that nothing else seems to matter; the experience is so enjoyable that people will do it even at great cost... It is the ability to control what happens in consciousness moment by moment and each person can achieve it on the basis of their own efforts and creativity.[25]

Flow happens as we become completely immersed and absorbed by whatever we are doing. We are fully engaged and fully participating. Our egos fall away, time flies and every action follows naturally from the last.

According to Mihaly the preconditions that can support working in Flow are: clear goals (that are challenging yet attainable and intrinsically rewarding); a loss of ego; a timelessness and serenity from complete absorption and immersion; and immediate feedback. Flow experiences can occur in different ways for different people. Working Wisely is working in Flow as much as possible. Mihaly uses the metaphor of a sailor to capture the essence of Flow when he writes:[26]

> Optimal experience is what the sailor holding a tight course feels when the wind whips through his/her hair, when the boat lunges through the waves like a colt – sails, hull, wind and sea humming a harmony that vibrates in the sailor's veins. Or it is what a painter feels when the colours on the canvas begin to set up a magnetic tension with each other, and a new thing, a living form, takes shape.

For this practice:

- Think back to a time when you felt in Flow.

- Ground and centre yourself. Reconnect with what was happening, how you felt and what had made this possible.

- Journal your felt experience.

- Now reconnect with a time when you did not feel in Flow. Revisit what was happening, how you felt and what had made this possible.

- Journal your felt experience.

- Capture ways in which you can connect more with finding your Flow as you work.

Practice 166
Inquiry: Working from the Whole

Working Wisely means working from the Whole. As James Gimian and Barry Boyce write:[27]

> The myriad details can never be fully counted, but we aspire to know them, and then go beyond the countable things to know the larger and deeper patterns in the phenomenal world. Then we can 'go with' these patterns to apply powerful and effective action, just as seafarers came to know the patterns of winds and ocean currents to chart their way across the vast featureless expanse of the ocean.

For this practice:

- Think back to a time when you felt that you were working from the Whole.

- Ground and centre yourself. Reconnect with what was happening, how you felt and what had made this possible.

- Journal your felt experience.

- Now reconnect with a time when you did not feel in you were working from the Whole. Revisit what was happening, how you felt and what had made this possible.

- Journal your felt experience.

- Capture ways in which you can connect more with working from the Whole.

Practice 167
Exercise: Working with How Life Is

'Working from How Life Is' means working with Nature. 'Biomimicry' is a term coined by Janine Benyus to describe an emerging discipline, which explores how nature works and how we can learn from nature to solve problems.[28] In Greek, 'Bio' means 'life' and 'mimesis' means 'imitation'. Biomimicry:

a. Uses Nature as Model: to inspire interventions which work in harmony with nature's laws.

b. Uses Nature as a Measure: learning from evolution to assess interventions which work, which are appropriate and which are sustainable.

c. Uses Nature as Mentor: which can teach us how to live.

Janine has worked with ecologists to articulate a very powerful set of Nature's Laws, which are:

1. Nature runs on sunlight

2. Nature only uses the energy it needs

3. Nature fits form to function

4. Nature recycles everything

5. Nature rewards co-operation

6. Natures relies on diversity and emergence

7. Nature demands local expertise

8. Nature curbs excesses from within

9. Nature tests the power of limits and limitations

Nature's organizing principles are based on Partnerships, Networking, Seasonality, Resilience, Diversity and Dynamic Balance. As Vaclav Havel, President of the Czech Republic wrote:[29]

We must draw our standards from the natural world. We must honour the humility of the wise boundaries of the natural world and the mystery, which lies beyond them, admitting that there is something in the order which exceeds our competence.

For this practice:

- Consider your reaction to Biomimicry – and why you have it.

- In your life and work, ask yourself if and how you could use:

  - Nature as Model

  - Nature as Measure

  - Nature as Mentor

- Ask yourself if and how you could bring Nature's Laws and Organizing Principles alive in your life and work.

- Journal your reflections.

- Ask yourself 'What is now needed from me?'

As Confucious reminds us:[30] 'He who is in harmony with Nature hits the mark without effort and apprehends the truth without thinking.'

Practice 168
Exercise: Using the Wisdom of Hindsight

This practice is an exercise in embodying a desired future state in the present, and learning from the questions 'What do I wish I had known?'

For this practice:

- Ground and centre yourself in the present.

- Envisage a compelling future state or goal for yourself and the date it will have been achieved.

- Now embody this future state in the present. Describe what it looks, feels and might taste like and the steps that you took to get you there, looking back in hindsight.

- Then return to now and reflect on the learning.

- Ask yourself 'what is needed from me?'

Practice 169
Exercise: From Ego to Eco Consciousness

Life should be a journey through and into deepening levels of awareness and consciousness. As adults we meet thresholds, which invite us into different levels of expansion, development and integration. This shifts the place within us from which we choose to live.

Working Wisely means being able to meet ourselves and others where they are at on their own journeys, rather than imposing our own frame of reference on them.

Many have written very extensively about Adult Stages of Development. These have included Robert Kegan,[31] Ken Wilbur,[32] Otto Laske,[33] Carol Pearson,[34] James Fowler,[35] Erik Erikson[36] and Don Beck and Christopher Cowan.[37]

I find it most useful to think in terms of five lenses which reveal WHO we are being, in our developing relationships with ourselves, others and the world. These inform HOW we act and HOW we choose to work. Working with more wisdom works from an Ego to an Eco consciousness.

- The Centre Self: I-in-Me
- The Rational Self: I-in-It
- The Relational Self: I-in-You
- The Authentic Self: I-in-Now
- The Transforming Self: I-in-Now and Us

For this practice:

- Ask yourself 'Who am I?

- For Yourself: Consider the impact this has on four key dimensions:

  i.   Your key relationships

  ii. How you relate to your experiences

  iii. How you see the world

  and

  iv. How you act in the work

- Journal your discoveries. Ask yourself 'What is needed for me to shift?'

- With Your Clients: Repeat this inquiry with clients. Invite them to consider 'Who am I? – for some of the time and for most of the time?' – and the impact this has for them on

i. Their key relationships

ii. How they relate to their experiences

iii. How they see the world

and

iv. How they act in the world

- Invite them to journal their discoveries. Invite them to consider what needs to shift.

As Martha Graham writes:[38]

> We learn by practice. Whether it means to learn to dance by practicing dancing or to learn to live by practicing living the principles are the same.

Practice 170
Exercise: From Technician to Alchemist

Developing our awareness and 'WHO we are being' maps across into different action logics – otherwise known as our worldview – which have been developed by a number of different writers and researchers. An action logic is defined as how we interpret our surroundings and how we react when our power or safety is challenged.

These different action logics therefore express how we work in the world – and the different levels of awareness and consciousness that we are working from. It is argued that each action logic represents an expanded level of awareness and personal development, whilst also incorporating our earlier action logics.

Peter Hawkins identified four levels from Experimentation to Eldership.[39] These Peter describes as:

1. The Action Logic of Experimentation where we focus on arriving, what we enjoy and want to do next.

2. The Action Logic of Experience Accumulation where we focus on deepening our experience along with establishing our credibility and traction in work.

3. The Action Logic of Full Leadership where we make a difference and want to leave a legacy.

4. The Action Logic of Eldership where want to enable others, share our wisdom and pass on our legacy.

Bill Torbert, Dalmar Fisher and David Rooke identified the seven action logics of: Opportunist,

Diplomat, Expert, Achiever, Individualist, Strategist and Alchemist.[40] Bill, Dalmar and David researched how these different action logics were distributed and how they equated to performance across a sampled leadership population. They found that Opportunists represented 5% of their cohort; Diplomats 12%; Experts 38%; Achievers 30%; Individualists 10%; Strategists 4%; and Alchemists 1%. They also found that:[41]

> Three types of leader, the Opportunists, Diplomats and Experts (some 55% of the sample) were associated with below average corporate performance. They also found that Opportunists, Diplomats and Experts were also significantly less effective at implementing organizational strategies than 30% of the sample who measured as Achievers. Moreover only 15% of managers in the sample (the Individualists, Strategists and Alchemists) showed consistently the capacity to innovate and to successfully transform their organizations.

Working Wisely is about appreciating your own – and others' – action logic. There is no right or wrong. This approach enables you to meet your clients where they are in their own journey and work with what is, as needed.

For this practice:

- Decide which set of action logics you find easiest to work with for this exercise. You can do the exercise for yourself and with your clients.

- For Yourself:

  - Reflect on your own developmental journey.

  - Ask yourself 'Where am I now?' and 'How do I know?'

  - Now ask yourself 'What is needed from me?' and 'How do I put in place the developmental experiences I need to help me to develop?'

- For Your Clients:

  - Invite your clients to reflect on their own developmental journeys.

  - Invite them to ask themselves 'Where am now I?' and 'How do I know?'

  - Invite them to consider what Practices 169 and 170 might mean for them.

  - Now invite your clients to ask themselves 'What is needed from me?' and 'How do I put in place the developmental experiences I need to help me to develop?'

- Create a Personal Development Plan.

Practice 171
Inquiry: Espoused and Actual Practice

Chris Argyris and Donald Schön identified the gap which can open up between what they called 'espoused theory' and 'theory-in-use' or actual practice.[42]

This is the gap between WHO we are being (how we *believe* our worldview and values inform our behaviours) and HOW we *actually* practice (how our worldview and values are actually expressed through our behaviour and actions).

Professional bodies have Codes of Ethics and Conduct, which set standards for practice. However it is in Donald Schön's 'swampy lowlands' of actual practice that practitioners need to be held to account.[43] The gap is closed through Working with Integrity – being open to what we do not know or cannot see, regularly self-assessing ourselves against our relevant professional codes, and ensuring that we review our work with a Supervisor.

Professor Roger Steare has developed the MoralDNA™ personality profile.[44] MoralDNA™ helps us to understand our moral values and how we prefer to make decisions and 'do the right thing'. From the three decision-making preferences of Law, Logic or Love our MoralDNA™ character is either Philosopher, Judge, Angel, Teacher, Enforcer or Guardian, and we are scored on the ten moral values of Wisdom, Fairness, Courage, Self Control, Trust, Hope, Humility, Care, Honesty and Excellence.

For this practice:

- Review your practice notes. Spot areas where there might have been a gap between your espoused theory and practice in action. Reflect and investigate further. Take to your supervisor for further exploration as necessary

- Periodically refresh yourself with your professional body's Codes of Ethics and Conduct. Assess yourself against each quality and/or competency. Take to your supervisor for further exploration as necessary.

- Refresh as necessary your own Codes of Practice.

- Refresh and update your Contract documentation.

- Design feedback processes with your clients to help you spot any gaps between your intention and how you are actually experienced or your actions interpreted.

Practice 172
Inquiry: Discerning and Discernment

The faculty of discernment sits at the heart of every wisdom tradition. Beyond assessment or judgement, it is the act of perceiving clearly and intuitive recognition. *The Oxford English Dictionary* defines discernment as follows:[45]

> To perceive clearly with mind or senses, to make out by thought or by gazing, listening etc. – of having quick or true insight …

Discernment is sorting the wheat from the chaff – what is more true or less true? Does this support or negate? Is this me and mine or not? This is captured in extracts from William Stafford's poem 'Deciding':[46]

> You hold all things or not, depending
> not on greed but whether they suit what
> life begins to mean.
>
> Like those workers [in a gold mine] you study what moves,
> what stays. You bow, and then, like them,
> you know –
>
> What's God, what's world, what's gold.

For this practice:

* Ask yourself 'What would it take for me to be more discerning?' and 'How might that show up in my life and in my work?'

* Ask yourself what William Stafford's poem might mean for you.

* Ask yourself 'How can I hone my faculty for discernment?'

* Journal your reflections.

Practice 173
Inquiry: Offering without Attachment v. Withholding

Working Wisely involves discerning when it is appropriate and timely for us to offer our insights or knowledge without attachment, and when that might be an act of ego or even superiority. Equally, withholding what we sense or know might be helpful is an act of control or power over another.

For this practice:

- Ask yourself 'How do I walk the fine line in my practice between offering with and without attachment?' and 'How do I know the difference?'

- Ask yourself 'When might I withhold or withdraw and why?'

- Be curious about your relationship with and to power.

- Be curious about deference and how this might show up in your life and work.

- Journal your reflections.

Practice 174
Inquiry: Using Self as Instrument

Working Wisely is bringing our whole selves to the work. 'People work' demands that we use our selves as instruments. We need to use all of our intelligences to tune in, to hear the notes, vibrations, tones, rhythms, spaces, cadences and silences within ourselves, as we work with others. The resonance – and dissonance – which can occur as we work gives us valuable data with which we can modulate or fine-tune our interventions. As Beethoven wrote:[47] 'Music is a higher revelation than all wisdom and philosophy. Music is the electrical soil in which the spirit lives, thinks and invents.'

For this practice:

- Consider the question 'What instrument am I in an orchestra?'

- Visualize yourself as this instrument.

- Ask yourself 'What do I look and feel like and what kind of noise do I make when I am in tune and also off key?'

- Consider how you can keep yourself fit for practice.

Practice 175
Exercise: 'Namaste'

'Namaste' is an ancient Sanskrit greeting. Roughly translated Namaste means 'I bow to the God in you' or 'the Spirit within me salutes the Spirit in you'. 'Namaste' is usually spoken with a slight bow and hands pressed together, palms touching and fingers pointing upwards, thumbs close to the chest. The blessing honours our shared humanity – that we are all made from the same divine consciousness.

For this practice:

*   Consider how you could bring this blessing or another form of blessing you might be more comfortable with into your work. This could be done silently or spoken out loud before or after a piece of work or incorporated into your email signature.

*   Start to collect your own scrapbook of blessings from different cultures across the world.

Practice 176
More Inspiration: Working Wisely

Here is some inspiration to support you in Working Wisely. Albert Einstein reminds us of the three rules of work![48]:

> Three Rules of Work:
> Out of clutter find simplicity;
> From discord find harmony;
> In the middle of difficulty lies opportunity.

As Epictetus writes:[49]

> There are three topics in philosophy, in which he/she who would be wise and good must be exercised: that of the desires and aversions, that he/she may not be disappointed of the one nor incur the other; that of the pursuits and avoidances, and in general, the duties of life, that he/she may act with order and consideration, and not carelessly; the third included integrity of mind and prudence, and in general, whatever belongs to judgement.

For Leo Tolstoy.[50]

It is a mistake to think that there are times when you can safely address a person without love. In the same way as you cannot work with bees without being cautious, you cannot work with people without being mindful of their humanity.

And finally, as John O'Donohue writes:[51]

May you know the wisdom of deep listening,
The healing of wholesome words,
The encouragement of the appreciative gaze,
The decorum of held dignity,
The springtime edge of the bleak question

* * * * *

Reflective Questions

1. Which of the twenty practices are you most drawn to and why?

2. Which of the twenty practices are you least drawn to and why?

3. What are you going to action now?

By three methods we may learn wisdom: first, by reflection, which is noblest; second, by imitation, which is easiest; and third by experience, which is the bitterest.

Confucius[1]

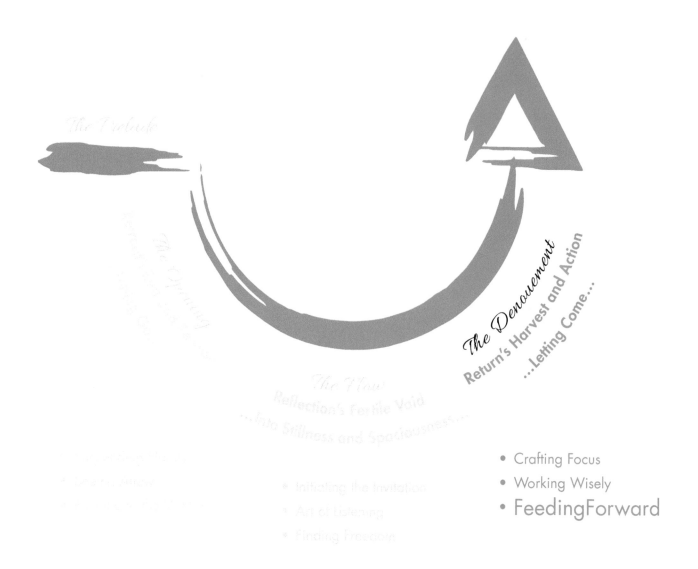

The Prelude

The Opening

The Denouement
Return's Harvest and Action
...Letting Come...

The Flow
Reflection's Fertile Void
...Into Stillness and Spaciousness...

- Initiating the Invitation
- Art of Listening
- Finding Freedom

- Crafting Focus
- Working Wisely
- FeedingForward

FeedForward reframes feedback. FeedForward gives us the intelligence we need to learn from the past and the intimations of the future in order to reshape or create wisely in the present here and now. The practices for Feedforward help us to learn from the past and the future without anxiety or shame.

FeedForward shows us how our intention is experienced both by ourselves and others. It provides us with our own navigational system, which tells us if and how we are on course and what needs to be altered, adjusted or stopped if we are not. It allows us to test who we are being, what we intend and how we are working in the world.

When given and received as a generous gift FeedForward can help us – and the people we work with – stay true to what we/they intend. It is a radical act of care for ourselves and others as we work. As the composer Peter Maxwell Davies wrote:[2] 'If you don't [know how you are doing] from your performers and your audience, you're going to be working in a vacuum.'

FeedForward involves feedback but is more than feedback. Nature thrives on complex feedback loops. These are called mutual causal interactions – nature's design for finding balance and building resilience. Every action has an equal and opposite action or reaction. When we act, the world acts back in a constant state of dialogue, exchange and co-creation. We shape the world and in turn are shaped by it. Closed systems atrophy. Open systems adapt and thrive.

However, feedback itself has been given a bad press. Negative feedback is amplified and positive feedback gets downplayed. Receiving feedback of any sort is often associated with memories of fraught educational, familial or other learning experiences where we felt criticized, shamed and/or judged by some external measures, which found us lacking in some way with clear instructions for improvement. FeedForward helps us to learn.

FeedForward is a set of practices for learning how to truly value data from the past and the present time as generous gifts of reciprocity, communication and exchange which are needed to keep us on track, in balance, resourced and resilient.

The FeedForward which we can give to ourselves – as well as that which we receive – often reveals more about the inner state of the giver than the receiver. Finding the generous, curious and appreciative space within ourselves – and what we intend – as we give and receive FeedForward determines its power to inspire change. As Tara Mohr writes:[3]

> Feedback doesn't tell you about yourself. It tells you about the person giving the feedback. In other words, if someone says your work is gorgeous, that just tells you about their taste. If you put out a new product and it doesn't sell at all, that tells you something about what your audience does or doesn't want. When we look at praise and criticism as information about the people giving it, we tend to get really curious about the feedback, rather than dejected or defensive.

For Vironika Tugaleva:[4]

There is a difference between judgment and feedback. Your critics use you as a mirror for their own hidden darkness. Your teachers hold up a mirror to yours.

FeedForward is a courageous act. FeedForward puts us in relationship with our own internal and external ecosystem, which will tell us if we are aligned and in flow or not. Crafting Focus and Working Wisely requires us to pay attention to our FeedForward so that we can create the conditions for our intentions to thrive and flex as we experiment and prototype. FeedForward should aim to inspire not shame – even when we have to hear difficult messages.

FeedForward appeals to our human need for appreciation and belonging. It also gives us the data to tell us what is working, and not working. FeedForward enables us to be responsible and thereby accountable to ourselves and others. It gives us the data we need to know how and when to start, stop or continue on a particular course.

As Winston Churchill wrote:[5] 'Success is not final, failure is not fatal: it is the courage to continue that counts.'

For Michael J. Gelb:[6] 'Champions know that success is inevitable, that there is no such thing as failure, only feedback. They know that the best way to forecast the future is to create it.'

Practices for FeedForward

There are many ways in which you can receive FeedForward. Here are twenty-one practices which work for me.

Practice 177
Reflection: What is your Relationship with Feedback?

Our past experiences of giving and receiving feedback can shape how we work with it. We can find ourselves amplifying what we perceive to be negative feedback and discounting the positive. This does not serve our own development. As Yehuda Berg writes:[7]

> If we were handling a bomb, which could go off at any minute as a result of our actions, we would mind ourselves and be delicate. Our words have the same power, yet we wield them around as though they were powerless and insignificant.

This practice invites you to explore your relationship with feedback in order for you to understand your own unconscious triggers and patterns so that you can open yourself up to the gifts of FeedForward.

For this practice:

- Centre and ground yourself.

- **Working with Negative Feedback**

  ○ You Receiving Negative Feedback

    ◊ Think back to a time when you received what you perceived to be negative feedback.

    ◊ Reconstruct the situation. Ask yourself 'What was happening – and what caused it to happen?', 'Where were you?', 'What was the context?', 'What was intended?', 'Was the feedback invited or not invited?' and 'Who was involved?'

    ◊ Reconnect with how, why and what you were thinking and feeling as you received the feedback, its impact on you and your relationship with the person.

    ◊ Reconnect with your voice. Reconnect with what you said or did not say.

    ◊ Return to the present and from the position of your wise adult self consider what you might like to have said or done but did not. Decide which part of the feedback is yours and what you need to work on and which part is not yours and you can give away.

  ○ You Giving Negative Feedback

    ◊ Think back to a time when you gave what you perceived to be negative feedback.

    ◊ Reconstruct the situation as above.

    ◊ Return to the present and from the position of your wise adult self consider what you might like to have said or done but did not.

  ○ Journal your lessons.

  ○ Repeat the exercise if needed to explore your patterns.

  ○ Release yourself with a self compassion and appreciation prayer.

- **Working with Positive Feedback**

  ○ You Receiving Positive Feedback

    ◊ Think back to a time when you received what you perceived to be positive feedback.

    ◊ Reconstruct the situation. Ask yourself 'What was happening – and what caused it to happen?', 'Where were you?', 'What was the context?', 'What was intended?', 'Was the feedback invited or not invited?' and 'Who was involved?'

    ◊ Reconnect with how, why and what you were thinking and feeling as you received the feedback. Ask yourself 'What did I do with the feedback? – Did I welcome it, allow it in, or discount it?'

◊ Return to the present and from the position of your wise adult self consider how you could become more open to positive feedback.

  ○ You Giving Positive Feedback

    ◊ Think back to a time when you gave what you perceived to be positive feedback.

    ◊ Reconstruct the situation

    ◊ Return to the present and from the position of your wise adult self consider what you might like to have said or done but did not.

  ○ Journal your lessons.

  ○ Repeat the exercise if needed to explore your patterns.

  ○ Release yourself with a self compassion prayer.

• Reflect on the 4 sets of inquiries and notice both your conscious and unconscious patterns. Ask yourself which metaphor comes to mind when you think of you receiving and giving what you perceive as both negative and positive feedback.

As Buddha reminded us:[8]

Whatever words we utter should be chosen with care for people will hear them and be influenced by them for good or ill.

Practice 178
Inquiry: Why Bother?

FeedForward can be welcome or unwelcome, irritating, derailing or empowering. Appreciating why we need FeedForward can help us invite, appreciate and work with it so that we stay on track. We are all fallible and cannot always see. FeedForward helps to hold the mirror to ourselves and our work. FeedForward wakes us up to what we are doing and the unintended consequences of our actions.

FeedForward is an essential part of learning and creativity. Without its nudges and messages we risk blindly blundering our way through the implementation of our projects or doggedly repeating past mistakes with the same results. We also risk becoming blind to the improvements, impact or contributions we are actually making. FeedForward helps us to know if we are Working Wisely.

For this practice:

• List your own reasons for engaging in FeedForward. Ask yourself:

  ○ 'What is my "why bother"?'

  ○ 'How does FeedForward support and serve me?'

and

- ○ 'What are the costs to me?'

- Consider how you tune into your own navigational system and what is being transmitted to you from both your internal and external landscapes.

- Consider how you welcome or dismiss these nudges. Ask yourself 'What do I typically prefer to pay attention to and what do I typically tend to ignore or discard?'

- Ask yourself:
  - ○ 'How do I tell the difference?'
  - ○ 'What do the different sensations feel like?'
  - ○ 'Where do they appear in my body?'
  - ○ 'How do I pay attention to them?'

  and

  - ○ 'Do I welcome or dismiss them – and how do I know the difference?'

- Journal what you notice.

- Consider how you can invite more FeedForward into your work and life.

- Decide on what actions you will now take.

Practice 179
Exercise: Reframing and Embracing FeedForward as a Gift

FeedForward is the engine for improvement and change. FeedForward is the gift, which wakes us up to WHO we are being and HOW we are being as we work. As Mark Bland writes:[9]

> Critique, feedback, reaction to one's work or the way they have presented it, regardless of intention, is a gift.

This practice invites you to reframe FeedForward as a gift – whilst appreciating that not all gifts come in pretty neat packages! A deep dive might be needed to find the pearl in the grit.

For this practice experiment and play:

- Ask yourself 'If I saw FeedForward as a present what wrapping paper, ties and bows would I use?'

- Ask yourself 'If I received an unwanted gift of FeedForward how would I be with both the gift and the person who gave me the gift?'

- Ask yourself 'If I received a wanted gift of FeedForward how would I be with both the gift and the person who gave me the gift?'

- Ask yourself 'What is different for me between the two scenerios?' and 'What do I need to learn from this in order to be a generous recipient of all FeedForward?'

- Consider how you can create the conditions you need to support you in your processing of whatever FeedForward you receive.

- Journal your reflections.

As Denise Morrison writes:[10] 'I think of feedback as constructive, not positive or negative. You choose to do what you want with it.'

Practice 180
Inquiry: The Caring Art of Giving and Receiving FeedForward

FeedForward is a radical act of care. What is key is how we first own our own perceptions and then how, with care, we connect with our intentions as we give or receive FeedForward. As Bill O'Brien observed:[11] 'The success of an intervention depends on the interior condition of the intervenor.'

David Whyte points to the art of giving when he writes:[12]

Giving is not done easily, giving is difficult; giving well is in fact a discipline that must be practiced and observed over years to be done properly. The art often involves giving the wrong thing to the wrong person and learning how to do the opposite through time and trial, it means getting beyond the boundaries of our own needs, it means understanding another and another's life, it acknowledges implicitly that we ourselves must be recipients of things we cannot often identify or even find ourselves … To give is to make an imaginative journey to put oneself in the body, the mind and anticipation of another.

For this practice:

- Invite yourself to consider the statement 'FeedForward is a radical act of care.' Study your thoughts, feelings and reactions as you contemplate the statement. Explore what is evoked and invoked in you and why.

- **Giving FeedForward**
  Think back to when you last gave FeedForward. Replay what happened in your mind. Now ask yourself:
  - 'What did I intend?'
  - 'What was my interior state?'
  - 'How did I/we contract or establish permission to offer FeedForward?'
  - 'How did I act and behave?'
  - 'What was the impact on myself and the other?'
  - 'What happened as a result of the FeedForward?'
  - Challenge yourself with the questions 'Is the FeedForward I offered life giving or stunting to both me and the other?'
  - Journal your reflections.

- **Receiving FeedForward**
  Think back to when you last received FeedForward. Replay what happened in your mind. Now ask yourself:
  - 'What was my interior state when I asked for FeedForward or when FeedForward was unsolicited?'
  - 'How did I/we invite the FeedForward? Or how did we contract for how the FeedForward would be given?'
  - 'How did I act and behave?'
  - 'What was the impact on myself and the other?'
  - 'What happened as a result of the FeedForward?'
  - Challenge yourself with the question 'Is the FeedForward I offered life giving or stunting to both me and the other?'
  - Journal your reflections.

- Ask yourself 'What would change if FeedForward became an act of love?'

A final thought from Atticus in *To Kill a Mockingbird* when Scout is trying to understand the town's reactions to the trial:[13] 'You never really understand a person until you consider things from his point of view ... until you climb into his skin and walk around in it.'

Practice 181
Exercise: Keeping Ourselves Safe

FeedForward is a also an act of vulnerability. This is because both the giving and receiving of FeedForward can challenge our assumptions and mindsets about what we think we know, or what others think they know. FeedForward requires us to show up and be seen, and this makes us vulnerable.

We might have to give or receive data which, in some way, is inconvenient, difficult, critical or upsetting to us, or to people we work with. Or we might have to give and receive data which supports and encourages us or the people we work with – which helps us or them to feel appreciated and encouraged. Either can challenge old identities or vindicate long struggles. FeedForward may provoke an emotional response deep within us which cannot be fully understood. This practice therefore invites us to explore how we can keep ourselves safe and supported as we work with FeedForward to create the pre conditions for learning.

For this practice:

- Consider how you currently contract to create a place of physical, psychological and emotional safety for the learning process of giving and receiving FeedForward.

- Ask yourself what permissions, protections and courtesies are in place which honour and respect all parties for the FeedForward in service of what is intended.

- Pay attention to the details. Consider:

  - What is intended?

  - What time and place best supports the work?

  - What style and mode of conversation best supports what is needed?

  - Do you understand each others' communication, learning and thinking styles sufficiently?

  - How can fear reactions be minimized or normalized?

  - What permissions are needed?

  - What protections are needed?

  - Where is compassion and self-compassion?

  - Are you in full relational presence with each other before commencing FeedForward?

- Remember that choice is always present. We can always choose how we are being and what we want to do with the FeedForward we receive.

Whilst remaining open to new information is how we learn, Eleanor Roosevelt also reminds us:[14] 'No one can make you feel inferior without your consent.'

Practice 182
Exercise: Ready, Steady, Go

Brene Brown has developed a Manifesto for Courageous Feedback.[15] Brene's work recognizes how important our intrinsic sense of worthiness – 'that we are not perfect but we are good enough' – is key to wholehearted living. Also how FeedForward can provoke feelings of shame and unworthiness, which can denude and disempower us.

Brene says that we are ready to give Feedback when we can say yes to all 10 items on the following checklist:

1. I am ready to sit next to you rather than across from you.

2. I am willing to put the problem in front of us rather than between us (or sliding it towards you).

3. I am ready to listen, ask questions, and accept that I do not fully understand the issue.

4. I want to acknowledge what you do well instead of picking apart your mistakes.

5. I recognize your strengths and how you can use them to address your challenges.

6. I can hold you accountable without shaming or blaming you.

7. I am willing to own my part.

8. I can genuinely thank you for your efforts rather than criticize your failings.

9. I can talk about how resolving these challenges will lead to your growth and opportunity.

10. I can model the vulnerability and openness that I expect to see from you.

For this practice:

* Review the Checklist.

* Identify which of the 10 are easy for you and which are more difficult.

* Reflect why this is for you.

* Design your own Checklist. Change or add to the list.

* Consider how your Checklist could be part of your future Contracting or Agreements with your client.

* Ask yourself 'What needs to change – and also change in me – to make sure I meet all 10 before I engage in FeedForward?'

This is crucial because, as Brene Brown says:[16]

> Shame works like the zoom lens on a camera. When we are feeling shame, the camera is zoomed in tight and all we see is our flawed selves, alone and struggling.

Practice 183
Reflection: Real-time FeedForward

FeedingForward in the moment keeps us in flow. Real-time FeedForward keeps us in conversation, a property and ally of the system, in service of what is emerging. Fractals reveal the whole. Small and immediate tweaks or corrections for the health of the whole become possible before a major issue occurs.

For this practice:

- Consider when you typically give FeedForward. Ask yourself 'Do I tend to give FeedForward in the moment or do I reserve FeedForward for staged set pieces?' and 'What influences my choices?'

- Ask yourself 'To what extent do I work lightly and gently with what I am noticing' and 'Where is my focus: on the specific behaviour or seeds which are emerging or on the person and their intentions?'

- Ask yourself 'What am I noticing about the impact of my choices?' and 'What is now needed from me?'

- Now notice when you typically prefer to receive FeedForward. Ask yourself 'Why?', 'Does it matter?' and 'What do I need to better support my learning and development?'

This is important because, as Fritjof Capra writes:[17]

> The phenomenon of emergence takes place at critical points of instability that arise from fluctuations in the environment, amplified by feedback loops. Emergence results in the creation of novelty, and this novelty is often qualitatively different from the phenomenon out of which it emerged.

As the African Proverb reminds us:[18] 'Examine what is said and not who speaks.'

Practice 184
Exercise: The 5:1 Appreciation–Criticism Formula

Nancy Kline recommends the 5:1 appreciation to criticism feedback formula. For Winston Churchill:[19] 'Criticism may not be agreeable, but it is necessary. It fulfils the same function as pain in the human body. It calls attention to an unhealthy state of things.'

The 5:1 formula invites us to begin and end with four appreciations, with one piece of negative feedback in the middle. This is because, as Nancy writes:[20]

> Appreciation keeps people thinking. Appreciation that is genuine, succinct and concrete is important not because it feels good or nice, but because it helps people to think for themselves on the cutting edge of an issue.

For this practice:

- Think back to a time when you had to give difficult or negative feedback to another person. Ask yourself 'What ratio of appreciation and criticism did I use?' Explore what your recipient might have felt and how you felt as you gave the feedback.

- Now think back to a time when you received difficult or negative feedback. Ask yourself 'What ratio of appreciation and criticism was used?' Explore how you felt as you received the feedback and how the giver might have felt as they gave you the feedback.

- Consider the similarities and differences between the two scenarios. Explore 'What were the intended and unintended impacts of both scenarios?' and 'What can I learn and now change as a result of my reflections?'

- Journal your actions.

As William James writes:[21] 'The deepest principle of human nature is the craving to be appreciated.'

Practice 185
Inquiry: Remembering 'I am OK; You are OK'

Working from the 'I am OK; You are OK' position in Transactional Analysis enables FeedForward to be deeply respectful, honouring and supportive of each other.

'I am OK; You are OK' keeps both parties responsible, accountable and proactive to themselves and towards each other whilst also preventing either or both from falling down the rabbit hole of victim and persecutor. It avoids one person slipping into 'I am OK; You are not OK', 'I am not OK; You are OK' or both feeling that together 'We are not OK'.

For this practice:

* Ask yourself 'What is my stance?', 'What do I assume?', and 'How do I behave?' when I both give and receive FeedForward.

* Consider a situation when you have stayed in the 'I am OK; You are OK' position when giving and receiving FeedForward. Ask yourself 'What, why and how was this made possible?'

* Now consider a situation when you did not stay in the 'I am OK; You are OK' (and slipped into 'I am OK; You are not OK', 'I am not OK; You are OK' or 'We are not OK') positions when giving and receiving FeedForward. Ask yourself 'What, why and how did this happen?' and 'What is needed from me to remain in the "I am OK; You are OK" position or to return to the "I am OK; You are OK" position as quickly as possible when I feel myself slipping?'

* Journal your insights.

* Action plan any changes you need to make.

Practice 186
Exercise: Everyone Gets an 'A'

Rosamund and Benjamin Zander recommend 'Giving an A'![22]. When Ben tested this with his students in orchestras he found that teaching was easier and progress was quicker. The 'A' was not about comparison with others or an expectation to live up to, but a possibility for each student to grow into. As they write:[23]

> When you give an 'A' (to anyone) you find yourself speaking not from a place of measuring how they stack up against your standards, but from a place of respect that gives then room to be themselves. Michelangelo is often quoted as saying inside every block of stone or marble dwells a beautiful statue;

one need only remove the excess to reveal the work of art within. If we were to apply this to education (or to performance) it would be pointless to compare one person with another. Instead all the energy would be focused on chipping away at the stone, getting rid of whatever is in the way of each person's developing skills, mastery and self-expression.

For this practice:

- Consider what getting consistent 'A's would mean for you and your clients.

- Consider how you might give consistent 'A's to yourself and your clients – and what this would mean for you and for them.

- Consider when giving a grade other than an A to someone might be appropriate and how you would deliver the news.

- Consider when receiving a grade other than an A might be appropriate and how you might receive the news.

- Journal your reflections and commitments.

Practice 187
Exercise: Tuning into Ourselves

FeedForward is about tuning in. FeedForward is tuning into our natural rhythms to match our energy to the tasks we have set ourselves for that day. It is also scanning our emotional, cognitive, psychological and spiritual selves for feedback, to ensure that we are in alignment and on track. Noticing when we are out of step with ourselves gives us valuable data about who we are being and how we are working in the moment – and what needs our attention. This helps us work and go with flow rather than trying to force matters with sheer willpower. Chogynam Trungpa compares this to riding a horse:[24]

> Even though the horse beneath you may move, you can still maintain your seat. As long as you have good posture in your saddle, you can overcome any startling or unexpected moves. And whenever you slip you simply regain your posture; you don't fall off the horse. In the process of losing awareness you regain it **because** of the process of losing it. Slipping in itself, corrects itself.

For this practice:

- Breathe deeply.

- Now imagine you are a flowing river or a turning wheel which is fed by the tributaries from your head, heart, gut and soul.

- Check in with each tributary. Notice if there is flow or if there are any hesitations, bumps or obstacles from any tributary.

- Pay attention to your felt sensations. Note them and inquire into them. Ask yourself 'What is the message here for me?'

- Act as necessary, which might include rest and doing nothing.

- Repeat the practice when you have acted to review.

Practice 188
Reflection: Listening to Our Shadows

As Johann Wolfgang von Goethe wrote:[25]

> There is strong shadow where there is much light. Our shadows can derail us but they can also keep us on track. When we notice our shadows we can choose to either ignore them or embrace the message, which they offer us.

The 'Shadow 7Cs' are:

- Criticizing

- Controlling

- Competing

- Comparing

- Complaining

- Complacency

- Closed

© Elaine Patterson

When we slip into any or some of these we need to become aware that we might no longer be Working Wisely. As Carl Jung wrote:[26]

> How can I be substantial if I do not cast a shadow? I must have a dark side also if I am to be whole. One does not become enlightened by imagining figures of light, but by making the darkness conscious. The latter procedure, however, is disagreeable and therefore not popular.

For this practice:

- Consider what each shadow means for you and/or for your clients. What is your default?

- Notice which of the shadows is your go-to place (or places) when you are triggered.

- Think back to a time when you were triggered. Ask yourself 'What happened?', 'Why did it happen?', 'How did I feel – and how might I have made the other feel?' and 'What resulted?'

- Now reflect on how you could catch your shadow earlier before its drama is enacted.

- Consider how you can pause, breathe and pay attention to its FeedForward message to turn the/your shadow into the light.

- Consider how you make a friend of your shadow(s).

- Journal your reflections.

Practice 189
Reflection: Working with the Law of Unintended Consequences

In the Social Sciences the Law of Unintended Consequences was popularized by Robert K. Merton. These unintended consequences are:

- An unexpected benefit

- An unexpected drawback

or

- A perverse result or backfire

This practice invites us to become aware of the possible unintended consequences of our actions in pursuit of our intentions.

For this practice:

- Think back to a time when you were the recipient of an action or set of actions which had unintended consequences for you – or for your team. Ask yourself 'What happened?', 'Why did it happen?', 'How did I feel – and how might I have made others feel?' and 'What resulted?'

- Now think back to a time when your actions or set of actions had unintended consequences. Ask yourself 'What happened?', 'Why did it happen?', 'How did I feel – and how might I have made others feel?' and 'What resulted?'

- Consider how you can create working environments which openly acknowledge and work with the Law of Unintended Consequences.

- Consider how you can use FeedForward to anticipate unintended consequences to both harness any unexpected benefits and manage any fallouts.

Practice 190
Reflection: The Art of Saying Sorry

Saying sorry when needed is an act of reparation, responsibility and accountability.

In our busy unpredictable and fast-paced world we can make mistakes and errors of judgement. Saying sorry when things go wrong honours the other as well as our shared humanity. FeedForward ensures that we tune into times when saying sorry is vital to restoring balance in service of the long-term health of a relationship or project. As Grace Poe writes:[27]

> It's always best to ask for forgiveness if you feel that you made a mistake. And again, asking for forgiveness is not just saying the words "I'm sorry"; it is also offering what you need to do.

For this practice:

- Ask yourself 'How do I see – and what is my relationship with – saying sorry?'

- Be curious about what has shaped and influenced this. Explore whether you view saying sorry as a weakness or a strength – and what circumstances make either so.

- Think back to a time when you chose not to say sorry. Ask yourself 'What happened?', 'How did I feel – and how might I have made others feel?', 'What resulted?' and 'What could have been different?'

- Think back to a time when you needed to receive an apology from another person. Ask yourself 'What happened?', 'How did I feel – and how might the other person have been feeling?', 'What resulted?' and 'What could have been different?'

- Reflect on how you can use FeedForward to alert you to when saying sorry is appropriate, kind or pragmatic.

Practice 191
Exercise: In the Company of Critical Friends

Critical friends are an important part of our support network as we start to make changes and make change happen. 'Critical' here does not mean criticizing. Emerging from the Critical Pedagogy reforms in the 1970s, a 'Critical Friend' is defined as:[28]

> A trusted person who asks provocative questions, provides data to be examined through another lens, and offers critiques of a person's work as a friend. A critical friend takes the time to fully understand the context of the work presented and the outcomes that the person or group is working toward. The friend is an advocate for the success of that work.

For this practice:

- Write down a list of the people in your support network.

- Who from your list act as your Critical Friend(s)?

- Consider how you invite their FeedForward and what more or different is needed.

- Consider who else you might need to invite into your network to help support and resource you.

- Consider how you might act as a Critical Friend to others and how you would fulfill this role.

As John MacBeath, Professor of Education Leadership at Cambridge University, writes:[29]

> The Critical Friend is a powerful idea, perhaps because it contains an inherent tension. Friends bring a high degree of unconditional positive regard. Critics are, at first sight at least, conditional, negative and intolerant of failure. Perhaps the critical friend comes close to what might be regarded as 'true friendship' – a successful marrying of unconditional support and unconditional critique.

Practice 192
Inquiry: Saving Ourselves from the Dangers of Groupthink

FeedForward saves us from one-dimensional thinking. FeedForward reminds us to invite different and diverse views into the mix so that we are not blindsided by our own focus or perspective.

Much has been written elsewhere on Group Dynamics. For this practice you are invited to:

- Consider how to invite and stay open to perspectives other than your own.

- Consider your own relationship to difference and diversity.

- Consider your reactions when something or someone different or diverse enters your field. Do you find yourself irritated by the intrusion or do you welcome the invitation? How might timing and context alter your reactions?

- Journal your insights and what is now needed from you.

Practice 193
Exercise: Working with Difficult Feedback

Not all FeedForward is welcomed, appreciated or even valid. Some FeedForward can be very negative, or even rock our foundations. This practice reminds us that we do not have to indiscriminately accept every piece of FeedForward we receive or which is offered to us. We are free to accept what is rightfully ours and reject what is not rightfully ours – and that responsibility rests with us. Remember that sometimes FeedForward which is meant to control us shows up that we are on track!

For this practice:

- When you find yourself receiving unexpected or difficult FeedForward remember to ground and centre yourself by breathing deeply.

- Imagine yourself as a giant sieve. Catch what you need in the sieve. Allow what is not yours to drain away.

- Calmly voice what you need to in the moment but try to avoid arguments, defensiveness or recriminations. Thank the person for their observations and move away.

- Get yourself to a calm, safe and if possible supported space where you can process your nuggets, feelings and reactions. Place one hand on your belly and your other hand on your heart. The hand on your belly provides you with the comfort and the courage to hear the meaning behind the words. Your hand on your heart gives you the self-compassion you need to take any learning that is yours and then release yourself from the encounter.

- Journal your insights and reflections. Then draw a line under your entry and move on.

This extract from John O'Donohue's poem 'After a Destructive Encounter' holds much wisdom:[30]

Withdraw into your own tranquility,
Loosen from your heart the new fester.
Free yourself of the wounded gaze
That is not yet able to see you.
Recognize your responsibility for the past.

Don't allow your sense of self to wilt.
Draw deep from your own dignity.

Practice 194
Exercise: Managing Strong Energies

FeedForward means that we have to manage strong energies and emotions. These may range from resistance and denial to celebration and overwhelm and everything in between. We therefore need to find ways to protect ourselves in order to continue to do our work.

This practice uses a metaphorical Hug in a Rug, which we can use at any time to centre ourselves if we feel depleted by strongly expressed emotions.

For this practice:

- Ground and centre yourself.

- Imagine you are sitting in the middle of a tubular blanket which is lying on the floor.

- When you need replenishment or protection imagine yourself reaching for your blanket and then pulling your blanket slowly over your legs and torso to your head. Stay in its warm protective shield for as long as you need before returning.

Practice 195
Exercise: Making Time and Space to Process FeedForward

Creating spaces, places and times to process our FeedForward is key to healthy practice and general wellbeing. Creating a space for ourselves in the midst of our busy lifestyles is the secret to Working Wisely.

Here are a few tactics which I have found work well for me:

- Designing core questions for Reflective Note-taking.
  Core questions might include:

  ○ What happened?

  ○ What was I **Thinking** and **Feeling** and how was I **Behaving**?

  ○ What are my Learning Points?

  ○ What are my Action Points now?

Or use the American Military After Action Review Process:

- ○ What happened?
- ○ Why did it happen?
- ○ How it can be done better?

Other options include using for example the 7-Eyed Model[31] or the 7Cs[32] to study what has taken place.

- Keep Topic Notebooks to capture and process FeedForward. This keeps the FeedForward project specific.

- Keep a 'Treasure Chest' of positive FeedForward which you can dip into if and when your confidence wavers.

- Make processing time a top priority. Diary it in to help to keep you grounded and centred.

Practice 196
Exercise: Writing your own Obituary

The ultimate FeedForward is writing your own obituary – or asking friends to write one for you. By projecting forward we can state how we intended to live and then use each day up until our death making choices which honour our intentions for ourselves.

For this practice:

- Choose a bright sunny day.

- Ground and centre yourself, connecting with your deepest intentions, your vision and your best version of yourself. Ask yourself 'How would I like to be remembered?', 'What is my legacy?', and 'What do I want to gift the world?'

- Write freely without punctuation.

- Take a break. Then review what you have written.

- Redraft as you need. Then live it!

Practice 197
More Inspiration: FeedForward

Here are some inspirational poems and quotes to support your FeedForward.

As David Whyte wrote in a poem called 'Loaves and Fishes':[33]

This is not
the age of information.

This is *not*
the age of information.

Forget the news,
and the radio,
and the blurred screen.

This is the time
of loaves
and fishes.

People are hungry,
and one good word is bread
for a thousand.

Roy T. Bennett reminds us in his poem 'Don't' Just...' that FeedForward is about reciprocity:[34]

Don't just learn, experience.
Don't just read, absorb.
Don't just change, transform.
Don't just relate, advocate.
Don't just promise, prove.
Don't just criticize, encourage.
Don't just think, ponder.
Don't just take, give.
Don't just see, feel.
Don't just dream, do.
Don't just hear, listen.
Don't just talk, act.
Don't just tell, show.
Don't just exist, live.

I want to finish with one of my own poems called 'Self Portrait' which focuses how FeedForward can support and resource us for good work and inspired living for a life well lived.

I am interested in what God or Gods comfort you.
I want to know how to live in ease, with peace and grace.
I want to know how to surrender to the joys of life and living,
Even when I do not feel like it.

I want to know how to feel the wind in my hair...
To dance in the rain,
To jump into the cold sea
To dwell in life's generosity and abundance...
To cherish a child's smile,
To always be open to delight and surprise,
To never stop wondering,
To truly listen,
To be courageous enough to ask for help before it is too late.

To remember who I am so I can be free to enable others to be who they truly are.
To learn how to be a generous citizen of loss.
To celebrate the gift which is each new day.
To practise appreciation and gratitude even when I am tired and grumpy.
To embrace all that is life.

I am not interested in your God or Gods.
I just want to know if we can meet each other in the place of our shared humanity
Where we sit with our pain and vulnerability, and also our endless possibility,
Where we can embrace the miracle of being alive
As guests on this precious earth
Honouring a golden line as inheritors and as creators which links us to all that has come before and is yet to come in this moment NOW.

* * * * *

Reflective Questions

1. Which of the twenty-one practices are you most drawn to and why?

2. Which of the twenty-one practices are you least drawn to and why?

3. What are you going to action now?

CHAPTER 14
Supervision

Dancing is the loftiest, the most moving, the most beautiful of the arts. For it is no mere translation or abstraction of life. It is life itself.

Henry Havelock[1]

Reflect to *Create's!* dance moves and steps can be danced alone. However, there are times when we can feel ourselves getting lost or stuck in the noise. We lose our enthusiasm, flow and rhythm for the dance as well as wonder if we belong on the dance floor at all. These are times when we need a partner to dance with us.

Supervision is Reflect to *Create's!* dance partner. A supervisor can accompany, partner, guide, support, resource, encourage and inspire their supervisee as they explore the rhythms, tones, nuances and cadences of their practice and life for new insights, learning and change.

A supervisor works with their clients to find the discordant notes, the hidden patterns, and the new choreography waiting to be revealed and worked with. A Supervisor can help find the notes which fuse WHO you are and WHO you are becoming with WHAT you want to create and HOW you choose to work. As Barbara de Angelis writes:[2] 'The moment in between what you once were, and who you are becoming, is where the dance of life really takes place.'

This is as true for you the practitioner as it is for the clients you work with.

For people professionals – other than for therapists – supervision is sometimes dismissed as irrelevant because it emerged from the worlds of therapy and counselling. Also, for many leaders and managers, supervision is often associated with conformity, correction, command and control. This is a major loss both for people professionals and those they serve.

As a leader in my twenties and thirties I would have benefited from working with a Supervisor who was also my 'dance partner'. As an Executive Director I knew I needed support and resourcing which was beyond coaching. Technical competence was assumed: what I needed was help to understand me in my role.

After adoption leave I subsequently trained as an Executive Coach, but it was not until I trained as a Coaching Supervisor with the Coaching Supervision Academy that I fully appreciated the transformative powers of supervision's relational presence, generative conversation and reflective learning. I have since worked with many wonderful people practitioners and this chapter explains how I now see Supervision as Reflect to *Create's!* Dance Partner.

What is Supervision?

Supervision is a co-created learning partnership for reflective inquiry, which has been choreographed by the Supervisor and Supervisee together.

The purpose of Supervision is to offer a 'super-seeing' of the Supervisee and their practice, to creatively inspire, support and resource both, in service of their clients or their teams.

Supervision helps to align and attune the Supervisee – the dancer – with the music of their experiences to make meaning from their experiences for wise and creative practice. The process of Supervision is orchestrated by and through Reflect to *Create's!* dance map. Supervision can take place 1:1 or as a group.

Says Michael Carroll of Supervision:[3]

> Supervision is always about the quality of awareness and what I choose to give my attention to. As I step outside my comfort zone and take an open stance, without blame or assumption and am open and indifferent to the outcome, what would I allow myself to think and reflect upon? Can I look beyond, beneath, above, below, against or for ....?

For Sheila Ryan:[4]

> Supervision interrupts practice. It wakes us up from what we are doing. When we are alive to what we are doing we wake up to what is, instead of falling asleep in the comfort of our routines and daily practice. We have profound learning difficulties when it comes to being present to our own moment-to-moment experiences. Disturb the stuck narrative. The supervisory voice acts as an irritator interrupting repetitive stories and facilitating the construction of new stories.

Dr. Alison Hodge defines Supervision as:[5]

> A co-created learning relationship that supports the supervisee in his or her development, both personally and professionally, and seeks to support him or her in providing best practice to his or her client. Through the process of reflecting on his or her work in supervision, the supervisee can review and develop his or her practice and re-energize him or herself.

Francis Inskipp and Brigid Proctor saw Supervision as fulfilling three functions: Normative (or managerial) to assure quality; Formative (or Educative) to support learning and development; and Restorative (or Supportive) to support the practitioners' own wellbeing and fitness to practice.[6] Edna Murdoch defines Supervision as a process of Reflection, Insight and Support. As Edna writes:[7]

> When I hire a Supervisor, I want someone who will walk with me, and create a reflective space in which I can become curious about all aspects of my work. One way of describing what Supervision does is to think of it as a process of **Reflection, Insight and Support**. Supervision enhances 'seeing' – the seeing into one's practice, the illumination of subtle processes in coaching conversations and of blind spots in oneself and in one's thinking.

Julie Hay writes that we need Supervision because we are human. We discount and therefore do not see what we do not see.[8] For Fiona Adamson Supervision is a safe space and place where:[9]

> We can step back from the action, reflecting, pondering, analysing, trying out new ways of working, getting feedback, exploring where we are vulnerable, sharing our mistakes, understanding the part that unconscious processes play in our work, learning to hold the creative tension, attending to the intuitive and imaginative parts of ourselves… being playful and experimental, allowing creative leaps and non linear transformations to emerge from the apparent chaos of the moment.

This is developed by Geraldine Holton when she writes:[10]

> Supervision provides a safe environment where both the practitioner and client are held. Supervision creates a container or transitional space for the emergence of a health selfhood, where all aspects of self – physical, spiritual, intellectual, personal and professional – are explored, reflected upon and integrated. It is the place (or a place) where personal and professional identity is formed and transformed. Supervision provides a safe holding environment where through wise conversation and creative attentiveness individuals and groups can co-create a deeper perspective and wisdom that can lead to transformation and effective practice.

The Supervisor meets the supervisee in the field of their shared humanity to help practitioners make meaning from all of their experiences, for use in creative leadership and professional practice.

A Reflect to *Create!* Supervisor's 'Dance Training'

Reflective Supervision is a distinct practice, which blends and integrates insights from the arts, sciences and humanities to support adult learning and development. In order to work as a Reflect to *Create!* Dance Partner, Supervisors need to be able to work from a foundational appreciation of our shared humanity and to live the disciplines and practices outlined in Part 2. Their training and ongoing Continuous Professional Development needs to eclectically combine insights from the contemplative traditions with the latest thinking and research from the fields of relational presence, dialogue practices, quantum physics, psychological mindedness, neurobiology, systems thinking, creativity, adult learning and change. A Supervisor also needs to be in Supervision themselves to stay refreshed, resourced and fit for practice.

I trained with the Coaching Supervision Academy.[11] I found the training transformational. The teaching I received on the Diploma in Coaching Supervision – together with my ongoing personal and professional supervision and development since qualification – has made this book possible.

What to look for in a Reflect to *Create!* 'Dance Partner'

The Reflect to *Create!* dance is liminal space where soul meets role. This is a deeply personal space where the supervisee can allow their true evolving selves to emerge – where they can re-Source themselves and re-Vitalise their practice. This is also a rich landscape full of light and dark: a landscape likely to be scattered with excitement, potential, and possibility as well as problems, pain and difficulty. Choosing a Dance Partner is key to being held in the dance. As Fiona Adamson writes:[12]

> Supervision gives me the space to ask and try to answer (my) questions. I have been enabled to transform my capacity to reflect, to open my mind to a range of perspectives without being wedded to one model or explanation, and to accept my strengths and weaknesses without judgment, to become curious and openhearted and to see myself as a soul on a journey, accompany others on theirs.

Questions to explore when you are considering working with a Supervisor over and above their qualifications and track record are:

- ✓ 'Do I feel seen?'
- ✓ 'Do I feel safe?'
- ✓ 'Do I trust?'
- ✓ 'Can I allow myself to be vulnerable here?'
- ✓ 'Do I feel accompanied?'
- ✓ 'Will I be both supported and stretched at the same time?'
- ✓ 'What is my intuition telling me?'
- ✓ 'Am I really ready to learn?'
- ✓ 'Is this what I need now?'
- ✓ 'How are we going to work together?'
- ✓ 'What do I – and we together – intend?'
- ✓ 'How will the sessions be typically structured?'
- ✓ 'Do I want to work 1:1 or in and with a group?'
- ✓ 'How can we FeedForward to each other?'
- ✓ 'How will this serve both me and my work?'

A contract can then attend to the finer details of costs, what, how and when. Supervisors will also normally be members of a professional association and will typically be accredited through a professional accreditation scheme. All will have professional indemnity.

How Reflect to *Create!* Supervision Works

Reflect to *Create!* Supervision is a relational practice. Reflect to *Create!* Supervision is the intentional use of the relationship, which is co-created through the dance partnership between Supervisor and Supervisee. As a result of it, their relationships with themselves, each other and the world are explored, allowing new insights and learning to emerge.

The four cornerstones of this Relational Practice are:

1.   Reflective Relational Presencing

2.   Reflective Witnessing

3.   Reflective Conversations

4.   Reflective Learning

Each of the four cornerstones will be discussed in turn.

1. Reflective Relational Presencing

As human beings we are programmed from our birth to seek attachment and relationship. We are relational beings and we are shaped by the relationships we seek, co-create and also leave.

Our evolution happens in and through the nature of our relationships.

A supervisory relationship where the supervisee feels seen, heard and understood therefore creates the attunement and the preconditions necessary for the dance of exploration, discovery, learning and change. From this attunement the Supervisor creates the invitation – quite literally holds their hand out to initiate the dance – and the Supervisee feels held and so finds the courage to enter the liminal space of the dance, and to then flow with the dance.

The relationship creates the container for exploring the Reflect to *Create!* dance map. The relationship is crafted through the Supervisor holding the process and the Supervisee working on their content. Here the supervisee is held in unconditional positive regard: with acceptance and free from judgement. As Rumi wrote:[13]

> Somewhere beyond right and wrong, there is a garden. I will meet you there.

Gestures of reciprocity then flow. A new choreography emerges. As Bill Critchley writes:[14]

Change happens in the crucible of relationship.

For Fiona Adamson:[15]

A relationship that truly attunes and resonates for both parties is transformational because it allows us to meet another at a soul level, free from the constraints that fear evokes in us, constraints that block our creativity and capacity to learn.

It is also a relationship where, as Nancy Kline writes:[16]

there is an opportunity to bring someone back to their own mind, to show them how good they can be.

Working in this way also means that, as Joan Wilmot writes:[17]

both people will be changed by the relationship and the conversation that happens between them … Supervision is a place for everyone in the system to be thought about or held in mind. It is a place to have deep conversations; it is a place to think creatively with a joined heart/mind perspective.

Becoming present to and with each other is facilitated through mindful awareness. Mindfulness supports our capacity to stay present within ourselves and with each other, within the ebbs and flows of the conversation in the session and over the life of the relationship. As John Welwood writes:[18]

Pure presence is the intimate engagement … [and] opens up spontaneous clearings in the experiential stream without any strategy or intention to create change. We become open and empty so that we discover inner sources of wisdom as we move from the realm of personality into the larger space of being. Unconditional presence is the most powerful transmuting force there is.

A variety of mindfulness practices are shared in Part 2.

2. Reflective Witnessing

A Supervisor is a Dance Partner – and also a Guide, Companion, Witness and Critical Friend – accompanying the Supervisee on their learning journey wherever that takes them both.

As Geraldine Holton writes:[19]

The Supervisor is the holder of the space – including reflective witness, facilitator of meaning making and knowledge construction – through a quality of mindful presence rather than knowledge bearer, expert or problem solver.

This is a shared exploration of how the Supervisee is supported in any way they need to explore their seeing – and where their journey of seeing is witnessed by another human being (who is also a skilled practitioner) who wholeheartedly cares for their wellbeing and development, made possible through their shared humanity. As Albert Camus wrote:[20]

> Don't walk behind me; I may not lead. Don't walk in front of me; I may not follow. Just walk beside me and be my friend.

This is a professional and boundaried companionship. It is captured by David Whyte in his thought piece about friendship which I have slightly adapted to express the essence of being with and walking with another:[21]

> The ultimate touchstone of friendship [and supervision] is not [necessarily] improvement, neither of the other nor of the self [although either is possible]: the ultimate touchstone is witness, the privilege of having been seen by someone and the equal privilege of being granted the sight of the essence of another, to have walked with them and to have believed in them, and sometimes just to have accompanied them for however brief a span, on a journey impossible to accomplish alone.

This is also captured by Anne Morrow Lindbergh when she writes:[22]

> A good relationship has a pattern like a dance and is built on some of the same rules. The partners do not need to hold on tightly, because they move confidently in the same pattern, intricate but gay and swift and free, like a country dance of Mozart's. To touch heavily would be to arrest the pattern and freeze the movement, to check the endlessly changing beauty of its unfolding. There is no place here for the possessive clutch, the clinging arm, the heavy hand; only the barest touch in passing. Now arm in arm, now face to face, now back to back – it does not matter which. Because they know they are partners moving to the same rhythm, creating a pattern together, and being invisibly nourished by it. The joy of such a pattern is not only the joy of creation or the joy of participation, it is also the joy of living in the moment. Lightness of touch and living in the moment are intertwined. One cannot dance well unless one is completely in time with the music, not leaning back to the last step or pressing forward to the next one, but poised directly on the present step as it comes. Perfect poise on the beat is what gives good dancing its sense of ease, of timelessness, of the eternal.

3. Reflective Conversations

Conversation is the medium of exploration. Words make explicit the implicit. Words are the energetic building blocks for sense making and meaning making.

Generative conversations always start with deep and attentive listening. Deep listening means paying attention to the musicality which surrounds us: the notes, rhythms, vibrations, cadences, beats, hums and silences – with ourselves as well as others. As Eckhart Tolle writes:[23]

> Listening is a field of true attention, a state of absolute receptivity and alert presence.

Profound listening ... is the arising of alert attention: the words are secondary. Far more important is the act of listening, the space of conscious presence that arises as you listen. That space is a unifying field of awareness in which you meet the other person without the separate barriers created by conceptual thinking.

This is reinforced by John O'Donohue who writes:[24]

One of the tasks of true friendship is to listen compassionately and creatively to the hidden silences. Often secrets are not revealed in words, they lie concealed in the silence between the words or in the depth of what is unsayable between two people.

John Welwood captured how the discipline of bracketing enables a deep connection between the listener and the speaker:[25]

An essential part of true listening is the discipline of bracketing, the temporary giving up or setting aside of one's own prejudices, frames of reference and desires so as to experience as far as possible the speaker's world from the inside, step in inside his or her shoes. This unification of speaker and listener is actually an extension and enlargement of ourselves, and new knowledge is always gained from this. Moreover, since true listening involves bracketing, a setting aside of the self, it also temporarily involves a total acceptance of the other. Sensing this acceptance, the speaker will feel less and less vulnerable and more and more inclined to open up the inner recesses of his or her mind to the listener. As this happens, speaker and listener begin to appreciate each other more and more, and the duet dance of love is begun again.

Conversation is artistry. For Peter Senge:[26]

The artistry of dialogue lies in experiencing the flow of meaning and seeing the one thing that needs to be said now. Like the Quakers, who enjoin members to say not simply whatever pops into their heads but only those thoughts that are compelling (and which cause the speaker to quake from the need to speak them).

It is through the Practices of Generative Conversation (described in Part 2) that we can change. The kind of conversation Theodore Zeldin is interested in,

Is one in which you start with a willingness to emerge a slightly different person ... it is always an experiment whose results are never guaranteed. It involves risk.[27]

4. Reflective Learning

The purpose of Reflect to *Create!* is discovery, insight and reflective learning: to both dance with and learn from all of our experiences. Reflect to *Create!* provides the dance map and process for our own individual journeys of lifelong learning as we evolve, adapt, grow and change as a result of our own experiences. Our evolving self shapes our evolving life and work. We come home to ourselves. As Florida Scott-Maxwell writes:[28]

> You need to claim the events of your life to make yourself yours. When you truly possess all you have been and done, which may take some time, you are fierce with reality.

Supervision gives us the space to catch up and anticipate our evolving self so we remain fit for purpose with the skills, training, support and resources we need to do the work we love to do. As Peter Hawkins and Robin Shohet wrote:[29]

> Supervision is a place where a living profession breathes and learns … [it] can be a very important part of taking care of oneself [and] staying open to new learning.

The power and beauty of what is possible is expressed in Edna Murdoch's poem 'I Sit With You':[30]

> I sit with you, new to me
> As I am new to you.
> Pleasantries at first, a gentle tease,
> Then a gradual easing into the work.
> We listen to each other,
> We speak,
> Careful words edging us closer
> To the touch of truth.
>
> As the protecting layers fall away
> From both of us
> And we sit in a larger space
> Than either of us had ever imagined,
> The room dissolves, my notes stop,
> My breath walks with your breath.
>
> Hearts and minds entrain
> This hour slows right down,
> And the deep comfort of thinking
> And creating together

Happens.

We have 'let go, to let come.'

What comes to me is peace –
And gift.

For you, relief that we can be this way
That this conversation can hold so much –
More than I will ever know.

Supervision gives us access to our Bodhicitta: 'Bodhi' means 'awake', free from our ordinary egocentric everyday strategizing mind and the illusion that we are all separate from each other, and 'Citti' means that which is conscious. For Pema Chodron,[31] 'According to Shantideva and the Buddha before him, the unbiased mind and good heart of bodhi hold the key to happiness and peace.'

Our ability to learn is the only capital we have. As Aristotle warned:[32] 'The more you know, the more you know you don't know.' And as Shanna La Fleur reminds us:[33] 'It takes an athlete to dance, but an artist to be a dancer.'

Supervision gifts us the time, space, and support to move through the Reflect to *Create!* dance map. Reflective learning is a radical act of creativity – of bringing the new into the world: the opportunity to change how we are being, what we are doing and how we are doing it. Reflective learning is exciting and it can also be tough. As Parker J. Palmer writes:[34]

> If we are willing to embrace the challenge of becoming whole … we cannot embrace that challenge all alone, at least not for long; we need trustworthy relationships to sustain us, tenacious communities of support, if we are to sustain the journey toward an undivided life.

Final thoughts belong to the dancer Samuel Lewis when he asks 'What does dance do for us?':[35]

> What does dance do for us? First and foremost, it inculcates the sense of rhythm and enhances our response to rhythm. This is really a response to life. It makes us more living, which is to say, more spiritual. It brings out beauty of form and movement, and envelops our personalities in the enjoyment of them. It takes us beyond ourselves, bringing an initial taste of the state of non-being, which is really a balm for the soul.

… and to a Hopi Indian saying:[36] 'To watch us dance is to hear our hearts speak.'

* * * * *

Reflective Questions

Here are some questions for you to consider:

1. What are you looking for in a Dance Partner?

2. Who do you want to create, build and sustain your working dance partnership?

3. How will you know if your dance partnership is working well – and if not what might need to change?

4. Does the Reflect to *Create!* dance map fill you with hope, fear, ambivalence or something else and why?

CHAPTER NOTES

Chapter Notes guide you to the references used in each chapter and should also be used in conjunction with the Bibliography.

Preface

1   Printed with permission from Many Rivers Press. Whyte, D. (2007) *Many Rivers: New and Selected Poems 1984–2007*. Langley Washington, Many Rivers Press. Pp52

2   Yeats, W. B. (1987) 'The Second Coming' in *The Collected Poems of W. B. Yeats*. Ware, Wordsworth Poetry Library

3   Rilke, R. M. (1903) *Letters to a Young Poet*. Chapter 4. Worpswede, near Bremen, July 16th, 1903. [Accessed] https://www.aracnet.com/%7Emaime/rilke4.html Downloaded 11th November 2016

4   Whyte, D. (2007) *Many Rivers: New and Selected Poems 1984–2007*. Langley Washington, Many Rivers Press. Pp 356

5   Johansen, B. (2012) *Leaders Make the Future: Ten New Leadership Skills for an Uncertain World*. San Francisco, Berrett-Koehler Publishers, Inc.

6   See Patterson, E. (2015) in the Bibliography

7   Havel, V. (1990) Speech delivered to a Joint Meeting of the US Congress. From *The Art of the Possible* by Vaclav Havel; tran. Paul Wilson et al (New York: Alfred A. Knopf, Inc. 1997) Pp 17–18

Introduction

On Work

1   Spock (1987) in a *Star Trek* episode. The quote has actually been misattributed. Although in one episode Mr Spock does refer to 'no life as we know it', the version now in use comes from the 1987 song 'Star Trekkin', sung by The Firm. See more at: https://oupacademic.tumblr.com/post/45375455323/misquotation-its-life-jim-but-not-as-we-know#sthash.SygwDekY.dpuf

2   Einstein, A. (1943) Quote cited in 'The Real Problem is in the Hearts of Men'. *New York Times* magazine 23rd June 1946. https://icarus-falling.blogspot.co.uk/2009/06/einstein-enigma.html. [Downloaded 25th May 2016]

3   Johansen, B. (2012) *Leaders Make the Future: Ten New Leadership Skills for an Uncertain World*. San Francisco, Berrett-Koehler Publishers, Inc.

4   Torbert, W., Rooke, D. and Fisher, D. (2000) *Personal and Organizational Transformations: Through Action Inquiry*. Boston, Edge/Work Press

5   PWC (2012) *Key Trends in Human Capital Management*. Available from: https://www.pwc.com/gx/en/hr-management-services/pdf/pwc-key-trends-in-human-capital-management.pdf. [Accessed 30th July 2014]

6   Corporate Board Executive 2005 . Recruiting Roundtable Survey. Arlington, VA: Corporate Executive Board

7   Gavett, G. and Berinato, S. *Harvard Business Review* (2013) *State of the Global Workplace*. Available from: https://hbr.org/2013/10/map-the-sad-state-of-global-workplace-engagement/ [Accessed 26th April 2016]

8   Finkelstein, S. (2004). *Why Smart Executives Fail: And What you Can Learn from their Mistakes*. New York: Portfolio Trade, an imprint of Penguin Group

9   Skiffigton, S. and Zeus, P. (1999) 'What is Executive Coaching?' *Management Today*, November 1999

10 Lodes, V. (2013) *75% of Companies Struggle with Overwhelmed Employees Three Tips to Cope*. Downloaded 11th November 2016. https://www.forbes.com/sites/vanessaloder/2015/04/24/75-of-companies-struggle-with-overwhelmed-employees-here-are-three-tips-to-cope/#3694cd6d4f0e

11 Meeker, M. (2014) *Global Internet Report: Mobile Evolution and Development of the Internet*. Published by Kleiner, Perkins, Caulfied and Byers. Downloaded 26th April 2016 https://www.internetsociety.org/globalinternetreport/?gclid=CMv08suarMwCFUKeGwodF8UDGQ

12 United Nations (2007) *Human Development Report: Fighting Climate Change – Human Solidarity in A Divided World*. New York, Palgrave Macmillan

13 Scharmer, O. and Kaufer, K. (2013) *Leading from the Emerging Future: From Ego-System to Eco-System Economies Applying Theory U to Transforming Business, Society and Self*. San Francisco, Berret-Koelher Publishers, Inc.

14 ?WHATIF! Innovation Partners (2015) *Eyes Wide Shut: Leading for Innovation in Post Recession Britain*. Downloaded 26th April 2016 from www.whatifinnovation.com

15 Gardner, H. (1993) *Frames of Mind*. London, Fontana Press

16 See Patterson, E. (2015) in the Bibliography

17 Murdoch, E. and Arnold, J. (eds) (2013) *Full Spectrum Supervision 'Who you are is how you supervise'*. Pp xxvii. Herts, Panoma Press

18 Jung, Carl G. *Psychological Reflections*. (1953) Pantheon Books, NY. Sands, Frederick. *Good Housekeeping*, 'Why I Believe in God' (Interview with Carl Jung, 1951)

On Reflection

19 Einstein, A. (1946) cited in Calaprince, A. (2005) *The New Quotable Einstein*. New Jersey, Princeton University Press

20 Lejuwaan, J. (2016) *A Story about the Dalai Lama* Downloaded from https://highexistence.com/a-story-about-the-dalai-lama/ [Accessed 18th November 2016]

21 Drucker, P. F. (1995) *Managing in Times of Great Change*. Abingdon, Oxon. Pp25 and cited in Hutchins, G. (2016) https://thenatureofbusiness.org/2014/05/28/a-new-logic-beyond-the-illusion-of-separation

22 Milne, A. A. (1926) *Winnie the Pooh*. Pp 1. Methuen, London

23 Whyte, D. (1994) *The Heart Aroused Poetry and the Preservation of the Soul in the Workplace*. Pp 5. New York, Random House

Chapter 1 The Dance

1 Marshall Pace, S. (2016) Downloaded from https://www.azquotes.com/author/53628-Stephanie_Pace_Marshall. Accessed on 18th November 2016

2 Downloaded 1st May 2018 from https://www.goodreads.com/quotes/62315

3 Scharmer, O. (2007) *Theory U: Leading from the Future as it Emerges. The Social Technology of Presencing*. Cambridge, MA. The Society for Organizational Learning Inc.

4 *Oxford English Dictionary* (1976) 6th Edition. Pp 961. Oxford, Clarendon Press

5 See Campbell, J. (2012) in the Bibliography

Chapter 2 On Creativity

1 Attributed to Picasso in *Time* Magazine. October 4, 1976, Modern Living: Ozmosis in Central Park, Note: The quotation appears as an epigraph at the beginning of the article. Quotation is slightly adapted from the original which reads: 'The problem is how to remain an artist once he grows up.'

2 Ulrich, D. (2002) T*he Widening Stream – The Seven Stages of Creativity*. Pp ix. Oregon, Beyond Words Publishing Inc.

3 O'Donohue, J. (2008) *To Bless the Space Between Us: A Book of Blessings*. USA, Sounds True Inc.

4 *Oxford English Dictionary* (1976) 6th Edition. Pp 239. Oxford, Oxford University Press

5 *Oxford English Dictionary* (1976) 6th Edition. Pp 240. Oxford, Oxford University Press

6 Mille de, A. (1991) As quoted in *Martha: The Life and Work of Martha Graham*. London, Random House

7 Bos, du C. (1922) *Approximations*. South Carolina, Nabu Press

8 Robinson, K. (2011) *Out of Our Minds. Learning to be Creative*. Pp 3. Chichester, Capstone Publishing Ltd.

9 Judkins, R. (2015) *The Art of Creative Thinking*. Pp 1. London, Hodder & Stoughton Ltd.

10 Udall, N. (2014) *Riding the Creative Rollercoaster: How Leaders Evoke Creativity, Productivity and Innovation*. Pp 8. London, Kogan Page

11 Judkins, R. (2015) *The Art of Creative Thinking*. Pp 1. London, Hodder & Stoughton Ltd.

12 Kochhar, A. 'The Failure Project – The Story Of Man's Greatest Fear'. Accessed 6th March 2017 from https://www.goodreads.com/work/quotes/50683918-the-failure-project–the-story-of-man-s-greatest-fear. Mumbai, Leadstart Publishing Pvt Ltd.

13 Rilke, R. M. (1903) *Letters to a Young Poet*. Chapter 4. Worpswede, near Bremen, July 16th, 1903. [Accessed] https://www.aracnet.com/%7Emaime/rilke4.html Downloaded 11th November 2016

14 Whyte, D. (2007) *'Tobar Phadraic' from Many Rivers Flow*. Pp 287. Langley, Many Rivers Press

15 Picasso, P. Unable to fully reference the quote. Found at https://www.ranker.com/list/a-list-of-famous-pablo-picasso-quotes/reference

16 Osho (1999) *Creativity: Unleashing the Forces Within*. New York, Osho International Foundation

17 Ulrich, D. (2002) *The Widening Stream – The Seven Stages of Creativity*. Pp xii. Oregon, Beyond Words Publishing Inc.

18 Cohen, L. (1992) 'Anthem'. From the album *The Future*. New York, Columbia Record.

19 Einstein, A. (1955) 'Old Man's Advice to Youth: "Never Lose a Holy Curiosity".' Pp 64. *LIFE* Magazine

20 Lemcke, E. cited in Scharmer, O. (2010) *Addressing the Blind Spot of Our Time: An Executive Summary of a New Book by Otto Scharmer Theory U: Leading from the Future as It Emerges*. Pp 10. Cambridge, MA, The Society for the Organisational Learning, Inc.

21 Karyn Prentice 'Invitation to the Music – the Transpersonal Note in Coaching Supervision' in Murdoch, E. and Arnold, J. (2012) *Full Spectrum Supervision 'Who you are is how you supervise'* Pp 179. St Albans, Panama Press

22 McGilchrist, I. (2012) *The Master and His Emissary: The Divided Brain and the Making of the Western World.* New Haven, Yale University Press Publications

23 Zohar, D. and Marshall, I. (2000) *Spiritual Intelligence: The Ultimate Intelligence.* London, Bloomsbury Publishing Plc.

24 Bennis, W. (1994) *On Becoming A Leader.* Pp 61. Reading, MA, Perseus Books

25 Hillman, J. (1996) *The Souls Code: In Search of Character and Calling.* Pp 6. New York, Grand Central Publishing

26 O'Donohue, J. (2008) *To Bless the Space Between Us: A Book of Invocations and Blessings.* USA, Sounds True Inc.

Chapter 3
Becoming a Reflect to *Create!* Reflective Practitioner

1 Palmer, P. J. Introduction from *Leading from Within Poetry that Sustains the Courage to Lead.* Pp xxx. San Francisco, Jossey-Bass

2 Palmer, P. J. Introduction *from Leading from Within Poetry that Sustains the Courage to Lead.* Pp xxx. San Francisco, Jossey-Bass

3 Gardner, H. (2006) *Frames of Mind.* Reading, MA, Perseus Books

4 Cited in Sharmer, O. (2013) *Dialogue on Leadership.* Available from https://www.presencing.com/dol/about.html [Accessed 24th September 2014]

5 Whyte, D. (1994) *The Heart Aroused Poetry and the Preservation of the Soul in the Workplace.* Pp 5. New York, Random House

6 Downloaded 10th March 2017. https://www.goodreads.com/quotes/146373-through-discipline-comes-freedom

7 Auden, W. H. Accessed 6th March 2017 at https://www.brainyquote.com/quotes/quotes/w/whauden101727.html?src=t_attention

8 Downloaded 10th March 2017 from https://www.leadershipnow.com/preparationquotes.html

9 See Armour, A. J. (2014), Bowlby, J. (1969), Gershon, M. (1998), McGilchrist, I. (2012), Kahneman, D. (2011), Siegel, D. (2007, 2010, and 2015), Van Der Kolk, B. (2000) and Zohar, D. et al (2014)

10 See Hutchins, G. (2012 and 2014) in the Bibliography

11 Downloaded 10th March 2017 from https://www.goodreads.com/quotes/tag/sow

12 Downloaded 10th March 2017 from https://quotationsbook.com/quote/7152/#F5A6YZdZToD861iD.99

13 Shunryu, S. (2011) *Zen Mind, Beginners Mindset: Informal Talks in Zen Meditation and Practice.* Pp 21. Massachusetts, Shambhala Publications, Inc.

14 Dionysuis cited in Osho (1999) *Creativity: Unleashing the Forces Within.* Pp 119. New York, Osho International Foundation

15 From presidential address by Joseph Henry on 24th Nov 1877 to the Philosophical Society of Washington. As cited by L.A. Bauer in his retiring president address on 5th Dec 1908 'The Instruments and Methods of Research', published in *Philosophical Society of Washington Bulletin*, 15, 103. Reprinted in William Crookes (ed.) *The Chemical News and Journal of Industrial Science* (30 Jul 1909)

16 Downloaded 17th June 2017 from https://goodreads.com/quotes/540671

17 Downloaded 17th June 2017 from https://goodreads.com/author/quotes/191925.Daniel.J.Siegel

18 Kornfield, J. (2016) *A Mind Like Sky.* Downloaded from https://jackkornfield.com/a-mind-like-sky/. 18th November 2016

19 Downloaded 20th March 2017 from https://www.goodreads.com/quotes/22534

20 Downloaded 14th March 2018 from https://www.wiseoldsayings.com/attention-quotes/

21 Downloaded 15th March 2017. Cited on website Therapist Self Care https://www.dmtselfcare.com/

22 Downloaded 15th March 2017. Cited at https://www.brainyquote.com/quotes/authors/a/arthur_ashe.html

Part 2 The Practices

1 Downloaded 10th March 2017 from https://www.goodreads.com/quotes/tag/practice

2 Downloaded 10th March 2017 from https://thinkexist.com/quotation/when_the_student_is_ready-the_teacher_will/181633.html

Chapter 4
Prelude to the Dance

1 Downloaded 23rd March 2017. Dejan Stojanovic cited at https://www.goodreads.com/author/show/6443586.Dejan_Stojanovic

2 Whyte, D. (2014) *Consolations: The Solace, Nourishment and Underlying Meaning of Everyday Words.* Pp 237. Langley, Many Rivers Press

3 Downloaded 25th March 2017. Traditional Zen Koan cited at https://bengtwendel.com/your-teacup-is-full-empty-your-cup/

4 Downloaded 25th March 2017. Tara Estacaan cited at https://www.goodreads.com/quotes/tag/pause

5 Downloaded 23rd March 2017. Dr. Elisha Goldstein's video is available at https://elishagoldstein.com/videos/the-stop-practice/

6 Davis, W. H. Cited in Barber, L. (ed.) *Poems for Life.* Pp 145. London, Penguin

7 Whyte, D. (2014) *Consolations: The Solace, Nourishment and Underlying Meaning of Everyday Words.* Pp 233. Langley, Many Rivers Press

8 Brown, B. (2010) *The Gifts of Imperfection: Let Go of Who You Think You're Supposed to Be and Embrace Who You Are. Your Guide to Wholehearted Living.* Pp ix. Minnesota, Hazelden

9 Russell, S. (1999) *Barefoot Doctor's Guide to the Tao: A Spiritual Handbook for the Urban Warrior.* Harmony, London. Quote downloaded 24th April 2017 at https://www.goodreads.com/work/quotes/451006-barefoot-doctor-s-handbook-for-heroes-a-spiritual-guide-to-fame-and-for

10 Brown, B. (2012) *Daring Greatly: How the Courage to Be Vulnerable Transforms the Way We Live, Love, Parent, and Lead.* Penguin, London. Quote downloaded 24th April 2017 at https://www.goodreads.com/quotes/tag/vulnerability

11 Oliver, M. (1994) *Poem 14 from Dream Work.* USA, Atlantic Monthly Press

12 Quindlen, A. (2005). *"Anna Quindlen's Commencement Speech".* Downloaded from https://www.mtholyoke.edu/offices/comm/oped/Quindlen.shtml; Anna Quindlen, *Being Perfect.* New York, Randon House

13 Germer, C. K. (2009) *The Mindful Path to Self Compassion: Freeing Yourself from Destructive Thoughts and Emotions.* New York, Guildford Press

The Opening
Retreat's Rest and Release

Chapter 5
Suspending Habits

1 Hans Bos. Downloaded 2nd May 2017 at https://www.searchquotes.com/quotation/While_I_dance_I_cannot_judge%2C_I_cannot_hate%2C_I_cannot_separate_myself_from_life._I_can_only_be_joyfu/3897/#ixzz4fuMVcWvG. It was used by Landra French as the heading quote for the Sept-Oct 1995 issue of *The Crescent Moon* (Volume 2, Issue 5)

2 Biography of Jon Kabat-Zinn Founding Executive Director of Centre for Mindfulness at Massachusetts University. Downloaded 5th May 2017 from https://www.umassmed.edu/cfm/About-Us/people/2-Meet-Our-Faculty/Kabat-Zinn-Profile/

3 Stone, J. D. (1994) *A Beginner's Guide to the Path of Ascension. The Ascension Series. Easy-To-Read Encyclopedia of the Spiritual Path.* Pp 162. Flagstaff, Light Technology Publishing

4 *Oxford English Dictionary* (1976) Sixth Edition. Pp 1164. Oxford, Clarendon Press

5 Wagoner, D. (1999) *From Traveling Light: Collected and New Poems by David Wagoner.* Illinois, University of Illinois Press. Printed with permission

6 Body Scan meditation is available from Jon Kabat-Zinn's official website which is https://www.mindfulnesscds.com/. Another option can be found on https://palousemindfulness.com/meditations/bodyscan.html

7 Kabat-Zinn, J. (2005) Extract from *Coming to our Senses.* New York, Hyperion Press. Downloaded from www.palousemindfulness.com

8 The exercise I cite can be found at www.wikihow.com but research your own and find what works for you

9 Kabat-Zinn, J. (1994) *Where You Go, There You Are – Mindfulness Meditation for Everyday Life.* Pp 32. London, Little, Brown Book Group. Jon says that the phrase was taken from a poster of a 70-ish yogi, Swami Satchitananada, on a surf board riding the waves off a Hawaiian beach!

10 Dalai Lama and van den Muyzenberg, L. (2008) *The Leader's Way.* Pp 14. London, Nicholas Brealey Publishing

11 Quote from the yogi B.K.S. Iyengar. Downloaded 10th May 2017 from https://www.azquotes.com/author/17706-B_K_S_Iyengar

[12] Dalai Lama (2011) *A Profound Mind – Cultivating Wisdom in Everyday Life*. Pp 43. London, Hodder & Stoughton

[13] Brown, J. (2012) Poem 'The Story That We Tell' was cited in *The Art and Spirit of Leadership*. Pp 302. USA, Trafford Publishing. Printed with permission

[14] Shakespeare, W. (Written sometime between 1599 and 1602) *Hamlet* Act 2, Scene 2. London, Wordsworth Editions

[15] Berne, E. (1964) *The Games People Play – The Psychology of Human Relationships*. USA, Grove Press, Inc.

[16] Jaworski, J. (2011) *Synchronicity – The Inner Path to Leadership*. San Francisco, Berrett-Koehler Publishers

[17] Senge, P., Scharmer, O., Jaworski, J., and Flowers, B. S. (2005) *Presence – Exploring Profound Change in People, Organisations and Society*. London, Nicholas Brealey Publishing

[18] Myles, P. and Shafran, R. (2015) *The CBT Handbook: A Comprehensive Guide to Using CBT to Overcome Depression, Anxiety, Stress, Low Self-Esteem and Anger*. London, Constable and Robinson Ltd.

[19] Quote from Pema Chodron. Downloaded 10th May 2017 from https://www.goodreads.com/author/quotes/8052.Pema_Ch_dr_n

[20] Quote Investigator says that the precise origin of this quote is unknown but is often attributed to Abraham Lincoln and Winston Churchill. Downloaded 10th May 2017 from https://quoteinvestigator.com/2014/06/28/success/

[21] Chodron, P. (2001) *Start Where You Are: A Guide to Compassionate Living*. USA, Shambhala Publications

[22] Holder, J. (1999) *Soul Purpose: Self Affirming Rituals, Meditations and Creative Exercises to Free Your Creative Spirit*. London, Judy Piaktus (Publishers) Ltd.

[23] Pope, A. (1710) *An Essay on Criticism. Part II*. Downloaded 11th May 2017 from https://en.wikipedia.org/wiki/An_Essay_on_Criticism

[24] Translated by Prof Tom Wright (2011) *New Testament for Everyone*. 1 Corinthians 6:19-20. London, Society for Promoting Christian Knowledge/

[25] Quote from the yogi B.K.S. Iyengar. Downloaded 10th May 2017 from https://www.azquotes.com/author/17706-B_K_S_Iyengar

[26] Downloaded 11th May 2017 from https://www.summertomato.com/great-thinkers-10-inspiring-quotes-for-healthy-living

[27] Downloaded 11th May 2017 from https://www.goodreads.com/quotes/tag/vulnerability

[28] Downloaded 11th May 2017 from https://www.goodreads.com/quotes/538827-beyond-our-ideas-of-right-doing-and-wrong-doing-there-is-a

[29] O'Donohue, J. (2008) *To Bless the Space Between Us: A Book of Blessings*. Pp125. USA, Sounds True Inc.

[30] Whyte, D. (2007) *River Flow New and Selected Poems 1984 – 2007*. Langley, Many Rivers Press

Chapter 6
Seeing Anew

[1] Quote downloaded 12th May 2017 from https://www.searchquotes.com/search/Fresh_Eyes/#ixzz4gwoNPBJV

[2] Whyte, D. (2007) *Many Rivers Flow*. Pp 351. Langley, Many Rivers Press

[3] Whyte, D. (2007) *Many Rivers Flow*. Pp 361. Langley, Many Rivers Press

[4] Quote downloaded 18th May 2017 from https://www.azquotes.com/author/37902-John_Welwood

[5] O'Donohue, J. (2008) *To Bless the Space Between Us: A Book of Blessings*. Pp 41. USA, Sounds True Inc.

[6] Welwood, J. (1998) *Journey of the Heart – Intimate Relationships and the Path of Love*. Pp 21-22. New York, Harper Collins Publishing Inc.

[7] Quote downloaded 18th May 2017 from https://en.wikiquote.org/wiki/Seneca_the_Younger

[8] Quote downloaded 18th May 2017 from https://www.azquotes.com/author/37902-John_Welwood

[9] Gendlin, E. (1978) *Focusing*. New York, Bantam Dell. For more information visit The Focusing Institute at https//www.focusing.org

[10] Gendlin, E. (1992) *Man and World Journal*. Reference: 25 (3-4) 341-353. PA, State College. Also downloadable from https://www.focusing.org/primacy.html

[11] Cornell, A. and McGavin, B. (2008) *Inter Relationship Focusing*. Pg 21 Available from https://www.focusing.org/folio/Vol21No12008/03_InnerRelatTRIB.pdf

[12] Cameron, J. (1994) *The Artist's Way – A Course in Discovering and Recovering Your Creative Self*. London, Pan Books

[13] Cameron, J. (1994) *The Artist's Way – A Course in Discovering and Recovering Your Creative Self*. Pp 18 & 20. London, Pan Books

14 *Oxford English Dictionary* (1976) *The Concise Oxford Dictionary of Current English. 6th Edition.* Pp 559. Oxford, Oxford University Press

15 Quote downloaded 23rd May 2017 from https://www.goodreads.com/quotes/tag/gratitude

16 Quote downloaded 18th May 2017 from https://www.azquotes.com/author/37902_John_Welwood

17 Quote downloaded 23rd May 2017 from https://www.goodreads.com/quotes/tag/sense

18 Quote downloaded 23rd May 2017 from https://quotationsbook.com/quote/30101/

19 Quote downloaded 23rd May 2017 https://www.goodreads.com/author/quotes/7190.Anais_Nin

20 See Coaching Supervision Academy website for details of their Diploma in Coaching Supervision Programmes which are run worldwide. Visit www.coachingsupervisionacademy.com

21 Quote downloaded 23rd May 2017 from https://www.brainyquote.com/quotes/quotes/h/henrydavid106041.htm

22 Downloaded 5th June 2017 from https://wwwgoodreads.com/quotes/tag/listening

23 Scharmer, O. (2007) *Theory U: Leading from the Future as it Emerges. The Social Technology of Presencing.* Pp 234. Cambridge, MA, The Society for Organizational Learning Inc.

24 Downloaded 5th June 2017 from https://www.cultureofempathy.com/References/Quotes/Listening.htm

25 Sharmer, O. (2007) *Addressing the Blind Spot of our Time: An Executive Summary of the new book by Otto Scharmer Theory U: Leading from the Future as It Emerges.* Downloaded 5th June 2010 from www.theoryu.com

26 Downloaded 5th June 2017 from https://www.goodreads.com/quotes/tag/talking

27 Downloaded 5th June 2017 from https://www.brainyquote.com/quotes/quotes/y/yehudaberg536651.html

28 Whyte, D. (2015) *Consolations: The Solace, Nourishment and Underlying Meaning of Everyday Words.* Pp 147. Langley, Many Rivers Press

29 Downloaded 5th June 2017 from https://www.goodreads.com/author/show/1461.Gustave_Flaubert

30 Bowlby, J. (1969) *Attachment and Loss.* New York, Basic Books.

31 Ainsworth, M. D. S., Blehar, M. C., Waters, E., and Wall, S. (1978). *Patterns of Attachment: A Psychological Study of the Strange Situation.* Hillsdale, NJ: Erlbaum

32 Siegel, D. (2015) *The Developing Mind – How Relationships and the Brain Interact to Shape Who we Are.* New York, Guildford Press

33 Adapted from: "*What is Your Attachment Style?*". Downloaded 12th June 2017 from https://www.psychalive.org/what-is-your-attachment-style/

34 Steiner, C. M. (1974) *Scripts People Live: Transactional Life Scripts.* New York, Grove Press

35 Downloaded 10th June 2017 from https://www.goodreads.com/work/quotes/1413589-i-know-why-the-caged-bird-sings

36 Downloaded 10th June 2017 from https://www.goodreads.com/quotes/tag/storytelling

37 Berne, E. (1964) *The Games People Play – The Psychology of Human Relationships.* USA, Grove Press, Inc.

38 Downloaded 13th June 2017 from https://www.brainyquote.com/quotes/quotes/confucious104254.html

39 Downloaded 13th June 2017 from https://www.brainyquote.com/quotes/quotes/m/marievoneb385420.html

40 For more information visit https://www.myersbriggs.org/myers-and-briggs-foundation/

41 For more information visit https://www.talentlens.co.uk/develop/peter-honey-learning-style-series

42 Argyris, C. (1990) *Knowledge for Action – Overcoming Organizational Defences: Facilitating Organizational Learning.* San Francisco, Jossey Bass Inc. Publishers

43 Wolinsky, S. (1993) *Quantum Consciousness: The Guide to Experiencing Quantum Psychology.* Pp35. Canada, Bramble Books

44 Nicoll, M. (1984) *Psychological Commentaries on the Teachings of Gurdjieff and Ouspensky. Vol 1.* Pp 59. Boulder/London, Shambhala Publications

45 Dearing, R. L. and Tangney, J. P. (2003) *Shame and Guilt (Emotions & Social Behavior).* New York, The Guildford Press

46 Downloaded 14th June 2017 from https://brenebrown.com/2013/01/14/2013114shame-v-guilt-html/

47 Downloaded 14th June 2017 from https://www.goodreads.com/quotes/tag/shame

48 Downloaded 14th June 2017 from https://www.quotes-inspirational.com/perspective.php

49 Lee, H. (1960) *To Kill A Mockingbird.* London, Pan Books Ltd.

50 Downloaded 14th June 2017 from https://www.goodreads.com/quotes/tag/perspective

51 Cottrell, A. P. (1998) The Resurrection of Thinking and the Redemption of Faust: Goethe's new scientific attitude. In D. Seamon and A. Zajonc (Eds.), *Goethe's Way of Science: A Phenomenology of Nature*. Pp. 257. Albany, NY: State University of New York

52 Downloaded 5th November 2018 from https://www.poemhunter.com/poem/senses

Chapter 7
Relating to the Wider Whole

1 Downloaded 16th June 2017 from https://www.azquotes.com/author/19933-Humberto_Maturana

2 Downloaded 16th June 2017 from https://www.quotes-positive.com/quotes/interrelatedness/

3 Cited in Lewis, T., Amini, F. and Lannon, R. (2001) *A General Theory of Love*. Pp 4. New York, Random House

4 Downloaded 19th June 2017 from https://www.goodreads.com/quotes/tag/compassion

5 Calaprice, A. (2005) *The New Quotable Einstein*. Pp 206. USA, Princeton University Press

6 Downloaded 19th June 2017 from https://www.dalailamaquotes.org/whether-one-is-rich-or-poor-educated-or-illiterate-religious-or-nonbelieving-man-or-woman-black-white-or-brown-we-are-all-the-same-physically-emotionally-and-mentally-we-are-all-eq/

7 Downloaded 19th June 2017 from https://www.goodreads.com/work/quotes/1096308-physiologie-du-mariage

8 Downloaded 19th June 2017 from https://www.goodreads.com/quotes/tag/compassion

9 Downloaded 19th June 2017 from https://www.brainyquote.com/quotes/quotes/d/dalailama101711.html

10 Palmer, P. J. (2017) *My Misgivings About Advice*. Downloaded 17th June 2017 from https://www.awakin.org/

11 Downloaded 19th June 2017 from https://www.goodreads.com/work/quotes/4489585-nesnesiteln-lehkost-byt

12 Downloaded 21st June 2017 from https://www.brainyquote.com/quotes/quotes/h/helenkeller101301.html

13 Downloaded 21st June 2017 from https://www.brainyquote.com/quotes/quotes/k/khalilgibr100753.html

14 Downloaded 21st June 2017 from https://www.goodreads.com/quotes/tag/heart

15 Downloaded 21st June 2017 from https://www.brainyquote.com/quotes/quotes/h/henrymille403026.html

16 Downloaded 21st June 2017 from https://www.goodreads.com/quotes/417396-we-cultivate-love-when-we-allow-our-most-vulnerable-and

17 See more in Lewis, T., Amini, F. and Lannon, R. (2001) *A General Theory of Love*. New York, Random House

18 Palmer, W. (1994) *The Intuitive Body – Discovering the Wisdom of Conscious Embodiment and Aikido*. Pp 24. California, Blue Snake Books

19 For more information visit https://www.ifaroma.org

20 For more information visit www.acupuncture.org.uk

21 For more information visit https://www.britreflex.co.uk

22 For more information visit https://www.reikiassociation.net/

23 Retold in McTaggart, L. (2001) *The Field*. Pp 5 & 6. London, HarperCollinsPublishers

24 Downloaded 23rd June 2017 from https://www.brainyquote.com/quotes/quotes/c/chiefseatt104989.html

25 Giono, J. (1954) Originally published in *Vogue* under the title *"The Man Who Planted Trees and Grew Happiness"*. London, Conde Naste Publications Ltd.

26 Downloaded 26th June 2017 from https://quotegarden.com/seasons.html

27 Downloaded 26th June 2017 from https://www.greatest-inspirational-quotes.com/inspirational-quotes-nature.html

28 Downloaded 26th June 2017 from https://quotegarden.com/seasons.html

29 Downloaded 26th June 2017 from https://www.greatest-inspirational-quotes.com/inspirational-quotes-nature.html

30 Prentice, K. (2020) *Nature's Way: Designing the Life You Want through the Lens of Nature and the Five Seasons*. UK, Milton Keynes

31 Poem 'In Blackwater Woods' by Mary Oliver, from *American Primitive*. USA, Back Bay Books, 1983

32 Whyte, D. (2015) *Consolations: The Solace, Nourishment and Underlying Meaning of Everyday Words*. Pp 233. Langley, Many Rivers Press

33 Richo. D. (2017) *The Five Longings: What We Have Always Wanted and Already Have – A Guide to Love, Meaning, Freedom, Happiness and Growth*. Colorado, Shambhala Publications Ltd.

34 Richo. D. (2017) *The Five Longings: What We Have Always Wanted and Already Have – A Guide to Love, Meaning, Freedom, Happiness*

and Growth. Pp 8. Colorado, Shambhala Publications Ltd.

36 Downloaded 27th June 2017 from https://www.azquotes.com/author/19899-David_Whyte

37 Downloaded 27th June 2017 from https://www.goodreads.com/author/quotes/10427.James_Baldwin

38 Patterson, E. (2020) Our Humanity@Work Working with the 7Cs – the 7 Human Capacities – for Insight, Learning and Change A New Lens for Coaching, Coaching Supervision and Executive Reflection. London, Centre for Reflection and Creativity Ltd.

39 Anderson, G. and Nadel, J. (2017) 'WE' A Manifesto for Women Everywhere. London, Thorsons

40 Downloaded 28th June 2017 from https://www.goodreads.com/author/quotes/17297.Marianne_Williamson

41 Adapted from Professor Mark Williams Befriending Meditation which can found at www.franticworld.com. There are many to chose from including Barbara Fredrickson at www.positivityresonace.com; Headspace at www.headspace.com; Insight Apps; or Kristina Neff at www.self-compassion.org

42 Downloaded 30th June 2017 from https://www.goodreads.com/work/quotes/38002-lovingkindness-the-revolutionary-art-of-happiness-shambhala-library

43 Downloaded on 30th June 2017 from https://www.brainyquote.com/quotes/quotes/m/martinluth403521.html

41 Downloaded on 30th June 2017 from https://www.brainyquote.com/quotes/quotes/y/yehudaberg536655.html

44 Downloaded 30th June 2017 from https://www.brainyquote.com/quotes/quotes/n/nhathanh591348.html

45 Extracted from Article 'Albert Einstein on the Interconnectedness of Our Fates and our Mightiest Counterforce Against Injustice'. Downloaded from https://www.brainpickings.org/2017/06/08/albert-einstein-human-rights/

46 Brown, J. (2012) The Art and Spirit of Leadership. Pp 292. USA, Trafford Publishing. Printed with permission

The Flow
Reflection's Fertile Void

1 Downloaded 4th July 2017 from https://www.goodreads.com/quotes/377058-to-be-creative-means-to-be-in-love-with-life

2 Whyte, D. (2015) Consolations: The Solace, Nourishment and Underlying Meaning of Everyday Words. Pp 214.Langley, Many Rivers Press

3 Scharmer, O. and Kaufer, K. (2013) Leading from the Emerging Future: From Ego-System to Eco-System Economies: Applying Theory U to Transforming Business, Society, and Self. Pp 469. San Francisco, Berrett-Koehler Publishers, Inc.

4 Perls, F. Hefferline, R. and Goodman, P. (1994) Gestalt Therapy: Excitement and Growth in the Human Personality. London, Souvenir Press

5 Frambach, L. (2003) The Weighty World of Nothingness: Salomo Friedlaender's 'Creative Indifference'.In M. Spagnuolo Lobb and N. Amendt-Lyon (eds), Creative License: The Art of Gestalt Therapy. New York: Springer-Verlag Wien. Pp 113–28

6 Wilbur, K. (1996) A Brief History of Everything. Boston, Shambhala Publications

7 Biesser, A. (1970) Paradoxical Theory of Change. In J. J. Fagan and I. E. Shepherd (eds), Gestalt Therapy Now. Palo Alto: Science and Behaviour Books. Pp 77–80

8 Downloaded 4th September 2017 from https://lorrainecohen.com/fertile-void/

Chapter 8
Initiating the Invitation

1 Caitlin Matthews cited in Cameron, J. (1994) The Artist's Way – A Course in Discovering and Recovering Your Creative Self. Pp 173. London, Pan Books

2 Downloaded 4th September 2017 from https://lorrainecohen.com/fertile-void/

3 Downloaded 4th September 2017 from https://www.brainpickings.org/2012/11/01/john-keats-on-negative-capability/

4 Downloaded 4th September 2017 from https://www.goodreads.com/quotes/481169-not-to-find-one-s-way-around-a-city-does-not

5 Solnit, R. (2017) A Field Guide to Getting Lost. Pp 10. New York, Viking Books

6 Beck, M. (2003) The Joy Diet. Essex, Piatkus

7 Downloaded 4th September 2017 from https://www.brainyquote.com/quotes/quotes/f/franzkafka134853.html

8 Downloaded 4th September 2017 from https://www.goodreads.com/quotes/17583-to-a-mind-that-is-still-the-whole-universe-surrenders

9 Downloaded 4th September 2017 from https://thinkexist.com/quotation/see_how_nature-trees_flowers_grass_grows_in/149761.

html

10 Downloaded 4th September 2017 from https://www.goodreads.com/quotes/73473-silence-is-the-great-teacher-and-to-learn-its-lessons

11 Downloaded 4th September 2017 from https://en.wikipedia.org/wiki/Monastic_silence

12 Downloaded 5th September 2017 from https://www.phrases.org.uk/meanings/silenceis-golden.html

13 'The Sound of Silence', originally 'The Sounds of Silence', is a song by the American music duo Simon & Garfunkel. The song was written by Paul Simon over a period of several months in 1963 and 1964

14 Whyte, D. (2007) *Many Rivers Flow*. Pp 288. Langley, Many Rivers Press.

15 Downloaded 5th September 2017 from https://www.brainpickings.org/2014/12/17/wendell-berry-pride-despair-solitude/

16 Downloaded 5th September 2017 from https://aeon.co/ideas/before-you-can-be-with-others-first-learn-to-be-alone

17 Whyte, D. (2015) *Consolations: The Solace, Nourishment and Underlying Meaning of Everyday Words*. Pp 1. Langley, Many Rivers Press

18 Thoreau, H. D. (1910) *Walden*. Pp 120. New York, Thomas Y Crowell & Co. Publishers

19 Fox, M. (2002) *Creativity – Where the Divine and Human Meet*. Pp 3 & 5. New York, Tarcher/Putman Books

20 Cited in Richo, D. (2017) *The Five Longings: What We Have Always Wanted and Already Have – A Guide to Love, Meaning, Freedom, Happiness and Growth*. Pp 22. Colorado, Shambhala Publications Ltd.

21 Find out more about Julia McCutchen's work at https://www.juliamccutchen.com/

22 Downloaded 16th September 2017 from https://www.sensationalcolor.com/color-meaning/color-meaning-symbolism-psychology/colors-chakras- #.Wb9r5K2ZOlM

23 Huffington, A. (2014) *Thrive: The Third Metric to Redefining Success and Creating and Happier Life*. USA, Harmony Books

24 Cited in Huffington, A. (2014) *Thrive The Third Metric to Redefining Success and Creating and Happier Life*. Pp 175. USA, Harmony Books

25 Downloaded 8th September 2017 from https://www.goodreads.com/author/quotes/9810.Albert_Einstein?page=30

26 Downloaded 8th September 2017 from https://www.goodreads.com/work/quotes/42104-thirst-poems

27 Downloaded 8th September 2017 from https://www.brainyquote.com/quotes/quotes/s/socrates101211.html

28 Downloaded 8th September 2017 from https://www.goodreads.com/quotes/tag/wandering?page=2

29 Downloaded 8th September 2017 from https://www.brainyquote.com/quotes/quotes/j/jkrowlin454009.html

30 Joseph Campbell, cited in Woodbury, D. (2013) *5 Tips for Creating a Sacred Space*. Downloaded 19th September 2017 from https://www.huffingtonpost.com/debbie-woodbury/sacred-space_b_3094267.html

31 Downloaded 17th September 2017 from https://www.brainpickings.org/2015/04/09/find-your-bliss-joseph-campbell-power-of-myth/

32 Grudin, R. (1990) *The Grace of Great Things: Creativity and Innovation*. London, Orion Hardbacks

33 Blake, W. (2010) 'Auguries of Innocence'. In *English Poetry II: From Collins to Fitzgerald*. Pp 356. The Harvard Classics 1909-14

34 Brown, J. (2012) *The Art and Spirit of Leadership*. Pp 46. USA, Trafford Publishing. Printed with permission

35 Brown, J. (2012) *The Art and Spirit of Leadership*. Pp 147. USA, Trafford Publishing. Printed with permission

Chapter 9
The Art of Listening

1 Downloaded 25th September 2017 from https://www.goodreads.com/quotes/tag/listening?page=3

2 Downloaded 25th September 2017 from https://www.classicfm.com/discover-music/latest/quotes-classical-musicians/alfred-brendel/

3 Downloaded 25th September 2017 from https://www.brainyquote.com/quotes/quotes/e/epictetus106298.html

4 Downloaded 25th September 2017 from https://www.leadershipnow.com/listeningquotes.html

5 Scharmer, O. (2007) *Theory U: Leading from the Future as it Emerges. The Social Technology of Presencing*. Cambridge, MA., The Society for Organizational Learning Inc.

6 Scharmer, O. (2007) *Theory U: Leading from the Future as it Emerges. The Social Technology of Presencing*. Pp 10. Cambridge, MA., The Society for Organizational Learning Inc.

7 Cited in Lebell, S. (1994) *Epictetus: The Classical Manual on Virtue, Happiness, and Effectiveness. A New Interpretation*. New York, HarperCollinsPublishers

8 Whyte, D. (2007) *Many Rivers Flow*. Pp 31. Langley, Many Rivers Press

9 Downloaded 26th September 2017 from https://www.goodreads.com/quotes/tag/listening

10 Downloaded 26th September 2017 from https://www.inc.com/dave-kerpen/15-quotes-to-inspire-you-to-become-a-better-listener.html

11 Downloaded 26th September 2017 from https://www.goodreads.com/quotes/tag/listening

12 Downloaded 26th September 2017 from https://www.inc.com/dave-kerpen/15-quotes-to-inspire-you-to-become-a-better-listener.html

13 Downloaded 26th September 2017 from https://www.brainyquote.com/quotes/quotes/h/hjacksonb100702.html

14 Silverstone, L. (1999) *Art Therapy the Person-Centred Way: Art and the Development of the Person*. London, Jessica Kingsley Publishers

15 Ferucci, P. (2009) *What We May Be. Techniques for Psychological and Spiritual Growth Through Psychosynthesis*. London, Jeremy P. Tarcher

16 This practice is adapted from an exercise which was designed by Susannah Conway. More of her work can be found at www.susannahconway.com

17 Downloaded 2nd October 2017 from https://www.azquotes.com/quote/694824

18 Downloaded 2nd October 2017 from https://www.goodreads.com/quotes/315733-i-write-because-i-don-t-know-what-i-think-until

19 Examples include:
Leadership Metaphor Explorer by the Centre for Creative Leadership available from www.ccl.org
Ho Cards by Ely Raman available from EoS Interactive Cards at oh-cards.com
ECCO cards by John David Ellis available from oh-cards.com
Blum, R. (1988) *The Rune Cards Sacred Play for Self Discovery*. London, Headline Book Publishing. Cards created by Jane Walmsley
Runes Oracle Cards by Bianca Luna available from www.loscarabeo.com

20 Adapted from Prentice, K. (2012) Chapter on the 'Invitation to the Music' In Murdoch, E. and Arnold, J. (eds) *Full Spectrum Supervision 'Who you are is how you supervise'*. St Albans, Panama Press who gained permission for inclusion of the Magic Gift Box in the chapter from Silverstone, L. (1999) *Art Therapy the Person-Centred Way: Art and the Development of the Person*. London, Jessica Kingsley Publishers

21 Downloaded 3rd October 2017 from https://www.brainyquote.com/quotes/quotes/a/anthonyjd384130.html?src=t_listen

22 Solnit, R. (2017) *A Field Guide to Getting Lost*. Pp 5. New York, Viking Books

23 Gabrielle Roth was the founder of the 5Rhythms Movement. Details can be found at www.5rhythms.com

24 Downloaded 3rd October 2017 from https://www.goodreads.com/author/quotes/875661.Jalaluddin_Rumi

25 Holden, R. (2017) I see you Blog post. Downloaded 4th October 2017 from https://www.healyourlife.com/i-see-you

26 Downloaded 4th October 2017 from https://thedailyquotes.com/look-at-the-world/

27 Full text can be found at https://www.huffingtonpost.com/2011/01/17/i-have-a-dream-speech-text_n_809993.html

28 Downloaded 5th October 2017 from https://quoteaddicts.com/1069161

29 Brown, J. with Issacs, D. (2005) *The World Café – Shaping our Futures through Conversations that Matter*. Pp 174. San Francisco, Berrett- Koehler Publishers

30 Cited in Brown, J. with Issacs, D. (2005) *The World Café – Shaping our Futures through Conversations that Matter*. Pp xii. San Francisco, Berrett- Koehler Publishers

31 Rilke, R. M (1903) *Letters to a Young Poet*. Chapter 4. Worpswede, near Bremen, July 16th, 1903. [Accessed] https://www.aracnet.com/%7Emaime/rilke4.html Downloaded 11th November 2016

32 Cited in 'A Tribute to John O'Donohue' by David Whyte https://www.bbc.co.uk/blogs/ni/2008/01/john_odonohue_the_death_of_a_s.html. Downloaded 30th October 2017

33 Paul Goodman quote Downloaded 4th July 2017 from https://vitalitymagazine.com/article/feeling-lost-and-confused-time-to-explore-the-fertile-void/

34 Downloaded 30th October 2017 from https://www.goodreads.com/quotes/552593-in-silence-there-is-eloquence

35 Downloaded 30th October 2017 from https://allteresting.com/these-5-quotes-prove-that-listening-is-one-of-the-best-things-you-can-do/

36 Palmer, P. J. (1990) *The Active Life – A Spirituality of Work, Creativity and Caring*. Pp 3. San Francisco, Jossey-Bass

37 Brown, J. (2012) *The Art and Spirit of Leadership*. Pp 42. USA, Trafford Publishing. Printed with permission

Chapter 10
Finding Freedom

1 Downloaded 31st October 2017 from https://www.goodreads.com/author/quotes/8567.Wendell_Berry

2 Tolle, E. (1999) *The Power of Now – A Guide to Spiritual Enlightenment*. Pp 9. USA, New World Library

3 Buechner, F. (1993) *Wishful Thinking: A Seeker's ABC*. Pp 119. San Francisco, HarperSanFrancisco

4 Whyte, D. (2015) *Consolations: The Solace, Nourishment and Underlying Meaning of Everyday Words*. Pp 237–239. Langley, Many Rivers Press

5 Palmer, P. J. (2000) *Let Your Life Speak – Listening for the Voice of Vocation*. Pp 80. San Francisco, Jossey-Bass

6 Palmer, P. J. (2004) *A Hidden Wholeness – The Journey Toward An Undivided Life, Welcoming Soul and Weaving Community in a Wounded World*. Pp 65. San Francisco, John Wiley and Sons, Inc.

7 Downloaded 1st November 2017 from https://www.goodreads.com/quotes/15920 love-is-what-we-are-born-with-fear-is-what

8 Downloaded 1st November 2017 from https://thinkexist.com/quotation/your_task_is_not_to_seek_for_love-but_merely_to/250294.html

9 Sarton, M. (1974) 'Now I Become Myself'. In *Collected Poems*, New York, Norton.

10 *Happy Feet* is a 2006 Australian–American computer animated musical family comedy film which was directed, produced, and co-written by George Millar and released by Warner Bros Pictures

11 Walcott, D. (1976) *Sea Grapes. New York*, Farrar, Straus and Giroux

12 *The Concise Oxford Dictionary* (1976). Pp 1095. Oxford, Oxford University Press

13 Palmer, P. .J. (2004) *A Hidden Wholeness – The Journey Toward An Undivided Life, Welcoming Soul and Weaving Community in a Wounded World*. Pp 33. San Francisco, John Wiley and Sons, Inc.

14 Palmer, P. J. (2004) *A Hidden Wholeness – The Journey Toward An Undivided Life, Welcoming Soul and Weaving Community in a Wounded World*. Pp 32. San Francisco, John Wiley and Sons, Inc.

15 Oliver, M. (1995) 'Maybe' in Robert Bly (ed.), *The Soul is Here for its Own Joy: Sacred Poems from Many Cultures*. Pp15. Hopewell, N. J., Ecco Press

16 Oliver, M. (2001) 'Low Tide' Pp 34. *Amicus* Journal, Winter 2001

[17] Downloaded 7th November 2017 from https://www.brainpickings.org/2017/09/25/e-e-cummings-advice/?utm_source=Brain+Pickings&utm_campaign=7d7ba39fed-EMAIL_CAMPAIGN_2017_09_29&utm_medium=email&utm_term=0_179ffa2629-7d7ba39fed-236356621&mc_cid=7d7ba39fed&mc_eid=2fe39422a2

[18] Whyte, D. (2007) *Many Rivers Flow*. Pp 351. Langley, Many Rivers Press

[19] Dr Maya Angelou interviewed by Bill Moyers on public television in 1973. Cited in Brown, B. (2017) *Braving the Wilderness – The Quest for True Belonging and the Courage to Stand Alone*. Pp 5. London, Vermilion

[20] Brown, B. (2017) *Braving the Wilderness – The Quest for True Belonging and the Courage to Stand Alone*. Pp 40. London, Vermilion

[21] Henley, William Ernest (1888). 'Invictus', published in A *Book of Verses*. Pp 56–7. London: D. Nutt

[22] Oliver, M. (2004) *New and Selected Poems* Vol. 1. USA, Beacon Press

[23] Machado, A. (2005) *Campos de Castilla*. Madrid, Ediciones Catedra, S.A.

[24] Downloaded 8th November 2017 from https://www.brainpickings.org/2016/01/19/seamus-heaney-commencement

[25] Downloaded 8th November 2017 from https://www.couragerenewal.org/

[26] Merton, T. and Dalai Lama XIV (2010) *The Way of Chuang Tzu*. New York, New Directions

[27] Palmer, P. J. (2004) *A Hidden Wholeness – The Journey Toward An Undivided Life Welcoming Soul and Weaving Community in a Wounded World*. Pp 47. San Francisco, John Wiley and Sons, Inc.

[28] Goswami, A. (2014) *Quantum Creativity – Think Quantum, Be Creative*. UK, Hay House

[29] Downloaded 20th November 2017 from https://www.goodreads.com/author/quotes/176832.Amit_Goswami

[30] Watts, A. (1951) *The Wisdom of Insecurity – A Message for an Age of Anxiety*. New York, Vintage Books

[31] Watts, A. (1951) *The Wisdom of Insecurity – A Message for an Age of Anxiety*. Pp 52 & 53. New York, Vintage Books

[32] Downloaded 21st November 2017 from Omid Safi 'The Prayer of the Heart' https://onbeing.us4.listmanage.com/track/

[33] Downloaded 21st November 2017 from https://www.goodreads.com/quotes/tag/choosing

[34] Printed with permission from Many Rivers Press. Whyte, D. (2007) *Many Rivers Flow*. Pp 354. Langley, Many Rivers Press

[35] Downloaded 21st November 2017 from https://www.goodreads.com/quotes/tag/follow-your-heart

[36] Downloaded 21st November 2017 from https://www.brainpickings.org/2015/04/09/find-your-bliss-joseph-campbell-power-of-myth/

[37] Downloaded 22nd November 2017 from https://www.huffingtonpost.com/jinna-yang/12-inspiring-quotes-about_1_b_6042312.html

[38] Printed with permission from Many Rivers Press. Whyte, D. (2016) 'To Break A Promise' from *The Sea In You: Twenty Poems of Requited and Unrequited Love*. Langley, Many Rivers Press

[39] Examples include Codes of Ethics and Practice from the Association of Coaching (at www.associationofcoaching.com), the European Mentoring and Coaching Council (at www.emcc.org) or British Association of Counselling and Psychotherapy (at www.bacp.org)

[40] Brown, B. (2017) *Braving the Wilderness – The Quest for True Belonging and the Courage to Stand Alone*. Pp 38. London, Vermilion

[41] Downloaded 8th December 2017. Cited in https://onbeing.org/blog/simplicity-on-the-other-side-of-complexity/

[42] Oliver, M. (2007) *Thirst: Poems*. Massachusetts, Beacon Press

[43] Handy, C. (1998) *The Hungry Spirit – Beyond Capitalism: A Quest for Purpose in the Modern World*. Pp 87. London, Random House Ltd.

[44] Richardson. C. (2009) *The Art of Extreme Self Care*. Pp xvi. London, Hay House UK Ltd.

[45] O'Donohue, J. (2007) *Benedictus – A Book of Blessings*. Pp 48. London, Transworld Publishers

[46] Cited in O'Donohue, J. (1998) *Anam Cara: A Book of Celtic Wisdom*. New York, Harper Perennial

[47] Whyte, D. (2007) *Many Rivers Flow*. Pp 347. Langley, Many Rivers Press

[48] Brown, J. (2012) *The Art and Spirit of Leadership*. Pp 39. USA, Trafford Publishing

The Denouement
Return's Harvest and Action

1 Downloaded 8th December 2017 from https://www.movemequotes.com/top-10-take-action-quotes/

2 Palmer, P. J. (1990) *The Active Life – A Spirituality of Work, Creativity and Caring.* Pp 15. San Francisco, Jossey-Bass

3 Palmer, P. J. (1990) *The Active Life – A Spirituality of Work, Creativity and Caring.* Pp 18. San Francisco, Jossey-Bass

4 Campbell, J. (1949) *The Hero with A Thousand Faces – The Collected Works of Joseph Campbell.* New York, Pantheon Books

5 Downloaded 8th December 2017 from https://www.dictionary-quotes.com/i-hear-and-i-forget-i-see-and-i-remember-i-do-and-i-understand-chinese-proverb/

Chapter 11
Crafting Focus

1 *The Concise Oxford Dictionary* (1976) 6th Edition. Pp 407. Oxford, Clarendon Press

2 Dalai Lama and van den Muyzenberg, L. (2008) *The Leader's Way.* Pp 13. London, Nicholas Brealey Publishing

3 Goleman, D. (2013) *Focus – The Hidden Dimension of Excellence.* London, Bloomsbury Publishing

4 Downloaded 8th December 2017 from https://www.movemequotes.com/top-10-take-action-quotes/

5 Downloaded 13th December 2017 from https://www.goodreads.com/quotes/tag/focus

6 Professor Barbara Oakley is co-teaching one of the world's largest online classes, 'Learning How to Learn', https://www.coursera.org/course/learning

7 Downloaded 13th December 2017 from https://www.goodreads.com/quotes/tag/focus

8 Downloaded 13th December 2017 from https://www.goodreads.com/work/quotes/22300682-the-one-thing-the-surprisingly-simple-truth-behind-extraordinary-result

9 Downloaded 20th December 2017 from https://www.goodreads.com/quotes/629613-people-think-focus-means-saying-yes-to-the-thing-you-ve

10 Seale, A. (2001) *Intuitive Living, A Sacred Path.* Pp 90. San Francisco, Red Wheel / Weiser

11 Downloaded 20th December 2017 from https://www.wiseoldsayings.com/starting-over-quotes/

12 Downloaded 20th December 2017 from https://www.wiseoldsayings.com/starting-over-quotes/

13 Downloaded 20th December 2017 from https://www.wiseoldsayings.com/starting-over-quotes/

14 With thanks to The Chaordic Alliance, cited in Szpakowski, S. (2010) *Little Book of Practice for Authentic Leadership in Action.* Canada, the ALIA Institute

15 Downloaded 10th January 2018 from https://www.goodreads.com/quotes/tag/intention

16 Downloaded 10th January 20168 from https://www.goodreads.com/quotes/tag/timing-is-everything

17 Downloaded 10th January 2017 from https://www.goodreads.com/quotes/tag/challenges

18 Stafford, W. (1980) 'You Reading This, Be Read' from Ask Me: *100 Essential Poems.* Copyright © 1980, 1998 by William Stafford and the Estate of William Stafford. Reprinted with the permission of The Permissions Company, Inc. on behalf of Graywolf Press, Minneapolis, Minnesota, www.graywolfpress.org

19 Cited in Szpakowski, S. (2010) *Little Book of Practice for Authentic Leadership in Action.* Pp 101. Canada, the ALIA Institute

20 Viewed 10th January 2018 at https://margaretwheatley.com/a-path-for-warriors-for-the-human-spirit/

21 Downloaded 12th January 2018 from https://tamingwickedproblems.com/quotes/

22 Sourced from Stacey, R. D. (2002) *Strategic Management and Organisational Dynamics: the Challenge of Complexity.* 3rd Edition. Harlow, Prentice Hall

23 Whyte, D. (2015) *Consolations: The Solace, Nourishment and Underlying Meaning of Everyday Words.* Pp 108. Langley, Many Rivers Press

24 Downloaded 15th January 2018 from https://www.goodreads.com/quotes/tag/rules

25 Downloaded 15th January 2018 from https://www.goodreads.com/quotes/558213-learn-the-rules-like-a-pro-so-you-can-break

26 Downloaded 15th January 2018 from https://www.goodreads.com/quotes/tag/patience

27 Downloaded 15th January 2018 from https://www.goodreads.com/quotes/558213-learn-the-rules-like-a-pro-so-you-can-break

28 O'Donohue, J. (2008) *To Bless the Space Between Us: A Book of Blessings*. Pp 14. USA, Sounds True Inc.

29 Oliver, M. (1984) *American Native*. UK, Little Brown

30 Downloaded 15th January 2018 from https://www.brainyquote.com/quotes/yehuda_berg_536650

31 Downloaded 15th January 2018 from https://www.goodreads.com/quotes/tag/focus

32 Downloaded 15th January 2018 from https://www.goodreads.com/quotes/tag/focus

33 Downloaded 15th January 2018 from https://www.goodreads.com/quotes/tag/focus

34 Downloaded 15th January 2018 from https://www.brainyquote.com/quotes/mary_wollstonecraft_204500

Chapter 12
Working Wisely

1 Downloaded 23rd July 2018 from https://lifehacker.com/the-way-a-person-does-one-thing-is-the-way-they-do-eve-1672939489

2 Downloaded 16th January 2018 from https://www.goodreads.com/quotes/69159-work-is-love-made-visible-and-if-you-can-t-work

3 *The Concise Oxford Dictionary* (1976) Pp 1338. Oxford, Oxford University Press

4 Downloaded 16th January 2018 from https://www.goodreads.com/quotes/tag/wisdom

5 Fox, M. (2002) *Creativity – Where the Divine and Human Meet*. Pp 98. New York, Tarcher/Putman Books.

6 Downloaded 16th January 2018 from https://www.thisdayinquotes.com/2011/03/power-without-responsibility.html

7 Downloaded 16th January 2018 from https://www.goodreads.com/quotes/tag/wisdom

8 Downloaded 16th January 2018 from https://www.goodreads.com/quotes/tag/wisdom

9 Downloaded 16th January 2018 from https://www.goodreads.com/quotes/tag/wisdom

10 Martin Luther King, Jr. AZQuotes.com. Wind and Fly LTD, 2018. 05 November 2018. https://www.azquotes.com/quote/525052

11 Greenleaf, R. K. (2002) *Servant Leadership A Journey into the Nature of Legitimate Power and Greatness*. 3rd edition. Pp 27. New Jersey, Paulist Press Ltd.

12 Frankl, V. (1959) *Man's Search for Meaning – The Classic Tribute to Hope in the Holocaust*. London, Rider

13 Downloaded 17th January 2018 from https://www.goodreads.com/quotes/150190-love-is-the-will-to-extend-one-s-self-for-the

14 Foster, J. (2013) *Falling in Love with Where You Are: A Year of Prose and Poetry on Radically Opening Up to the Pain and Joy of Life*. Salisbury, Non Duality Press

15 Foster, J. (2013) *Falling in Love with Where You Are: A Year of Prose and Poetry on Radically Opening Up to the Pain and Joy of Life*. Pp viii. Salisbury, Non Duality Press

16 Forster, E. M. (1908) *A Room with a View*. London, Penguin Classics

17 Downloaded 17th January 2018 from https://www.poemhunter.com/poem/what-we-need-is-here/

18 Downloaded 17th January 2018 from https://gratefulness.org/resource/you-reading-this-be-ready/

19 Printed with permission from Many Rivers Press. Whyte, D. (2012) *Pilgrim*. Pp 20. Langley, Many Rivers Press

20 Whyte, D. (2015) *Consolations: The Solace, Nourishment and Underlying Meaning of Everyday Words*. Pp 201. Langley, Many Rivers Press

21 Patterson, E. & Prentice, K. (2018) *The Compass Rose: Coming Home to Ourselves through Reflective Practice*. Published in *Coaching Today* Issue July 2018 by British Association of Counselling and Psychotherapy

22 Downloaded 18th January 2018 from https://quoteinvestigator.com/2011/12/18/happiness-balance/

23 Downloaded 18th January 2018 from https://www.janakingsford.com/balance-is-not-something-you-find-its-something-you-create/

24 Csikszentmihalyi, M. (1992) *Flow – The Classic Work on How to Achieve Happiness*. USA, Harper and Row

25 Csikszentmihalyi, M. (1992) *Flow – The Classic Work on How to Achieve Happiness*. Pp 4. USA, Harper and Row

26 Csikszentmihalyi, M. (1992) *Flow – The Classic Work on How to Achieve Happiness*. Pp 3. USA, Harper and Row

27 Cited in Szpakowski, S. (2010) *Little Book of Practice for Authentic Leadership in Action*. Pp 85. Canada, the ALIA Institute

28 Benyus, J. (2002) *Biomimicry: Innovation Inspired by Nature*. New York, Harper Perennial

29 Havel, V. (1984) *Politics and Conscience*. In an author's note, Havel writes, 'This speech was written for the University of Toulouse, where I would have delivered it on receiving an honorary doctorate, had I attended.' Havel had no passport and could not travel abroad. At the ceremony at the University of Toulouse-Le Mirail on May 14, 1984, he was represented by the English playwright Tom Stoppard

30 Downloaded 23rd January 2018 from https://www.azquotes.com/quote/796737

31 Kegan, R. (1982) *The Evolving Self: Problem and Process in Human Development*. Massachusetts, Harvard University Press

32 Wilbur, K. (1996) *A Brief History of Everything*. Boston, Shambhala Publications

33 Laske, O. E. (2005) *Measuring Hidden Dimensions: The Art and Science of Fully Engaging Adults*. Medford, MA, Interdevelopmental Institute Press

34 Pearson, C. S. (1991) *Awakening the Heroes Within: Twelve Archetypes to Help Us Find Ourselves and Transform Our World*. New York, HarperOne

35 Fowler, J. W. (1981) *Stages of Faith: The Psychology of Human Development and the Quest for Meaning*. New York, HarperCollins Publishers

36 Erikson, E. H. (1994) *Identity and the Life Cycle*. New York, W. W. Norton & Co.

37 Beck, D. E. and Cowan, C. C. (1996) *Spiral Dynamics Mastering Values, Leadership and Change*. Oxford, Blackwell Publishing

38 Downloaded 23rd January 2018 from https://www.azquotes.com/quote/353014

39 Hawkins, P. and Smith, N. (2006) *Coaching, Mentoring and Organisational Consultancy – Supervision and Development*. Maidenhead, Open University Press

40 Torbert, W., Rooke, D. and Fisher, D. (2000) *Personal and Organisational Transformations: Through Action Inquiry*. Boston, Edge/Work Press

41 Downloaded 24th January 2017 from https://hbr.org/2005/04/seven-transformations-of-leadership

42 Argyris, C., & Schön, D. (1978) *Organisational Learning: A Theory of Action Perspective*. Reading, Mass: Addison Wesley

43 Schön, D, A. (1983) *The Reflective Practitioner: How Professionals Think in Action*. New York: Basic Books

44 More information can be found at https://moraldna.org/

45 *Oxford English Dictionary* (1976) New Edition. Pp 293. Oxford, Oxford University Press

46 Downloaded 24th January 2017 from https://hudsonreview.com/authors/william_stafford/

47 Downloaded 24th January 2018 from https://www.sapphyr.net/songlyrics/quotes-music.htm

48 Downloaded 24th Janaury 2018 from https://wisdomquotes.com/albert-einstein-quotes/

49 Epictetus. *Discourses*, Book 11:5

50 Tolstoy, L. (1908). From the entry for April 21st in *A Calendar of Wisdom: Daily Thoughts to Nourish the Soul*. London, Scribner

51 O'Donohue, J. (2008) *To Bless the Space Between Us: A Book of Blessings*. Pp 153. USA, Sounds True Inc.

Chapter 13
FeedForward

1 Downloaded 29th January 2018 from https://www.goodreads.com/author/show/15321.Confucius

2 Downloaded 29th January 2018 from https://www.brainyquote.com/quotes/peter_maxwell_davies_332213

3 Downloaded 29th January 2018 from https://www.goodreads.com/work/quotes/40236441

4 Downloaded 29th January 2018 from https://www.goodreads.com/author/show/7355063.Vironika_Tugaleva

5 Downloaded 29th January 2018 from https://www.brainyquote.com/quotes/winston_churchill_124653

6 Downloaded 31st January 2018 from https://www.azquotes.com/author/38107-Michael_J_Gelb

7 Downloaded 31st January 2018 from https://www.azquotes.com/quote/750932

8 Downloaded 31st January 2018 from https://www.brainyquote.com/quotes/buddha_118669

9 Downloaded 31st January 2018 from https://www.brainyquote.com/quotes/mark_brand_862888

10 Downloaded 31st January 2018 from https://www.brainyquote.com/quotes/denise_morrison_8534114

11 Downloaded 1st February 2018 from https://www.dailygood.org/

12 Whyte, D. (2015) *Consolations: The Solace, Nourishment and Underlying Meaning of Everyday Words*. Pp 84. Langley, Many Rivers Press

13 Lee, H. (1960) *To Kill A Mockingbird*. Pp 35. London, Pan Books Ltd.

14 Downloaded 1st February 2018 from https://quoteinvestigator.com/2012/04/30/no-one-inferior/

15 Downloaded 1st February 2018 from https://brenebrown.com/wp-content/uploads/2013/09/DaringGreatly-EngagedFeedback-8x10.pdf

16 Brown, B. (2010) *The Gifts of Imperfection: Let Go of Who You Think You're Supposed to Be and Embrace Who You Are. Your Guide to Wholehearted Living.* Pp 68. Minnesota, Hazelden

17 Capra, F. (2014) *The Systems View of Life: A Unifying Vision.* Pp 319. Cambridge, Cambridge University Press

18 Downloaded 1st February 2018 from https://www.cognology.com.au/49-best-quotes-on-feedback/

19 Downloaded 1st February 2018 from https://www.cognology.com.au/49-best-quotes-on-feedback/

20 Kline, N. (1999) *Time to Think: Listening to Ignite the Human Mind.* Pp 62. London, Ward Lock

21 Downloaded 1st February 2018 from https://thinkexist.com/quotation/the_deepest_principle_in_human_nature_is_the/15218.html

22 Zander, R. and Zander B. (2000) *The Art of Possibility: Transforming Personal and Professional Life.* New York, Penguin

23 Zander, R. and Zander B. (2000) *The Art of Possibility: Transforming Personal and Professioanl Life.* Pp 26. New York, Penguin

24 Cited in Szpakowski, S. (2010) *Little Book of Practice for Authentic Leadership in Action.* Pp 105. Canada, the ALIA Institute

25 Downloaded 5th February 2018 from https://www.goodreads.com/quotes/tag/control

26 Downloaded 5th February 2018 from https://www.goodreads.com/author/show/38285.C_G_Jung

27 Downloaded 5th February 2018 from https://www.brainyquote.com/quotes/grace_poe_755607

28 Costa, A. and Kallick, B.(1993) 'Through the Lens of a Critical Friend'. *Educational Leadership* Vol 51, Issue 2, Pp 49-51

29 Downloaded 5th February 2018 from https://www.aoc.co.uk/sites/default/files/Being a critical friend_0.pdf

30 O'Donohue, J. (2008) *To Bless the Space Between Us: A Book of Blessings.* Pp 174. USA, Sounds True Inc.

31 Hawkins, P. and Smith, N. (2006) *Coaching, Mentoring and Organisational Consutlancy – Supervision and Development.* Maidenhead, Open University Press

32 Patterson, E. (2018) 'The 7 Cs of a Shared Humanity'. *Coaching at Work* magazine. Vol 13, Issue 4, Pp 50-52

33 Printed with permission from Many Rivers Press. Whyte, D. (2007) *Many Rivers Flow.* Pp 358. Langley, Many Rivers Press

34 Downloaded 5th February 2018 from https://www.goodreads.com/quotes/tag/listening

Chapter 14
Supervision

1 Downloaded 6th February 2018 from https://www.curatedquotes.com/inspirational-quotes/dance/

2 Downloaded 6th February 2018 from https://www.brainyquote.com/quotes/barbara_de_angelis_389754

3 Carroll, M. 'Supervision: A Journey of a Lifelong Learning'. In Shohet, R. (ed.) *Supervision as Transformation – A Passion for Learning* Pp 22. London, Jessica Kingsley Publishers

4 Ryan, S. (2004) *Vital Practice.* Portland, Sea Change Publications

5 Hodge, A., cited in Murdoch, E. and Arnold, J. (2012) *Full Spectrum Supervision 'Who you are is how you supervise'.* Pp 4. St Albans, Panama Press

6 Inskipp, F. and Proctor, B. (1993) *Making the Most of Supervision: Part 1 The Art, Craft and Skills of Counseling Supervision.* Middlesex, Cascade Publications

7 Murdoch, E. (2018) *What is Coaching Supervision?* Downloadable at https://coachingsupervisionacademy.com/what-is-coaching-supervision/

8 Downloaded 5th February 2018 from https://new.coachingnetwork.org.uk/article/supervision-or-super-vision/

9 Adamson, F. (2010) *Definitions of Supervision.* Unpublished. CSA Diploma Student Handbook

10 Benefiel, M. and Holton, G. (2010) *The Soul of Supervision – Integrating Practice and Theory.* Pp 4. New York, Moorhouse Publishing

11 Visit www.coachingsupervisionacademy.com

12 Adamson, F. (2011) *The Tapestry of My Approach to Transformational Learning in Supervision.* In R. Shohet (ed.) *Supervision as Transformation – A Passion for Learning.* Pp 90. London, Jessica Kingsley Publishers

13 Downloaded 9th February 2018 from https://www.goodreads.com/quotes/1319497-somewhere-beyond-right-and-wrong-there-is-

a-garden-i

[14] Critchley, B. and Sills, C. (2017) *A Relational Approach to Executive Coaching.* Association of Coaching Global Bulletin January 2017

[15] Adamson, F. (2011) *The Tapestry of My Approach to Transformational Learning in Supervision.* In Shohet, R. (ed.) *Supervision as Transformation – A Passion for Learning.* Pp 87. London, Jessica Kingsley Publishers

[16] Kline, N. (1999) *Time to Think: Listening to Ignite the Human Mind.* Pp 28. London, Ward Lock

[17] Wilmot, J. (2011). 'If You Want to Go Faster, Go Alone. If You Want to Go Further, Go Together: Work as Transformation through Supervision. In Shohet, R. (ed.) *Supervision as Transformation – A Passion for Learning.* Pp 69. London, Jessica Kingsley Publishers

[18] Downloaded 9th February 2018. Sourced from www.coachingsupervisionacademy.com

[19] Benefiel, M. and Holton, G. (2010) *The Soul of Supervision – Integrating Practice and Theory.* Pp 8. New York, Moorhouse Publishing

[20] Downloaded 6th February 2018 from https://quotesgram.com/albert-camus-quotes/

[21] Whyte, D. (2015) *Consolations: The Solace, Nourishment and Underlying Meaning of Everyday Words.* Pp 74. Langley, Many Rivers Press

[22] Downloaded 9th February 2018 from https://www.beliefnet.com/columnists/beyondblue/2008/02/anne-morrow-lindbergh-the-danc.html

[23] Downloaded 9th February 2018 from https://inner-growth.info/power_of_now_tolle/eckhart_tolle_stillness_speaks.htm

[24] O'Donohue, J. (1998) *Anam Cara: A Book of Celtic Wisdom.* New York, Harper Perennial

[25] Adapted from a talk given at the California Institute of Integral Studies in San Francisco. Copyright 2008 by John Welwood

[26] Downloaded 9th February 2018 from https://www.goodreads.com/work/quotes/254029-the-fifth-discipline-the-art-practice-of-the-learning-organization

[27] Quoted in Goss, S. (2014) *Open Tribe.* London, Lawrence and Wishart Ltd.

[28] Downloaded 10th February 2018 from https://www.goodreads.com/author/quotes/550910.Florida_Scott_Maxwell

[29] Hawkins, P. and Shohet, R. (2009) *Supervision in the Helping Professions.* Maidenhead, McGraw-Hill Education

[30] Murdoch, E. (2014) from www.coachingsupervisionacademy.com

[31] Chodron, P. (2007) *No Time to Lose.* Pp 1. USA, Shambhala Publications Inc.

[32] Downloaded 9th February 2018 from https://www.goodreads.com/quotes/526642-the-more-you-know-the-more-you-know-you-don-t

[33] Downloaded 6th February 2018 from https://www.curatedquotes.com/inspirational-quotes/dance/

[34] Downloaded 10th February 2018 from Parker J. Palmer, Author, Activist and https://www.couragerenewal.org/young-leaders/

[35] Downloaded 10th February 2018 from https://www.dancesofuniversalpeacena.org/na/images/DUP-poster.pdf

[36] Downloaded 10th February 2018 from https://dancingstorytellers.com/

GLOSSARY

Acorn Theory:	The Acorn Theory was described by the late James Hillman. It states that every acorn has within it the blueprint for a mighty and majestic oak tree. For it to grow it needs to drop into dark soil and, with huge effort, move through this into the light.
Alpha Brainwaves:	This frequency range bridges the gap between our beta (conscious) thinking and theta (subconscious) mind.
Artist Date:	Coined by Julia Cameron this is an appointment with oneself to find inspiration in art, beauty or nature.
Attachment Theory:	As defined by John Bowlby, Attachment Theory explores the importance of secure and trusting bonds between a child and their primary care giver/s for a child's development and wellbeing. Our earliest history of attachment can impact on our lives.
Beginner's Mindset:	Assuming nothing.
Blocks:	Obstacles which prevent free flow, restrain, constrain or stop us.
Body Scan:	A full body mindfulness and awareness exercise or practice.
Change Breath:	A practice of pausing and breathing to interrupt or change a dynamic.
Cognitive Behavoural Therapy:	A solution-focused talking therapy. CBT seeks to replace negative self-talk with a more realistic and adaptive strategy.
Conscious:	Able to perceive, apprehend or notice with a degree of controlled thought or observation.
Consciousness:	Quality or state of being aware and awake.
Creativity:	Bringing the new into the world or reshaping what already exists into new forms.

Criticality:	The questioning of experience, which challenges deeper held assumptions, mindsets and values. Holds the possibility for deeper change and transformation.	**God Spot:**	The place where our brains are connected to the universe.
Critical Reflection:	Reflective learning which challenges core mindsets, basic premises or underlying assumptions.	**Human Energy Field:**	Sometimes called the Aura, this is a complex combination of overlapping energy patterns, which define the unique spiritual, mental, emotional and physical makeup of an individual. A person's Human Energy Field (HEF) is that part of the Universal Energy Field (UEF) associated with that specific individual.
Dance Map:	The Reflect to *Create!* dance map, which consists of four moves: The Prelude, The Opening, The Flow and The Denouement, and their nine supporting dance steps.		
Drivers:	A set of five unconscious controllers of our behaviour. They are Be Perfect, Hurry Up, Please People, Be Strong and Try Hard.	**Intellectual Intelligence:**	When we are guided by our head brain's intelligence.
Enabling Ecosystem:	Conditions and preconditions for growth.	**Internal Thermometer:**	Our internal barometer sensing when we are in balance (or not).
Epistemology:	The philosophical exploration of what it means to know and how knowledge is created.	**Journaling:**	A regular writing practice to capture ideas, reflections and experiences.
		Mind:	A process that regulates the flow of energy and information which is both embodied and relational.
Fertile Void:	The Universe's infinite space of emergence, potential and possibility.	**Mindfulness:**	An act of placing intentional attention onto self or other in the present moment, in the here and now.
Field:	The total set of connections which are mutually interdependent.		
Generative Thinking:	To build or co-create new or different thinking from what has gone before.	**Neurons:**	The body's basic brain cells.
Gestalt Therapy:	A client-centred approach to psychotherapy that helps clients focus on the present and understand what is really happening in their lives right now, rather than what they may perceive to be happening based on past experience. Instead of simply talking about past situations, clients are encouraged to experience them, perhaps through re-enactment, to become more aware of how their own negative thought patterns and behaviours are blocking true self-awareness and making them unhappy.	**Open Heart:**	To access our Emotional Intelligence and use it as an organ of perception.
		Open Mind:	The capacity to suspend judgement and see with fresh eyes.
		Open Will:	The capacity to let go of old self and let come our emerging authentic or essential self. To access our sources of Spiritual Intelligence.
		Personality Type:	The psychological classification of different types of individual characteristics or traits.
		Presencing:	Presencing blends the words 'presence' and 'sensing' to work from our deepest source in the fertile void.

Reflection:

The term stems from the Latin meaning 'to bend back, to stand apart, to stand outside of'. Here reflection means to pause from whatever is happening (either as it is happening or after the event or in anticipation of an event), to retreat into an inquiry or questioning of that experience. From here we can learn and create meaning from that inquiry and return to apply this to life, practice and/or the workplace.

What is the difference between 'Thinking' and 'Reflection'?

'Thinking' and 'Reflection' are often confused. Reflection is a particular form of structured thinking but thinking might not be reflective. Reflection is thinking about our thinking and being aware of our awareness. Reflection is therefore a particular kind of meta thinking.

What is the difference between 'Reflection' and 'Mindfulness'?

Mindfulness is an act of giving intentional attention to the present moment. Mindfulness helps us to notice what is in the present moment without attachment or the desire to control. Mindfulness – in its many forms and varieties – is therefore key to creating and supporting some of the conditions for reflection and reflective learning. In and of itself it does not necessarily result in learning.

Reflection in Action:

Reflecting on the experience as it is happening in the moment to be able to choose how to respond.

Reflection on Action:

Reflecting on experiences which have already occurred in the past in order to learn from that experience and apply the learning to future practice.

Reflective Learning:

Learning from reflection on experience.

Reflective Practice:

Developing a discipline or consistent habit or routine to create space and focus for reflection.

Reflective Practitioner:

A leader or professional for whom reflection has become a way of being. One who has intentionally and consciously developed disciplines of reflective practice or practices into their work/life.

Reflexivity:

Finding strategies for critical reflection on experience to question our own mindsets, values, assumptions, habitual reactions and processes.

Resonance:

Responding to vibrations of a particular frequency.

Self-Care:

Taking care and attending to one's own needs and wellbeing.

Sensing:

Sensing is the view from within the Whole when you start to see the interrelatedness and interconnectedness of all living things.

Social Constructivism:

An approach that sees knowledge as co-created and constructed in dialogue with experience. People construct their own meaning though exploring their stories and social interactions with the world.

Soul:

The spiritual or immaterial part of us which is held to survive death.

Spiritual Intelligence:

When we are guided by our soul's intelligence.

S.T.O.P:

Created by Elisha Goldstein, S.T.O.P is an acronym for Stop, Take a few breaths, Observe and Proceed.

Strategic Withdrawal:

A withdrawal from something or someone in order to renew and step forward.

Sutta:

A collection of aphorisms or maxims relating to some aspect of the conduct of living.

Thinking:	To consider; to be of the opinion; to exercise the mind otherwise than by the passive reception of another's ideas.
Thought:	A 'process or power of thinking'.
Tonglen:	A Tibetan word which mean 'sending and taking' or 'giving and receiving'. [...] used in Buddhist meditation [...] [...] ith one's discomfort.
Transactional Analysis (TA):	A vast field of modern psychology which examines a person's relationships and interactions.
Transference:	The unconscious redirection of the feelings a person has about a second person to a third.
U Curve:	A shape commonly used to describe a change process. Theory U was popularized by Otto Scharmer and colleagues and encourages leadership from the emerging whole. It was a major inspiration for this book.
VUCA:	Acronym coined by Bob Johansen where 'V' means Volatility, 'U' means Uncertainty, 'C' means Complex and 'A' mean Ambiguous.
Whole – the:	The interrelatedness and interconnectedness of all living things.
Zen Kōan:	A kōan is a story, dialogue, question or statement used to provoke the 'great doubt' and thereby test a student's progress in Zen practice.

BIBLIOGRAPHY

Anderson, G. and Nadel, J. (2017) *'WE' A Manifesto for Women Everywhere*. London, Thorsons

Argyris, C. (1974) *Theory into Practice: Increasing Professional Effectiveness*. San Francisco, Jossey-Bass Inc.

Armour, A. J. (2014) *Neurocardiology: Anatomical and Functional Principles*. E-Book downloadable from: www.store. heartmath.org/s.nl/it.A/id.109/.f

Atavar, M. (2011) *12 Rules of Creativity*. London, Kiosk Publishing

Bager-Charleson, S. (2010) *Reflective Practice in Counselling and Psychotherapy*. London, Learning Matters Ltd.

Beck, D. E. and Cowan, C. C. (1996) *Spiral Dynamics Mastering Values, Leadership and Change*. Oxford, Blackwell Publishing

Belenky, M. F., Clinchy, C. M., Goldberger, N. R., & Tarule, J. M. (1986) *Women's Ways of Knowing*. New York, Basic Books

Benefiel, M. and Holton, G. (2010) *The Soul of Supervision – Integrating Practice and Theory*. New York, Moorhouse Publishing

Bennis, W. (1994) *On Becoming A Leader*. Reading, MA, Perseus Books

Benyus, J. (2002) *Biomimicry: Innovation Inspired by Nature*. New York, Harper Perennial

Berne, E. (1964) *The Games People Play – The Psychology of Human Relationships*. USA, Grove Press, Inc.

Blum, R. (1988) *The Rune Cards Sacred Play for Self Discovery*. London, Headline Book Publishing

Bohm, D. (1996) *On Creativity*. Oxon, Routledge

Bolton, G. (2010) *Reflective Practice Writing and Professional Development*. London, Sage Publications Ltd.

Bowlby, J. (1969) *Attachment and Loss*. New York, Basic Books

Brown, B. (2010) *The Gifts of Imperfection: Let Go of Who You Think You're Supposed to Be and Embrace Who You Are. Your Guide to Wholehearted Living*. Minnesota, Hazelden

Brown, B. (2012) *Daring Greatly: How the Courage to Be Vulnerable Transforms the Way We Live, Love, Parent and Lead*. London, Penguin Group

Brown, B. (2017) *Braving the Wilderness – The Quest for True Belonging and the Courage to Stand Alone*. London, Vermilion

Brown, J. (2006) *Reflective Practices for Transformational Leaders*. futureAge May/June 2006

Brown, J. (2008) *A Leader's Guide to Reflective Practice*. USA, Trafford Publishing

Brown, J. (2012) *The Art and Spirit of Leadership*. USA, Trafford Publishing

Brown, J. with Issacs, D. (2005) *The World Café – Shaping our Futures through Conversations that Matter*. San Francisco, Berrett- Koehler Publishers

Brown, P. and Brown, V. (2012) *Neuropsychology for Coaches – Understanding the Basics*. Berkshire, Open University Press

Buber, M. (1958) *I and Thou*. New York, The Scribner Library

Cameron, J. (1994) *The Artist's Way – A Course in Discovering and Recovering Your Creative Self*. London, Pan Books

Cameron, J. (1996) *The Vein of Gold – A Journey to Your Creative Heart*. USA, Tarcher/Putman

Cameron, J. (2016) *It's Never Too Late to Begin Again – Discovering Creativity and Meaning at Midlife and Beyond*. New York, Tarcherperigree

Campbell, J. (2012) *The Hero with a Thousand Faces. 3rd Edition*. San Francisco, New World Library

Carr, N. (2010) *The Shallows – How the Internet is Changing the Way We Think, Read and Remember.* New York, W.W. Norton & Company Inc.

Carroll, M., and Gilbert, M. C. (2005) *On Being a Supervisee: Creating Learning Partnerships.* London, Vukani Publishing

Carroll, M. (2010) 'Levels of Reflection: On learning reflection'. *Psychotherapy in Australia Volume 16 No. 2*, February 2010, Pp 28 – 35

Cashman, K. (2008) *Leadership from the Inside Out; Becoming a Leader for Life.* San Francisco, Berrett-Koehler Publishers Inc.

Chodron, P. (1994) *Start With Where You Are: How to Accept Yourself and Others.* London, HarperCollinsPublishers

Chodron, P. (2001) *Start Where You Are: A Guide to Compassionate Living.* USA, Shambhala Publications

Chodron, P. (2016) *When Things Fall Apart: Heart Advice for Difficult Times.* USA, Shambhala Publications

Christensen, T. (2015) *The Creativity Challenge.* MA, Adams Media

Csikszentmihalyi, M. (1996) *Creativity – The Psychology of Discover and Invention.* New York, Harper Collins Publishers.

Csikszentmihalyi, M. (1992) *Flow – The Classic Work on How to Achieve Happiness.* USA, Harper and Row

Dalai Lama (2011) *A Profound Mind – Cultivating Wisdom in Everyday Life.* London, Hodder & Stoughton

Dalai Lama and van den Muyzenberg, L. (2008) *The Leader's Way.* London, Nicholas Brealey Publishing

Densten, I. and Gray, J. (2001) 'Leadership Development And Reflection: What Is The Connection?' *The International Journal of Educational Management.* No. 15/3 Pp 119–24.

Dewey, J. (1938) *Experience and Education.* New York, Touchstone

Einzig, H. (2017) *The Future of Coaching – Vision, Leadership and Responsibility in a Transforming World.* Oxon, Routledge

Erikson, E. H. (1994) *Identity and the Life Cycle.* New York, W. W. Norton & Co.

Fook, J. (2006) 'Beyond Reflective Practice: Reworking the "Critical" in Critical Reflection'. *Proceedings for Professional Lifelong Learning: Beyond Reflective Practice 3rd July 2006.* [Internet]. Available from: https://mcgraw-hill.co.uk/openup/fook&gardner/resources/5.c.pdf. [Accessed 1st February 2013]

Fook, J. and Gardner, F. (2007) *Practising Critical Reflection: A Resource Handbook.* Berkshire, Open University Press

Foster, J. (2013) *Falling in Love with Where You Are: A Year of Prose and Poetry on Radically Opening Up to the Pain and Joy of Life.* Salisbury, Non Duality Press

Fowler, J. W. (1981) *Stages of Faith: The Psychology of Human Development and the Quest for Meaning.* New York, HarperCollins Publishers

Fox, M. (2002) *Creativity – Where the Divine and Human Meet.* New York, Tarcher/Putnam Books

Frankl, V. (1959) *Man's Search for Meaning – The Classic Tribute to Hope in the Holocaust.* London, Rider

Frederickson, B. (2014) *Love 2:0.* New York, Penguin

Gendlin, E. (1978) *Focusing.* New York, Bantam Dell

George, B. with Sims, P. (2007) *True North Discover Your Authentic Leadership.* San Francisco, Jossey-Boss

Germer, G. (2009) *The Mindful Path to Self Compassion.* New York, The Guildford Press

Gershon, M. (1998) *The Second Brain: The Scientific Basis of Gut Instinct and a Groundbreaking New Understanding of Nervous Disorders of the Stomach and Intestines.* London, Harper Collins

Gilbert, E. (2015) *Big Magic – Creative Living Beyond Fear.* London, Bloomsbury Publishing

Gilchrist, I. (2012) *The Master and His Emissary: The Divided Brain and the Making of the Western World.* Yale University Press Publications.

McGilligan, S. and Dilts, R. (2009) *The Hero's Journey: A Voyage of Self Discovery.* Carmarthen, Crown House Publishing Ltd.

Giono, J. (1995) *The Man Who Planted Tress.* Massachusetts, Shambhala Publications Ltd.

Goffee, R. and Jones, G. (2006) *Why Should Anyone Be Lead By You? What It Takes To Be An Authentic Leader.* Massachusetts, Harvard Business Review Press

Goleman, D. (2013) *Focus: The Hidden Driver of Excellence.* London, Bloomsbury Publishing Plc.

Goleman, D., Boyatzis, R., and McKee, A. (2002) *The New Leaders.* London, Little Brown

Gompertz, W. (2015) *Think Like An Artist... and Lead a More Creative, Productive Life.* UK, Penguin Random House

Goswami, A. (2014) *Quantum Creativity – Think Quantum, Be Creative.* UK, Hay House

Greenleaf, R. K. (2002) *Servant Leadership A Journey into the Nature of Legitimate Power and Greatness.* 3rd ed. New Jersey, Paulist Press Ltd.

de Haan, E. (2008) *Relational Coaching.* Chichester, John Wiley

Handy, C. (1998) *The Hungry Spirit – Beyond Capitalism A Quest for Purpose in the Modern World.* London, Random House Ltd.

Harris, M. (2017) *Solitude – In Pursuit of a Singular Life in a Crowded World.* London, Random House Books

Hassad, C. and Chambers, R. (2014) *Mindful Learning – Reduce the Stress and Improve Brain Performance for Effective Learning.* Wollombi, Exisle Publishing Pty Ltd.

Hawkins, P. (2011) *Leadership Team Coaching: Developing collective transformational leaders.* London, Kogan Page

Hawkins, P. and Smith, N. (2006) *Coaching, Mentoring and Organisational Consultancy – Supervision and Development.* Maidenhead, Open University Press

Hawkins, P. and Shohet, R. (2009) *Supervision in the Helping Professions.* Maidenhead, McGraw-Hill Education

Hewson, D. and Carroll, M. (2016) *Reflective Practice in Supervision.* Bristol, Minuteman Press

Hewson, D. and Carroll, M. (2016) *The Reflective Practice Toolkit – Companion Volume to Reflective Practice in Supervision.* Bristol, Minuteman Press

Hillman, J. (1996) *The Soul's Code: In Search of Character and Calling.* New York, Grand Central Publishing

Holder, J. (1999) *Soul Purpose: Self Affirming Rituals, Meditations and Creative Exercise to Free Your Spirit.* London, Judy Piatkus (Publishers) Ltd.

Huffington, A. (2014) *Thrive The Third Metric to Redefining Success and Creating and Happier Life.* USA, Harmony Books

Hutchins, G. (2012) *The Nature of Business – Redesigning Business for Resilience.* Devon, Green Books Ltd.

Hutchins, G. (2014) *The Illusion of Separation – Exploring the Cause of our Current Crisis.* Edinburgh, Floris Books

Hutchins, G. (2016) *Future Fit.* Self published

Inskipp, F. and Proctor, B. (1993) *Art, Craft and Tasks of Counselling Supervision: Making the Most of Supervision Pt. 1: Professional Development for Counsellors, Psychotherapists, Supervisors and Trainees Paperback.* No longer in print

Intrator, S. & Scribner, M. (2007) *Leading from Within – Poetry That Sustains the Courage to Lead.* San Francisco, Jossey-Bass

Jarvis, P. (2006) *Towards a Comprehensive Theory of Human Learning.* Oxon, Routledge

Jaworski, J. (2011) *Synchronicity – The Inner Path to Leadership.* San Francisco, Berrett-Koehler Publishers

Johns, C. (2004) *Becoming a Reflective Practitioner.* Oxford, Blackwell Publishing

Judkins, R. (2015) *The Art of Creative Thinking.* London, Hodder & Stoughton Ltd.

Kabat-Zinn, J. (1994) *Where You Go, There You Are – Mindfulness Meditation for Everyday Life.* London, Little, Brown Book Group

Kabat-Zinn, J. (2005) *Coming to our Senses.* New York, Hyperion Press

Kagge, E. (2017) *Silence in the Age of Noise.* London, Viking

Kahneman, D. (2011) *Thinking, Fast and Slow.* London, Penguin Books

Kegan, R. (1982) *The Evolving Self: Problem and Process in Human Development.* Massachusetts, Harvard University Press

Kolb, D. (1984). *Experiential Learning: Experience as the Source of Learning and Development.* Englewood Cliffs, New Jersey: Prentice Hall

Kline, N. (1999) *Time to Think: Listening to Ignite the Human Mind.* London, Ward Lock

Kline, N. (2009) *More Time to Think – A Way of Being in the World.* Poole-In-Wharfdale, Fisher King Publications

Laloux, F. (2014) *Reinventing Organizations: A Guide to Creating Organizations Inspired by the Next Stage in Human Consciousness.* Belgium, Nelson Parker

Laske, O. E. (2005) *Measuring Hidden Dimensions: The Art and Science of Fully Engaging Adults.* Medford, MA, Interdevelopmental Institute Press

Lewis, T., Amini, F. and Lannon, R. (2001) *A General Theory of Love.* New York, Random House

May, R. (1975) *The Courage to Create.* New York, W.W. Norton & Company

McTaggart, L. (2001) *The Field.* London, HarperCollins

Mezirow, J. (1991) *Transformative Disciplines of Adult Learning.* San Francisco, Jossey-Bass

Moon, J. (2004) *A Handbook of Reflective and Experiential Learning Theory and Practice.* Oxon, Routledge-Farmer

Murdoch, E. and Arnold, J. (2012) *Full Spectrum Supervision 'Who You Are is How You Supervise'.* St Albans, Panama Press

Neff, K. (2011) *Self-Compassion: Stop Beating Yourself Up and Leave Insecurity Behind.* Hodder and Stoughton Ltd, London

O'Donohue, J. (1998) *Anam Cara: A Book of Celtic Wisdom.* New York, Harper Perennial

O'Donohue, J. (2007) *Benedictus – A Book of Blessings.* London, Transworld Publishers

O'Donohue, J. (2008) *To Bless the Space Between Us: A Book of Blessings.* USA, Sounds True Inc.

O'Neill, M. (2000) *Executive Coaching with Backbone and Heart.* Chichester, John Wiley & Son

Osho (1999) *Creativity: Unleashing the Forces Within.* New York, Osho International Foundation

Palmer, P. J. (1990) *The Active Life – A Spirituality of Work, Creativity and Caring.* San Francisco, Jossey-Bass

Palmer, P. J. (2000) *Let Your Life Speak – Listening for the Voice of Vocation.* San Francisco, Jossey-Bass

Palmer, P. J. (2004) *A Hidden Wholeness – The Journey Toward An Undivided Life Welcoming Soul and Weaving Community in a Wounded World.* San Francisco, John Wiley and Sons, Inc.

Palmer, P. J. (2007) *The Courage to Teach: Guide for Reflection and Renewal.* San Francisco, Jossey-Bass

Palmer, P. J. (2007) *Introduction from Leading from Within Poetry that Sustains the Courage to Lead.* San Francisco, Jossey-Bass

Palmer, W. (1994) *The Intuitive Body – Discovering the Wisdom of Conscious Embodiment and Aikido.* California, Blue Snake Books.

Parlett, M. (2015) *Future Sense – Five Explorations of Whole Intelligence for a World That's Waking Up.* Leicestershire, Matador Books

Patterson, E. (2008) *Reflective Practice: The Key to Transformational Learning.* Oxford, *The OJM Journal* Spring 2008

Patterson, E. (2011) Chapter 8: 'Presence in Coaching Supervision.' In *Supervision in Coaching – Supervision, Ethics and Continuous Professional Development.* Jonathan Passmore (ed.). London, Kogan Page

Patterson, E. (2013) Chapter 4: 'Reflective Learning and the Reflective Practitioner'. In: *Full Spectrum Supervision 'Who You Are is How You Supervise'* St Albans, Panama Press, Pp. 93–120

Patterson, E. (2015) 'What are Leaders' Experiences of Reflection?' What leaders and leadership developers need to know from the findings of an exploratory research study, *Reflective Practice*, Volume 16 Number 5, Pp. 636–51 [Internet] https://dx.doi.org/10.1080/14623943.2015.1064386

Patterson, E. (2017) Chapter 1: 'Waking up to the Power of Reflection to Unlock Transformation in People, Teams and Organisations in Contemporary Leadership Challenges' edited by Aida Alvinius. Download from: https://www.intechopen.com/books/contemporary-leadership-challenges/waking-up-to-the-power-of-reflection-to-unlock-transformation-in-people-teams-and-organizations. Hard Copies available from orders@intechopen.com

Pearson, C. S. (1991) *Awakening the Heroes Within: Twelve Archetypes to Help Us Find Ourselves and Transform Our World.* New York, HarperOne

Pellicer, L. O. (2008) *Caring Enough to Lead: How Reflective Practice leads to Moral Leadership. 3rd ed.* Thousand Oaks, SAGE Publications

Penman, D. (2015) *Mindfulness for Creativity. Adapt, Create and Thrive in a Frantic World.* London, Piatkus

Perls, F. Hefferline, R. and Goodman, P. (1994) *Gestalt Therapy: Excitement and Growth in the Human Personality.* London, Souvenir Press

Pert, C. (1999) *Molecules of Emotion – Why You Feel The Way You Do.* London, Pocket Books

Richardson, C. (2009) *The Art of Extreme Self Care.* London, Hay House UK Ltd.

Richo, D. (2017) *The Five Longings: What We Have Always Wanted and Already Have – A Guide to Love, Meaning, Freedom, Happiness and Growth.* Colorado, Shambhala Publications Ltd.

Rilke, R. M. (1929) *Letters of a Young Poet.* New York, Dover Publications

Robinson, K. (2011) *Out of Our Minds. Learning to be Creative.* Chichester, Capstone Publishing Ltd.

Rock, D. and Page, L. J. (2009) *Coaching with the Brain in Mind: Foundations of Practice.* New Jersey, John Wiley & Sons, Inc.

Rogers, C. (1961) *On Becoming A Person: A Therapist's View of Psychotherapy.* London, Constable and Company Ltd.

Rogers, C. (1980) *A Way of Being.* New York, Houghton Mifflin Company

Rogers, C. R. and Freiburg, H. J. (1994) *Freedom to Learn.* California, Merrill

Rozenthuler, S. (2012) *Life-Changing Conversations – 7 Strategies for Talking About What Matters Most.* London, Watkins Publishing

Salzberg, Sh. (2002) *Loving Kindness – The Revolutionary Art of Happiness.* Massachusetts, Shambhala Publications

Sandberg, S. (2013) *Lean In – Women, Work and the Will to Lead.* New York, Random House

Scharmer, O. (2007) *Theory U: Leading from the Future as it Emerges. The Social Technology of Presencing.* Cambridge, MA. The Society for Organizational Learning Inc.

Scharmer, O. (2018) *The Essentials of Theory U – Core Principles and Applications.* California, Berrett-Koehler Publishers Inc.

Scharmer, O. and Kaufer, K. (2013) *Leading from the Emerging Future: From Ego-System to Eco-System Economies: Applying Theory U to Transforming Business, Society, and Self.* San Francisco, Berrett-Koehler Publishers, Inc.

Schien, E. (2011) *Helping – How to Offer, Give and Receive Help: Understanding Effective Dynamics in One-to-One, Group and Organisational Relationships.* San Francisco, Berrett-Koehler Publishers, Inc.

Schön. D. (1983) *The Reflective Practitioner: How Professionals Think In Action.* US, Basic Books Ltd.

Seale, A. (2001) *Intuitive Living – A Sacred Path.* San Francisco, Red Wheel/Weiser

Senge, P. M. (1990) *The Fifth Discipline: The Art and Practice of the Learning Organisation.* London, Random House Business Books

Senge, P., Scharmer, O., Jaworski, J., and Flowers, B. S. (2005) *Presence – Exploring Profound Change in People, Organisations and Society.* London, Nicholas Brealey Publishing

Senge, P. M., Smith, B., Kruschwitz, N., Laur, J., and Schley, S.(2008) *The Necessary Revolution: How individuals and organisations are working together to create a sustainable world.* New York, Doubleday

Shohet, R. (ed.) (2008) *Passionate Supervision.* London, Jessica Kingsley Publishers

Shohet, R. (ed.) (2011) *Supervision as Transformation – A Passion for Learning.* London, Jessica Kingsley Publishers

Shunryu, S. (2011) *Zen Mind, Beginners Mindset: Informal Talks in Zen Meditation and Practice.* Massachusetts, Shambhala Publications, Inc.

Siegel, D. (2007) *The Mindful Brain: Reflection and Attunement in the Cultivation of Wellbeing.* New York, W. W. Norton and Company

Siegel, D. (2010) *Mindsight: Transform your Brain with the New Science of Kindness.* London, Oneworld Publications

Siegel, D. (2015) *The Developing Mind – How Relationships and the Brain Interact to Shape Who we Are.* New York, Guildford Press

Silverstone, L. (1999) *Art Therapy the Person-Centred Way: Art and the Development of the Person.* London, Jessica Kingsley Publishers

Smith, A. and Shaw, P. (2011) *The Reflective Leader: Standing Still to Move Forward.* Norwich, Canterbury Press

Solnit, R. (2017) *A Field Guide to Getting Lost.* New York, Viking Books

Steare, R. (2011) Ethicability® *How to Decide What's Right and Find the Courage to Do It.* UK: Roger Steare Consulting Ltd.

Steiner, C. M. (1974) *Scripts People Live: Transactional Life Scripts.* New York, Grove Press

Strock, J. (2010) *Serve to Lead.* UK, Amazon Digital Services Ltd.

Szpakowski, S. (2010) *Little Book of Practice for Authentic Leadership in Action.* Canada, the ALIA Institute

Tippet, K. (2016) *Becoming Wise – An Inquiry into the Mystery and Art of Living.* US, Penguin Press

Tolle, E. (1999) *The Power of Now – A Guide to Spiritual Enlightenment.* USA, New World Library

Torbert, W., Rooke, D. and Fisher, D. (2000) *Personal and Organisational Transformations: Through Action Inquiry.* Boston, Edge/Work Press

Turkle, S. (2015) *Reclaiming Conversation – The Power of Talk in a Digital Age.* New York, Penguin Press

Udall, N. (2014) *Riding the Creative Rollercoaster: How Leaders Evoke Creativity, Productivity and Innovation.* London, Kogan Page

Udall, N. and Turner, N. (2008) *The Way of Nowhere – 8 Questions to Release Our Creative Potential.* London, HarperCollinsPublishers.

WEBSITE REFERENCES

Here are suggestions for further resources for support and inspiration. Themes are organized in alphabetical order.

All the website addresses were correct at the time of printing.

Please add to the list as you make your own discoveries. These lists cannot be exhaustive as they are based on what has worked for me and are necessarily UK and Europe based. They have been designed to stimulate and inspire you to search out sources of inspiration.

Please email me with further ideas which can then be added to the book's website and which will be included in the 2nd edition.

Ulrich, D. (2002) *The Widening Stream – The Seven Stages of Creativity.* Ppix. Oregon, Beyond Words Publishing Inc.

Van der Kolk, B. (2014) *The Body Keeps the Score: Brain, Mind, and Body in the Healing of Trauma.* New York, Viking Penguin Group

Watts, A. (1951) *The Wisdom of Insecurity – A Message for an Age of Anxiety.* New York, Vintage Books

Welwood, J. (1998) *Journey of the Heart – Intimate Relationships and the Path of Love.* New York, HarperCollins Publishing Inc.

West, L. and Milan, M. (2001) *The Reflecting Glass: Professional Coaching for Leadership Development.* Basingstoke, Palgrave

Wheatley, M. J. (1999) *Leadership and the New Science – Discovering Order In A Chaotic World.* San Francisco, Berrett-Koehler Publishers

Wheatley, M. J. and Kellner-Rogers, M. (1999) *A Simpler Way.* San Francisco, Berrett- Koehler Publishers

Whyte, D. (1994) *The Heart Aroused Poetry and the Preservation of the Soul in the Workplace.* New York, Random House

Whyte, D. (2001) *Crossing the Unknown Sea: Work as a Pilgrimage of Identity.* New York, Riverhead Books

Whyte, D. (2007) *Many Rivers Flow.* Langley, Many Rivers Press

Whyte, D. (2009) *The Three Marriages – Reimagining Work, Self and Relationship.* USA, Riverhead Books

Whyte, D. (2012) *Pilgrim.* Langley, Many Rivers Press

Whyte, D. (2015) *Consolations: The Solace, Nourishment and Underlying Meaning of Everyday Words.* Langley, Many Rivers Press

Whyte, D. (2016) *The Sea In You: Twenty Poems of Requited and Unrequited Love.* Langley, Many Rivers Press

Wilbur, K. (1996) *A Brief History of Everything.* Boston, Shambhala Publications

Williams, M. and Penman, D. (2013) *Mindfulness: A Practical Guide to Finding Peace in a Frantic World.* London, Piatkus

Wilson, E. O. (2017) *The Origins of Creativity.* UK, Allen Lane

Wolinsky, S. (1993) *Quantum Consciousness: The Guide to Experiencing Quantum Psychology.* Canada, Bramble Books

Zander, R. and Zander, B. (2000) *The Art of Possibility: Transforming Personal and Professional Life.* New York, Penguin

Zohar, D. (1997) *Rewiring the Corporate Brain – Using the New Science to Rethink How We Structure and Lead Organisations.* San Francisco, Berrett-Koehler Publishers Inc.

Zohar, D. and Marshall, I. (2000) *Spiritual Intelligence: The Ultimate Intelligence.* London, Bloomsbury Publishing Plc.

Activities

National Cycle Network
https://www.sustrans.org.uk

National Trails
https://www.nationaltrail.co.uk

Nordic Walking Association
https://www.inwa-nordicwalking.com

Surfing
https://www.thesurfingsite.com

Creative Experiences

5Rhythms
https:// www.5rhythms.com

GalleriesNow: International Gallery Guide & Exhibition
Listings
https://www.galleriesnow.net/

Good Food Guide
https://www.thegoodfoodguide.co.uk

International Association of Conscious and Creative
Writers
https://www.iaccw.com

International Association of Journal Writing
https://www.iajw.org

Jazz Clubs Worldwide
https://www.jazz-clubs-worldwide.com

National Association of Decorative And Fine Arts
https://www.nadfas.org.uk

Orchestras Live
https://www.orchestraslive.org.uk

Public Monuments and Sculpture Association
https://www.pmsa.org.uk

Creative Spaces

British Library
https://www.bl.uk/

English Heritage
https://www.english-heritage.org.uk

National Trust
https://www.nationaltrust.org.uk

Retreats
https://www.amazon.co.uk/Good-Retreat-Guide
https://www.goingonretreat.com
https://www.retreatfinder.com
https://www.theretreatcompany.com

Sawday's Special Places to Stay
https://www.sawdays.co.uk

Tourist Information Centres
https://www.visitengland.com

Guided Meditations

Barbara Fredrickson
www.positivityresonance.com

Headspace
www.headspace.com

Insight App
https://www.insighttimer.com/meditation-app

Kristina Neff
www.self-compassion.org

Professor Mark Williams
www.franticworld.com

Holistic Therapies

British Academy of Crystal Healing
https://www.britishacademyofcrystalhealing.co.uk

British Acupuncture Council
www.acupuncture.org.uk

British Reflexology Association
https://www.britreflex.co.uk

Complementary and Natural Heathcare Council
https://cnhc.org.uk

Federation of Holistic Therapies
https://fht.org.uk

International Association of Aromatherapists
https://www.ifaroma.org

International Association of Reiki Practitioners
www.iarp.org

Reiki Association
https://www.reikiassociation.net/

Inspiration

Alternatives – Events Inspiring Heart, Mind and Soul
https://www.alternatives.org.uk

Authentic Leadership Centre at Naropa University
https://www.naropa.edu

BBC 4 Desert Island Discs
https://www.bbc.co.uk

Edinburgh Fringe Festival
https://www.edfringe.com

Edinburgh International Festival
https://www.eif.co.uk

Headspace – Meditation Made Simple
https://www.headspace.com

International Association of Conscious and Creative Writers
https://www.iaccw.com

The Musical Brain – Arts, Science and the Mind
https://www.themusicalbrain.org

National Theatre
https://www.nationaltheatre.org.uk

Network for Grateful Living
https://gratefulness.org

Nic Askew Soul Biographies
https://nicaskew.com/

On Being
https://onbeing.org/

Pema Chodron Heart Advice
https://www.shambhala.com/heartadvice

Presencing Institute
https://www.presencing.com

Rambert Contemporary Dance Company
https://www.rambert.org.uk

Royal Horticultural Society
https://www.rhs.org.uk/

Royal Opera House
https://www.roh.org.uk

Royal Society of the Arts
https://www.thersa.org/

Sadlers Wells Theatre – London's Dance House
https://www.sadlerswells.com

Shakepeare's Globe Theatre
https://www.shakespearesglobe.com

Society for Organisational Learning
https://www.solonline.org

Susannah Conway, Author and Photographer
www.susannahconway.com

TED Talks – Ideas Worth Spreading
https://www.ted.com

TEDx Talks – Ideas Worth Spreading
https://www.ted.com/watch/tedx-talks

Inspirational People

Dalai Lama
https://www.dalailama.com

Jack Kornfield – Author, Buddhist Practitioner
https://jackkornfield.com

Parker J. Palmer – Centre for Courage and Renewal
https://www.couragerenewal.org

Speeches That Changed the World
https://www.amazon.co.uk/Speeches-that-Changed-World

David Whyte
https://www.davidwhyte.com

Professional Associations

For Coaching

Association for Coaching
https://www.associationforcoaching.com

European Mentoring and Coaching Council
https://www.emccouncil.org

International Coaching Federation
https://www.coachfederation.org

For Counselling

Association of Transpersonal Psychology
https://www.atpweb.org

British Association of Art Therapists
https://www.baat.org

British Association for Counselling and Psychotherapy
https://www.bacp.co.uk

British Association of Drama Therapists
https://www.badth.org.uk

For HR Professionals

Chartered Institute of Personnel and Development
https://www.cipd.co.uk

For Supervision

Association of Professional Executive Coaching and Supervision
https://www.apecs.org

Training Bodies for Coaches and Supervisors

Academy of Executive Coaching
https://www.aoec.com

The Bath Consultancy Group
https://www.bathconsultancygroup.com

British Psychology Society
https://beta.bps.org.uk/

Centre for Counselling and Psychotherapy Education
https://ccpe.org.uk

Centre for Supervision and Team Development
https://www.cstdlondon.co.uk

Coaching Development
https://www.coachingdevelopment.com

Coaching Supervision Academy
https://www.coachingsupervisionacademy.com

Henley Business School
https://www.henley.ac.uk

The Hudson Institute of Coaching
https://www.hudsoninstitute.com

The OCM
https://www.theocm.co.uk

Oxford Brookes University
https://www.brookes.ac.uk

Said Business School
https://www.sbs.ox.ac.uk

Sheffield Hallam University
https://www.shu.ac.uk

Other Resources

16PF (Personality Factors)
https://www.16pf.com

Action for Happiness
https://www.actionforhappiness.org/

Breathe Magazine
https://www.breathemagazine.co.uk/

Coaching@Work
https://www.coaching-at-work.com/

CPI 260 California Pscyhological Inventory
https://www.opp.com/en/tools/cpi-260

DISC Profiling (Dominance, Influence, Steadiness and Conscientiousness)
https://www.discprofile.com

FIRO B (Fundamental Interpersonal Relationships Orientation)
https://www.cpp.com/products/firo-b/index.aspx

Headspace
https://www.headspace.com

Heartmath
https://www.heartmath.org

Hogan Personality Inventory
Hogan Development Survey
https://www.hoganassessments.com

Honey and Mumford Learning Styles Questionnaire
https://www.talentlens.co.uk/develop/peter-honey-learning-style-series

Insights Discovery™
https://www.insights.com/

Labyrinth Society
https://labyrinthsociety.org/

Metaphor Cards. Selections include:
• Leadership Metaphor Explorer by the Centre for Creative Leadership available from www. ccl.org

Mind Gym
https://themindgym.com

• Ho Cards by Ely Raman available from EoS Interactive Cards at oh-cards.com

• ECCO cards by John David Ellis available from oh-cards.com

• Blum, R. (1988) *The Rune Cards Sacred Play for Self Discovery*. London, Headline Book Publishing. Cards created by Jane Walmsley

• Runes Oracle Cards by Bianca Luna available from www.loscarabeo.com

Myers Briggs Foundation™
https://www.myersbriggs.org/myers-and-briggs-foundation/

Psychologies Magazine
https://www.psychologies.co.uk/

School of Life
https://www.theschooloflife.com/

Strengths Finder
https://strengths.gallup.com

TKI Thomas-Kilman Conflict Management Tool
https://www.opp.com/en/tools/TKI

STAYING IN TOUCH

Reflect to *Create!* is a holistic philosophy and set of reflective practices designed to free your innate creativity and humanity to craft wise, compassionate and skillful leadership, professional practice and supervision.

The Centre for Reflection and *Creativity* has been established to support this work.

Different ways of staying in touch and getting the ongoing inspiration and support you need are suggested below:

1. Join the Reflect to *Create!* Community

Stay in touch by:

- Visiting my website at **www.elainepattersonexecutivecoaching.com** for my latest blogs, audios and resources which also includes our range of Reflect to *Create!* journals, pens, prompt cards and workbooks.

- Sign up for my newsletter via my website.

- Follow me on Pinterest, LinkedIn and Twitter.

2. Join us on Reflect to *Create!* Workshops, Learning Circles and Retreats

Join us on our range of 1:1 reflective conversations and supervision, experiential workshops, small learning circles and retreats in beautiful locations throughout the world to deepen your understanding and application of the Reflect to *Create!* philosophy and its practices.

And a final thought from David Whyte from his poem 'Santiago' in his book of poetry *Pilgrim*

The road seen, then not seen, the hillside
hiding then revealing the way you should take,
the road dropping away from you as if leaving you
to walk on thin air, then catching you, holding you up,
when you thought you would fall,
and the way forward always in the end
the way that you followed, the way that carried you
into your future, that brought you to this place,
no matter that it sometimes took your promise from you,
no matter that it had to break your heart along the way:
the sense of having walked from far inside yourself
out into the revelation, to have risked yourself
for something that seemed to stand both inside you
and far beyond you, that called you back
to the only road in the end you could follow, walking
as you did, in your rags of love and speaking in the voice
that by night became a prayer for safe arrival,
so that one day you realized that what you wanted
had already happened long ago and in the dwelling place
you had lived in before you began,
and that every step along the way, you had carried
the heart and the mind and the promise
that first set you off and drew you on and that you were
more marvellous in your simple wish to find a way
than the gilded roofs of any destination you could reach:
as if, all along, you had thought the end point might be a city
with golden towers, and cheering crowds,
and turning the corner at what you thought was the end
of the road, you found just a simple reflection,
and a clear revelation beneath the face looking back
and beneath it another invitation, all in one glimpse:
like a person and a place you had sought forever,
like a broad field of freedom that beckoned you beyond;
like another life, and the road still stretching on.